Cher

ALL I REALLY WANT TO DO

Daryl Easlea and Eddi Fiegel

Cher ALL I REALLY WANT TO DO
Daryl Easlea & Eddi Fiegel

A BACKBEAT BOOK
First edition 2013
Published by Backbeat Books
An imprint of Hal Leonard Corporation
7777 West Bluemound Road
Milwaukee, WI 53213
www.backbeatbooks.com

Devised and produced for Backbeat Books by
Outline Press Ltd
2A Union Court, 20-22 Union Road,
London SW4 6JP, England

ISBN: 978-1-61713-452-4

A catalogue record for this book is available from the British Library.

Editor: Tom Seabrook
Design: Paul Cooper Design

Printed by Everbest Printing Co. Ltd, China

13 14 15 16 17 5 4 3 2 1

Contents

PART 1 1946–1979 BY DARYL EASLEA

CHAPTER 1 Birth Of An Icon 5

CHAPTER 2 Look At Us 15

CHAPTER 3 Catch The Wind 27

CHAPTER 4 Good Times 39

CHAPTER 5 3614 Jackson Highway 53

CHAPTER 6 All I Ever Need 64

CHAPTER 7 Mama Was A Rock & Roll Singer 79

CHAPTER 8 The Hard Way 94

CHAPTER 9 Take Me Home 129

PART 2 1980–2012 BY EDDI FIEGEL

CHAPTER 10 A Rock Singer Is Born 143

CHAPTER 11 Getting My Act Together 150

CHAPTER 12 I Found Someone 166

CHAPTER 13 Turn Back Time 178

CHAPTER 14 Love Hurts 189

CHAPTER 15 Walking In Memphis 201

CHAPTER 16 If You Believe 213

CHAPTER 17 Living Proof 224

CHAPTER 18 You Haven't Seen The Last Of Me 248

Selected Discography 261

Bibliography & Sources 264

Index 269

PART 1

1946–1979

BY DARYL EASLEA

CHAPTER 1

Birth Of An Icon

Cherilyn Sarkisan—better know today simply as Cher, and as one of the most enduring stars of modern times—was born on May 20 1946 in the otherwise unremarkable city of El Centro, California.

El Centro, a city since 1908, is situated 128 miles east of San Diego and ten miles north of the Mexican border, on the southernmost tip of California. The county seat for Imperial County, it lies fifty feet below sea level and is surrounded by thousands of acres of farmland. It was here that Cher's father, John Paul Sarkisan, worked in a variety of jobs, most notably as a farmer and a truck driver. Born in March 1926, Sarkisan was of striking appearance. He was of Armenian extraction, and provided the young Cherilyn with her distinctive looks.

Cher's mother was born Jackie Jean Crouch in Arkansas in 1927. She was of Cherokee, English, and French origin, which contributed to Cher's coloring. The young Jackie Crouch had a troubled childhood and made her living from the age of seven singing in saloons around the Midwest with her father, Roy Crouch. Her mother, Lynda Inez Gully, had walked out on them when Jackie was five. At the age of six, she had performed on an Oklahoma City radio station; by ten, she was singing with bandleader Bob Wills & His Texas Playboys.

Roy Crouch's dream was to get to Hollywood, but when he and his daughter arrived, it was not all he had hoped for. Within a year, Jackie was living with her father and brother in a one-bedroom apartment in impoverished circumstances. Undoubtedly talented, the young Crouch missed an opportunity to audition for Ethel Meglin's entertainment school Meglin's Kiddies—where Shirley Temple made her name—because her father couldn't afford to buy her new shoes.

When Roy sank into a trough of alcoholic despair, Jackie's mother, Lynda, attempted to retain custody of the children. Roy retaliated by trying to gas himself, and them, in their apartment. Although Lynda saved Jackie from this tragedy, times were still tough. Over the next five years, Cher's mother enrolled at a variety of schools and worked as a maid.

It was while working in a donut shop in Fresno that Jackie Crouch first encountered John Sarkisan. "Johnny was very charming and could talk you into anything," she told *People* magazine in 1978. Within a matter of weeks this strong, mysterious man had persuaded Jackie to marry him in a quick ceremony in Reno.

The marriage was to last, initially, for only one day. "I knew I didn't want to be married," Jackie continued. "But he told me to try it for three months, and if I didn't like it, then I could walk out. Well, before three months was out I was pregnant with Cher."

With a start like this, it was clear that Cher's was not to be a settled childhood. Her parents split up soon after her birth, and she was raised solely by her mother. She lived in a number of different homes, including an early spell in an orphanage while her mother scraped together enough money to live by singing and working in a diner. Cher would later describe her childhood as "pretty rocky. I felt like an outsider, the black sheep."

She did not meet her father until she was eleven years old. "He was in prison for a long time," she later recalled. While working as a truck driver, he had turned to heroin and petty theft, and would end up spending four terms in jail for drug possession. In 1980 he told the *National Enquirer* that he had been "away from home most of the time hauling produce. I'd only see Cher now and then because her mother was married several times in between all that. And [she] always told me that it was better if I stayed away."

In a vain attempt at stability, Cher's mother was to marry a total of eight times—and three of them were to Sarkisan. In 1949, Jackie Crouch became Georgia Holt, a name that seemed to her to be more glamorous, more professional, more showbiz. In September 1951, during her marriage to John Southall, she had another daughter, Georganne (or 'Gee' as she was to become known). Georgia's itinerant lifestyle meant that Cher effectively brought up her half-sister. "I actually raised my sister," she later said, "and that's why I think she's so normal and good."

The young Cherilyn was star-struck. "When I was a little girl, I saw *Cinderella* with my mother," she told *Parade* in 2010. "I started singing the songs from it, and I told her: this is what I am going to do. I was three, and I never changed my mind." Her talent for singing became apparent in the fifth grade when she almost single-handedly put on a production of *Oklahoma!*, and by the age of twelve she was practicing her autograph.

After relocating to Hollywood, Georgia Holt began to get work as an actress, picking up bit parts in shows such as *The Bob Cummings Show* and *The Adventures Of Ozzie And Harriet*. She made it clear to her daughters that they were special: they were princesses; she was the queen. She was conscious that Cherilyn looked unusual, compared with the other girls in her class, and did what she could to bolster her daughter's ego. But her comments would not always have the desired effect.

"My mother once told me something," Cher later recalled, "that has stayed with me through thick and thin: Honey, you're not the prettiest or most talented, so make the most of what you've got. At the time, that hurt. I felt so ugly, while my sister was so beautiful, with this white-blond hair and green eyes, like my mom."

Everything suddenly made sense to Cher when she met her father for the first time in 1957. She saw his dark colorings and knew straightaway where her look came from. "He was very showy," she later recalled. "He was flashy. When I saw this dark man walking into the house for the first time, I thought: OK, now I understand everything. This is where I came from."

Sarkisan attempted to rekindle his relationship with his ex-wife through yet another remarriage, but after six months the father-daughter relationship that Cher had so craved was in tatters. He would nonetheless play a recurring role in her life until his death from cancer in 1985.

Cher would watch the roller coaster relationship between her mother and father in awe. "I knew my mother and my father were crazy about each other, but they also tortured each other," she later noted in her autobiography, *The First Time*. "They were young, jealous, and immature; kind of like Sean and Madonna."

It was a pivotal period in the young Cher's life. In 1957, as an eleven-year-old, she first began to hear and appreciate rock'n'roll music. The first record that she bought was 'Tequila' by The Champs, and she thought Ray Charles's 'Georgia On My Mind' was one of the best things she had ever heard. Seeing Elvis on *The Ed Sullivan Show* sealed the deal.

Cher was clearly different. Her nascent style was all her own; her opinions were unlike anyone else's. At an early age she realized she was staunchly Democrat in her outlook. She was enamored—as were so many young Americans—by John Kennedy's youth and vitality. And she was horrified when her mother campaigned for Nixon.

"Mortified would have been about a hundred steps up from the utter humiliation I was feeling," she later wrote. "My mom even wore a straw hat that said 'NIXON' above the brim. Was she out of her fucking mind? I could not believe a member of my family was doing this." Although she would later smile benignly when her husband, Sonny Bono, savaged Jimmy Carter on primetime television, Cher remained on the left.

In 1960, Georgina Holt married for the fifth time. Her new husband, a banker named Gilbert LaPiere, subsequently adopted Cherilyn and Georganne, which is why, when her career took off, Cher was initially known as Cher LaPiere. Although the marriage didn't last, it did offer a period of financial stability to the family.

Cher's already striking exterior masked a deeply conservative interior. She had dabbled with drugs only once, when she was fourteen, and rarely drank alcohol. She was, however, deeply interested in men from an early age. During a brief relocation with her family to New York City, she found herself drawn to older men, and seemed to thrive on this peculiar turbulence.

"When I was little," she later recalled, "my mother used to say: Oh, I wish I could find someone nice so we could settle down and have a normal everyday life. And I used to think: Boy, I hope that doesn't happen! Because the way we lived seemed like so much more fun. Maybe it was crazy, but it seemed like fun."

It was when Cher returned to Hollywood that she encountered an actor on the rise: Warren Beatty. At this juncture, Beatty was considered to be pure Hollywood cheesecake, having begun to make a name for himself in films such as *Splendor In The Grass*. He met Cher after a traffic accident outside

Schwab's Drugstore on Sunset Boulevard, when Cher was driving her stepfather Gilbert's car.

"When I was sixteen years old, I fucked Warren Beatty," she later recalled with typical matter-of-factness. "Just like that. Of course, I'm one of a long list. And I did it because my girlfriends were crazy about him, and so was my mother. I saw Warren, he picked me up, and I did it ... and what a disappointment! Not that he wasn't technically good, or could be good, but I didn't feel anything. So, for me, I felt, there [was] no reason to do that again."

And that was that, apart from a proposed follow-up of pure Beatty quality that Cher later recounted in her autobiography. "I hadn't seen or talked to Warren for about eight months," she wrote. "When Warren called out of the blue and asked me to meet him for dinner, I told him I couldn't meet him because I was in love ... he said: '*Great*. How about lunch?'"

By now, Cher had left school and moved out of the family homestead. Never a talented academic, she had struggled with undiagnosed dyslexia and left Fresno High School at the age of sixteen. In late 1962 she set up with one of her girlfriends, Melissa Melcher, on Fountain Avenue in Hollywood. Some of their friends wanted to introduce Cher to her new next-door neighbor, who was supposedly "kinda famous."

Cher had her first encounter with the neighbor soon after in Aldo's coffee shop on Hollywood Boulevard. "I saw him walk through the door [and] everyone else just faded away," she told *Playboy* in 1975. "This thin guy with long black hair, Beatle boots, and a gold chain around his hand ... I didn't think he was handsome, but I'd never seen anyone with long hair and boots and stuff like that." She didn't know quite what she was looking at. "Something is different now," she later wrote. "You're never going to be the same."

C

Not conventionally handsome by any stretch of the imagination, Sonny Bono is often portrayed as the dual hero and villain in the Cher story. There is, however, little doubt that without him, her ascent to the summit of pop would simply not have happened.

Salvatore Phillip Bono was born in Detroit, Michigan, on February 16 1935, the youngest of three children. His family relocated to Los Angeles in 1942; his father worked on a factory line and his mother had a job as a beautician. After leaving school, Sonny took a variety of jobs—including driving a tug and working in grocery stores—so that he could pursue his dream of becoming a songwriter. He didn't have a tremendous natural ability for it, but he could at least string together a passable tune. Married young to Donna Allen, and with a baby daughter, Christy, Bono knew he was going to have to work hard.

In the late fifties, Bono started working at Specialty Records for A&R man Harold Battiste, where he wrote hits such as 'I'll Keep Coming Back To You' and 'Things You Do To Me' for Sam Cooke. Buoyed up with a little money, he tried to launch himself as a solo singer under the name Don Christy (an amalgam of his wife and daughter's names) but to little avail. It was while working for his friend, Los Angeles-based producer Jack Nitzsche, that he co-wrote 'Needles And Pins,' which became a huge smash for Jackie DeShannon in the USA and then for The Searchers in the UK.

Through Nitzsche, Bono came to the attention of wunderkind songwriter and producer Phil Spector, who was at the time just beginning to build his empire. Spector could see that Bono's talents as a writer and performer were limited but felt that his diligence, hard work, and overall *chutzpah* would make him an ideal candidate to work with him in promotion for Philles Records.

Bono would frequently add percussion or vocals to Spector's recordings, but more often than not he was the gofer. As Richard Williams put it in his groundbreaking biography of Spector, *Out Of His Head*, Bono "worshipped Phil." Or, as Philles co-founder Lester Sill notes in Mick Brown's book *Tearing Down The Wall Of Sound*, "Sonny had his nose up Phil's ass a mile."

Bono may have struggled with his position in the LA music scene, but by the time he met Cher he had certainly cut a swath and outwardly acted the star. "Sonny's lifestyle was so exciting," Cher said in 1992. "It was so interesting and I felt so great being a part of it and I really liked him very much."

When Cher and Bono first spoke, there was little spark, let alone any sexual chemistry. But there was something. A double date followed with Melcher—whom Bono was crazy about—and Cher's then-boyfriend, jazz musician Red Baldwin. Sonny and Cher danced, but that was it.

When it became apparent that Cher could not cover the rent on her apartment because Melcher had moved out, she enquired about whether she could room with Bono. He agreed to let her move in but downplayed the idea of them ever having a relationship and often criticized her physique. "I need someone to cook and clean," he told her, "and also, I don't find you terribly attractive."

Cher had always been independent, but living with Sonny—recently divorced with a five-year-old daughter—was proper adult stuff. She initially hid all evidence of him when her mother came to visit the apartment, but when Holt found out that the pair had become romantically involved she moved Cher back to the family home in Encino. Cher was furious and refused to speak to her mother. Finally, Holt relented and invited Sonny over to meet the family, beginning a cordial if at times uneasy relationship with him.

Bono may have taken some time to warm up to the idea of a relationship with Cher but he knew a striking look and distinctive voice when he heard it, and was determined to make her a star. He started to bring Cher with him into Gold Star Studios on Santa Monica Boulevard in Los Angeles, and soon she was on the microphone.

Cher had met Phil Spector already, when she briefly dated the singer Nino Tempo, a close friend of the producer. Legend has it that Spector's opening line to Cher, in French, was: "Do you want to go to bed with me?" Without missing a beat, Cher is said to have replied, also in French: "Yes—for money." As she would later note in her autobiography, she and Spector "had a very weird relationship from the start."

It was as a session singer that Cher fully came to grips with the recording studio. The experience she gained working with Spector during their fractious, uneasy liaison was invaluable. But Bono wanted to make something more of her. As Mick Brown notes in his book on Spector: "Cher—the messy, pimply, lazy girl who slept for endless hours back in his apartment and rarely changed her underwear—was going to be his Diana, Tina, Ronnie."

Cher got her break when Darlene Love was late to sing backing vocals on The Ronettes' 'Be My Baby'; Spector encouraged her to step up to the microphone to take Love's place. He was impressed enough to retain her as part of his vocal team for the next year, and took to calling Sonny and Cher his 'funk.'

Cher sang on a number of landmark Spector recordings: *Phil Spector's Christmas Album*, 'Da Doo Ron Ron' by The Crystals, and The Righteous Brothers' 'You've Lost That Lovin' Feelin'.' Her strident vocals were quickly spotted. According to Mick Brown: "Cher had a honking voice, so powerful that whenever she sang Larry Levine would move her to the back of the group, away from the microphone, so that she wouldn't drown out the other voices."

Cher was amazed at the studio hands and session players' stamina, and the amount of time they would devote to the project. "I was pretty naïve then," she said in 1985. "I just couldn't understand why everyone else could stay awake for a month without sleep [while] I was nearly dying. I didn't realize they were taking just about everything there was to stay awake. I was only sixteen."

Spector and Bono saw a lot of potential in this strange-looking, bohemian teenager. It was time for Cher to be made into a singing star. And if he was to record with her, Bono might finally get his performing break, too.

It was not to be a flying start for this strange duo on record, however. The first time Cher was heard on record as a solo singer was on the extreme curio 'Ringo, I Love You,' performed by one 'Bonnie Jo Mason.' A great bit of mock-Merseybeat, it sounds more like a garage band than The Beatles. Cher sings about wanting to run her fingers through Ringo's hair and show the drummer how much she cares. Written by Phil Spector with Paul Case, Peter Anders, and Vini Poncia (who would later work with Ringo himself), the song was one of the first US Beatles cash-ins. It was released in March 1964—a month after the Beatles phenomenon hit the USA.

Spector sold the song to Sceptor Records. Radio stations were confounded by Cher's low vocals, however—legend has it that many thought Bonnie Jo Mason was a man. Given the sensitivities over the length of The Beatles' hair in a deeply conservative America, this would never do. "I sounded too much like a boy," Cher later said. "Everyone thought it was a faggot song."

After 'Ringo' flopped, Sonny and Cher decided to see how well they would fare together. They decided to rechristen themselves Caesar & Cleo, then very *à la mode* thanks to the 1963 Richard Burton/Elizabeth Taylor film (which proved to be one of the costliest flops in Hollywood history). Cher explained how Bono looked like Caesar with his long, brushed-forward hair—a look that would frequently get him into trouble in public. To emphasize her role as Cleopatra, Cher began to accentuate her eye makeup.

Caesar & Cleo's debut single, 'The Letter,' was recorded for Vault Records in late 1963. It was a cover version of the 1957 Don & Dewey hit, which Bono had promoted while working at Specialty Records. Sonny was able to secure a three-single deal with Mo Ostin at Reprise Records. Caesar & Cleo continued with covers of 'Love Is Strange,' 'Let The Good Times Roll,' and 'Do You Wanna Dance,' all of which were interesting but hardly groundbreaking. The jangle of The Beatles was mutating, with the influence of Bob Dylan in America, to folk-rock. Caesar & Cleo's records were mired in the doo-wop styles of another era altogether.

Through their studio connections, Bono and Cher met managers Charlie Greene and Brian Stone, who encouraged them to record under their own names. Phil Spector suggested that Cher LaPierre reduce her name simply to Cher as he felt that her full name would sound too foreign to US audiences. Sonny Bono penned and produced the track 'Baby Don't Go,' a fabulous record that actually showed they had their own voice. It was predominantly a solo vehicle for Cher, but Bono's support gave the track its distinctive flavor. It certainly highlighted their potential.

Sonny sold the song back to Reprise, who had no idea that Sonny & Cher and the act they had already signed, Caesar & Cleo, were one and the same. 'Baby Don't Go' was released at the same time as the final Caesar & Cleo singles and became a minor hit on the West Coast. The record was certainly strong enough to get the duo wider exposure. It showed that all that time Bono had spent close to his idol, Phil Spector, had paid off; the expansive, faders-up noise sounded very much like Spector himself.

The success of the single proved that the duo should be known as Sonny & Cher. The record came to the attention of Ahmet Ertegun, the founder of Atlantic Records. He was aware of Caesar & Cleo, and realized that there may just be enough potential to add them to his roster. Greene and Stone contacted Ertegun and informed him that their deal with Mo Ostin was coming to a close. And so, at the start of 1965, Sonny & Cher signed to Atlantic.

CHAPTER 2

Look At Us

In 1965, on a promotional trip to Los Angeles, The Rolling Stones spent some time staying with Sonny and Cher. The British group's word-of-mouth support was a great boon for the fledgling duo's popularity. And they were about to get very popular indeed.

Sonny Bono was good at his day job. As a record company promotions man, he met the Stones off their plane at LAX in 1965. Their charismatic manager, Andrew Oldham, was deeply impressed. "Sonny Bono greeted us at the airport with an open heart and hand to La-La Land," he later wrote. "There was hope yet. Thirty-something Salvatore Bono looked as whacked as the Stones—and he worked for a living! Bono was all Sicilian LA heart, clad in barber-pole striped trousers."

Managers Brian Stone and Charlie Greene worked tirelessly with Sonny to get Sonny & Cher into the public eye. Stone and Greene were old-school hucksters and crafty businessmen. They had started out as publicists, and had worked with Phil Spector. Stone was the behind-the-scenes moneyman; Greene was the charming front man.

"We had these managers who lived in the prop room on one of the big motion-picture company lots and they went around in prop clothing, which we had to borrow too," Cher recalled in 1985. "The only reason we could afford to make 'I Got You Babe' was that they hawked all this film equipment. I don't even know if it was theirs." (With their showmanship and front—learned from the Hollywood characters with whom they mingled—it very probably wasn't.)

Atlantic Records supremo Ahmet Ertegun was smitten with the duo. "[Stone and Greene] called me up and told me they were managing Sonny & Cher," he later recalled. "I said really? They said yeah, they're not getting on too well with Mo Ostin of Warner Bros. They have forgotten to pick up their option, we haven't said anything, time has passed and now they are free.

"I said well, we'll sign them up," Ertegun continued. "At that time I had no relationship with Warners, and no thought of ever selling my company. So I signed Sonny & Cher, and our first record with them, 'I Got You Babe,' was not only a territorial hit, it was a nationwide hit and an international hit—I mean nothing like we had experienced before."

As always, however, it wasn't quite as straightforward as that.

It took one song, written by Sonny Bono in the style of his idol, Bob Dylan, to establish Sonny & Cher as a transatlantic phenomenon. 'I Got You Babe' is one of the greatest and most unmistakable pop singles of all time. Delivered with such outright sincerity and passion, it struck a universal chord with millions of sweethearts the world over. It neatly brought the sexual and teenage revolutions together: for this couple, love is strong and ever lasting. Although it arrived a full two years ahead of the Summer of Love, it was a record that outlined a manifesto of love and freedom, wrapped up in Bono's Spector-lite production.

It was recorded quickly at Gold Star Studios on July 7 1965, with Bono using every Spector reference possible to turn it into the kind of 'pocket symphony' that was fashionable at the time. Harold Battiste arranged, Hal Blaine played drums, and as many musicians as possible crammed themselves into the tiny studio.

"We stretched the capacity limit for musicians in the studio, that's for certain," Battiste later said. "Sonny got that from Phil Spector. If the fire marshal had come and seen how many musicians were squeezed into the studio, we'd all have been arrested. I used to say that the real technical achievement wasn't in recording Sonny & Cher, it was in getting everyone into that studio and still finding room for instruments and mics."

Bono pushed Cher into delivering take after take—something he'd seen Spector do with his wife, Ronnie. As a result, he was able to wring out all possible passion.

Bono had written 'I Got You Babe' in the basement of the apartment he shared with Cher. "We didn't have much ten years ago," he recalled from the stage in Las Vegas in 1973, "but we had each other. I bought a piano for $85 dollars and we bought a brass bed from a junk store. And that's all we had. But we had each other, and we had this philosophy ... it was so nice because we always believed that no matter how rough things got, and as long as we had each other and we hung in there, everything would work out. It was the first time in my life that I wanted to write down what I felt ... it shows how one thing can change your whole life for you, and our life changed completely in about four days."

On 'I Got You Babe,' Bono sang in the way the mainstream wished Bob Dylan would sing: more melodically. The song also contained the youth culture buzzword of the time: 'babe.' Sonny & Cher had taken Dylan's template and sweetened it. "At the time Dylan was doing his 'babe' this, 'babe' was all over the streets," Bono later recalled. "I thought, man, that's a hook if you ever use it right. Philip [Spector] would always play that kind of 6/8 rhythm, so I could duplicate it. You play and sing until a hook came in ... and 'I Got You Babe' came in. I knew the hook was real strong. I knew that was the one."

The record kept everything in perspective: it was Spector without the excess; Dylan without the grating delivery. It was the counterculture you could have in your middle-class suburb. Sonny wrote something that spoke of the universality of love with an open heart.

When Cher first heard the track, however, she was not keen. Sonny woke her in the night to play it to her. Although she was impressed that he had written something with modulation in the middle-eight, she was unsure about the lyric. More worryingly, new label boss Ertegun was similarly reluctant. He was smitten with another song the duo had cut: a fine, gritty, bluesy number entitled 'It's Gonna Rain.' But there was something about 'I Got You Babe,' this keening ballad with its hip lyrics, that separated it from Sonny's previous compositions—even the glory of 'Needles And Pins.'

Bono knew a hit when he heard one. He took 'I Got You Babe' to twenty-seven-year-old Honolulu-born disc jockey Ron Jacobs, the program director and star DJ at Los Angles radio station KHJ ('Kindness Happiness & Joy,' aka the groundbreaking Boss Radio). Sonny knew Jacobs well from his days in radio promotion. Jacobs's clout was such that when he selected 'I Got You Babe' as an exclusive, Atlantic had little option but to release it as the single's A-side.

The record was simply irresistible. Pop historian Colin Larkin would later describe it as "a majestic example of romanticized folk-rock and one of the best-produced discs of it time." It also made Dave Marsh's book *The Heart Of Rock And Soul: The 1001 Greatest Singles Ever Made*, in which Marsh writes that the record suggests: "Love redeems everything, no matter how ridiculous, moronic or grotesque. Noisy and misshapen as those declarations may be, they're also an essence of what rock'n'roll brought to pop music that hadn't been there before: a sense of democracy, fun, and possibility."

C

With 'I Got You Babe' starting to break in the USA, managers Greene and Stone felt that, in order to capitalize on this early success, Sonny & Cher should head to London. The managers put veteran UK publicist Larry Page in charge of publicity for their visit. When they arrived in London at the end of August 1965, they found that the UK accepted the duo warmly; with Britain fiercely proud of its pop exports, it was time to welcome some US newcomers to the fray. A controversial early incident—allegedly set up by Charlie Greene—during which the duo were thrown out of the Hilton Hotel in London's fashionable Park Lane guaranteed them acres of press coverage, and they were overnight stars. A photo shoot was arranged to capture the duo pitching their wigwam in Hyde Park.

The UK press was full of them: their look, their style, and their hair were all debated and discussed. The duo performed live at the 100 Club and garnered lots of good press. They shopped in Carnaby Street, cruised the Kings Road, and made friends. Soon they were drinking at the Scotch Of St James with sundry Beatles and Stones. Appearances on *Top Of The Pops* and *Ready Steady Go!* guaranteed the chart success of 'I Got You Babe.' "The people in England loved it," Cher recalled. "They didn't even think we were American. You know, American rock'n'roll at that time was zilch. Everything was The Beatles, and Dave Clark, and the Stones."

The duo's dress sense became a hot topic of conversation. Cher designed her own outfits and Sonny adopted a unique 'Neanderthal man' look with outfits made from animal pelts. This look marked out their otherworldliness, with Cher allegedly popularizing the craze for bell-bottom slacks. Working with her dressers, Colleen and Brigit, whom Cher would later describe as "real space cadets," she adapted some pantsuits that she had bought mail order from the UK.

Sonny wanted to make it clear that they were not bandwagon jumpers. "I've always dressed like this," he told Keith Altham at the *New Musical Express*. "We've got this little beatnik girl called Brigit, who I chained to a sewing machine back in our Hollywood home. She makes our clothes. My hair was this length when The Beatles first appeared in *Time* magazine. People brought me photographs and said: Look, they've got hair like yours." (Sonny was also somewhat aggrieved that the London cognoscenti wanted to spend more time with Cher than with him.)

On August 14, while Sonny and Cher were still in the UK, 'I Got You Babe' hit the US number one spot amid a plethora of British Invasion artists, coming after Herman's Hermits' 'I'm Henry VIII, I Am' and just before The Beatles' 'Help!' For three weeks, all-American pop had reclaimed the summit. It reached the UK peak on August 26 of the same year, after 'Help!' and before The Rolling Stones' '(I Can't Get No) Satisfaction.' It was a golden time for popular music, and here were these outsiders, arriving smack dab in the middle of it.

The UK trip had been a great success. "When we got to England, we got famous," Cher said in 1985. "And then we went back to the States and everybody thought we were English, so we got famous there too." Cher was a nervous performer and did not take to the stage easily, but Greene and Stone got the duo booked on bills in the USA and UK.

As Sonny & Cher topped the charts in their home country, the warmth they had enjoyed in the UK was not always replicated in the USA. It was one thing dealing with longhairs as they breezed in from the UK with their bad teeth, strange looks, and funny hairstyles, but to have two homegrown singers—and a thirty-year-old divorced man and a teenager at that—plying their own strange bohemia stuck in the craw of the deeply conservative US broadcasters. Sonny had a strange bohemian cool that was at once awkward and outlandish.

This coupled with Cher's otherworldly appearance meant that, despite their deeply conservative interior, the duo remained outside the mainstream.

According to Cher, the USA was "still suffering from a bad case of Doris Day and Rock Hudson. We were thrown out of every fucking place you can imagine. People were constantly trying to punch Sonny out because of the way he looked."

Nancy Sinatra had remarked that they looked like clowns. Someone told manager Charlie Greene that he had got himself "a great little circus act." But Greene could see that there was good business to be made out of this. "Yeah, I know," he replied, "and I'm gonna make big stars out of these clowns—and a lot of money off them, too."

Away from the establishment, Sonny and Cher quickly became totemic figures for young married couples. From shaky beginnings, the couple now seemed happier than ever. This was partially true and partially good for business. Every press article made mention of the fact that they were married. "When he finally proposed," Cher told *Rave* magazine in, "We went out and bought an enormous box of paints. Then we went back to my place and I painted a girl, which was very good. Sonny painted a purple candle in an iron wrought frame. It was terrible but I told him it was good so as not to hurt his feelings."

They said they had wed by eloping—of course—to Tijuana, Mexico, on October 27 1964. It was, in fact, a ceremony conducted in their bathroom with two gold-plated rings bought from an Indian Trading shop in Hollywood, and was neither official nor legally binding. It then became a case of keeping silent, as Bono was rightfully concerned that the press would be all over them if they tried to get married. Managers Greene and Stone urged them to make it official, and for the next few years it became a topic for speculation. Various dates and times were suggested for their union; in reality, they weren't wed until 1969.

Appearing 'married' to the world at large, however, was excellent for business. "Although our life is so hectic, I think we have a big advantage," Cher gushed in a September 1965 interview with *Disc Weekly*. "That's in being married. There's no 'bye honey, see you in two months time.' Wherever we go through work, we go together. That's the way it should be. We love each other. And we hate to be apart."

In the increasingly permissive society of the sixties, it was refreshing to hear a couple espousing such traditional values, no matter how wayward they looked. Cher would talk about Sonny being her best friend. "I don't have any regrets about getting married," she said in 1965. "I married Sonny because I wanted to, and there's never been a day when I wished I hadn't."

She expanded on this in an interview with *Rave* magazine, which followed the duo around the UK while they were filming for US television. "While we've got one another nothing can really hurt us," she said. "We called ourselves Caesar & Cleo, Napoleon & Josephine, and now we're Sonny & Cher. The only difference is that now we're a success, but all we really need is us. That's what our songs are all about. We're simply saying we're glad to be together. 'I Got You Babe,' 'Laugh At Me,' 'All I Really Wanna Do,' and 'Baby Don't Go' just say we're in love!"

It was this very public love that propelled them into the very top echelon of fame, very quickly.

C

The album that accompanied 'I Got You Babe,' *Look At Us*, was a bold if naïve statement of intent that established the formula that would make the duo the house hippies for middle-of-the-road America. Released on Atco in August 1965, its very title was a fantastic political declaration—an invitation to the mass market to gaze at two people who were clearly outside the mainstream.

The cover art captured them perfectly. Designed by Bono and Warner Bros art man Haig Adishian, it was appropriately 'in your face' for the time: the two of them against the world. Cher stares straight at the camera, living up to her 'little red Indian' look, while Sonny looks up and out of the frame, waiting for something that may never happen, or something that he knows is happening. In its rural setting, with Sonny looking every inch as if he had stepped out of his cave, they appear to embody the central tenet of the hippie ethos, the rejection of material values. The bits of bark and grass on Sonny's elbow suggested either that he had just completed some hard woodsman labor, or perhaps that the duo had recently performed something altogether more earthy.

The back cover runs through the key players in the Sonny & Cher organization under the heading "Look At ... Our Family," immediately turning convention on its head. Sonny & Cher were here in the mainstream, and had brought along their team for inspection. Harold Battiste—Bono's former boss at Specialty and now his right hand man with arrangements— is seen smiling among the players on the album. The fact that Battiste is African-American is not referenced at all. "Look at Harold Battiste," the notes scream. "He plays piano on all of our records. He's laughing at Sonny's hair but he's really jealous because he doesn't have any of his own."

The notes made clear that if you were to join Sonny & Cher's club, you were taken purely on your on merits, whatever your ethnic origination. The fact that Battiste could laugh simply at the nationwide joke of Bono's hair marked him out as being no different to any of the other players on the album.

It's clear how important mangers Charlie Greene and Brian Stone were to the operation: they get the first credit on the back of the LP. Greene is described as "the mouse that roars," while Stone is "so skinny he has to run round in the shower to get wet." In another break with tradition, clothing designers Colleen & Brigit are listed, making this more like a Hollywood film cast list than the back of an album: "Look at ... Colleen & Brigit—they sew all of our clothes." And this was a good two years before The Beatles were opening boutiques. Then, after giving "our very special thanks to all of our musicians who played their hearts out for us," they list all 16 players on the album, including lead guitarist Don Peake, who was singled out for a photograph alongside Battiste, Green, and Stone.

Between the covers is a sweet serenade of the love shared by this unconventional couple comprising four Bono originals and eight covers. Sonny repays his debt of gratitude to Phil Spector by covering two of his former boss's numbers, 'Then He Kissed Me' and 'Why Don't They Let Us Fall In Love.' The album also includes the duo's first Caesar & Cleo single, 'The Letter.'

Look At Us is a strange confection, one foot in vaudeville and the other in the folk scene. With its oompah beat, accordion, tubular bells, and wearisome interjections by Sonny in French, 'Sing C'est La Vie' is not a great moment, but it sets the template for Cher's style of storytelling in song. It also hit number one in Belgium, thus opening up a European fan base. There is a fairly straight reading of 'Unchained Melody' and an anemic take on 'You Really Got A Hold On Me,' the Miracles tune since popularized by The Beatles.

Of the Bono originals, the 'I Got You Babe' B-side 'It's Gonna Rain' is a superior slice of groove, somewhat discordant on vocals, but something that could easily slip into a *Nuggets* collection. 'Just You' is sweet and light, and was slated to be the duo's first Atlantic single.

Look At Us highlights the possibilities of Sonny & Cher's music but also their limitations as vocalists. Biographer J. Randy Taraborelli is scathing about the duo's vocal prowess. "Cher's tonal quality was interesting because she had one of those voices that went 360 degrees around a note but never really centered on it," he writes. "Sonny never even came close to the note." However, he concedes that when they do come together, they somehow sound "warm."

With its incorporation of folk, soul, and early psychedelia, *Look At Us* took elements of the counterculture's music into homes that would not dream of listening to anything darker or stronger. People strove to define this new sound: some wanted to call it pop; others wanted to call it folk. Cher, while still shy and uneasy in interview situations, could come up with a passable turn of phrase. "What do we sing?" she asked in 1965. "We call it folk'n'roll—a sort of folk music with a rocking beat. But with a smile. Ours is happy music—we haven't any message to impart."

The mid sixties was a time when the message meant everything. With the speed of the duo's success, it became apparent that serious rock stars and fans viewed them as a joke. For the time being, however, this was hardly an issue. *Look At Us* was a huge success on both sides of the Atlantic.

It was during this first wave of success that Cher's father, John Sarkisan, reappeared, asking for a position within the Sonny & Cher organization. Bono, Greene, and Stone had a deep-seated suspicion of him, but in a thinly veiled attempt to suppress tales of Sarkisan's life—which could have been potentially damaging—and keep him under close watch, it was decided that he could join as road manager.

C

In the meantime, there were other ventures to attend to. It was never going to be long before for an act as hot as Sonny & Cher got into the movies. Elvis Presley's films had demonstrated how a star's fame could be spread worldwide onscreen in lieu of a tour, while in 1964, Richard Lester had redefined the genre of the film musical with *A Hard Day's Night*. As a vehicle for The Beatles, it showed how wit, storyline, and excitement could be effectively added to the spectacle.

Richard Lester created a credible masterpiece. Sonny & Cher's motion picture debut was not, by any stretch of the imagination, a credible masterpiece. It is, to say the very least, a slender vehicle that briefly showcases their talents amid a plethora of other acts. Directed by Maury Dexter, *Wild On The Beach* is in the style of the beach-party movies that proved so lucrative for American International Pictures (AIP) in the sixties. The studios found they had a cash cow in their hands with these lightweight entertainment films starring the likes of Frankie Avalon and Annette Funicello.

The first of these surprise hits was the 1963 film *Beach Party*, in which the action is centered on a beach, with various teen melodramas taking place and the protagonists breaking into song every few minutes. Soon AIP was cranking out sequels, with other studios keen to get in on the act. By 1965, the genre had reached its apogee.

Although it is possibly the only beach film shot in black-and-white, *Wild On The Beach* is a competent bauble of the era. Dexter, a former actor, had cut his directing teeth on shocky B-movies such as *The Day Mars Invaded Earth* and *Police Nurse* before dipping his toe in the teen ocean with 1964's *Surf Party*.

Funded by prolific Hollywood producer Robert Lippert's Lippert Pictures Inc, *Wild On The Beach* stars Frankie Randall and Sherry Jackson. When a student (Jackson) inherits a beach house, he decides to turn it into a girls' boarding home. Then, of course, the boys turn up, led by Randall, who states that he, too, has a claim on the property. Much mirth ensues as the girls try to mask the boys' arrival. Artists turn up to play as both girls and boys have scheduled a party on the same weekend. And, naturally, romance blossoms between the male and female leads.

Appearing alongside artists such as Sandy Nelson and Jackie & Gayle, and for just over two of the film's seventy-seven minutes, Sonny & Cher perform Sonny's classic 'It's Gonna Rain.' Backed by Colorado-based surf band The Astronauts—and with a low key "and now, here's Sonny & Cher" intro—the duo look uncomfortable as they begin their work, standing in front of the stage in the beach house singing to frankly uptight-looking students in their buttoned-down plaid shirts. At best, there is some dancing in the seats. Cher looks beautiful in her white T-shirt and Sonny does his customarily awkward dancing. And then they are gone.

No one would make any great claims for the film, yet it has an élan absent from similar films of the genre. The *New York Times* would later offer the backhanded compliment that the film is "so third-rate and low-budget that an unintentional sense of 'realism' creeps into it"; the *NME Guide To Rock Cinema* describes it as a "lightweight teen farce."

Maury Dexter went on to become one of the leading directors on the long-running US television show *The Little House On The Prairie*. Sonny & Cher, who clearly had bigger cinematic ambitions in their sights, could have done a whole lot worse than appear—albeit briefly—in this enjoyable, freak-beat relic.

By the end of 1965, the duo's success was guaranteed. Their name was such that they were even invited to play a small function for John Kennedy's widow, Jacqueline, that September. The party was held at New York's Waldorf-Astoria Towers. The duo dressed in their trademark bell-bottoms and caveman chic for what would be a performance in front of a grand total of eighteen people. Stone saw it as a perfect opportunity to gain maximum publicity. It was clearly an opportunity for the elite to gawp at the latest pop sensation, and Sonny & Cher rose to the challenge.

"We were really honored," Sonny told the *NME*. "I flew all my musicians out there. Cher and I performed in this small front room. Mrs Kennedy asked us to repeat our performance, which we did, and then she talked to both Cher and myself. She said that I looked 'rather Shakespearian.' Then she went over and talked to my musicians." Cher on the other hand demonstrated her youth by being upset that she was not invited to have dinner with Kennedy but merely to meet her afterward. That said, the function had a very positive end result: it was their introduction to high society, and Jackie Kennedy loved the performance.

At the party, Cher met fashion doyen Diana Vreeland, who was captivated by the singer's appearance, putting her hand on top of Cher's head and exclaiming: "My dear, you're *lovely*. You have a pointed head." Vreeland also introduced Cher to Richard Avedon, who photographed her for *Vogue* magazine. *Newsweek* reported the evening with disdain: "The only way to distinguish man from wife was that Sonny's hair ended at his shoulders, and Cher's fell to her waist."

The year 1965 had been remarkably kind to Sonny & Cher. Aside from a transatlantic chart-topping single and a US top-three album, Cher's solo career had taken off as well. When the duo played lived, hysteria ensued. When they appeared at San Francisco's Cow Palace, they had to be escorted out of the building by the police.

"We had about a hundred policemen escorting us away from the stadium, and suddenly the kids spotted us," Sonny said. "They jumped on the car, under the car, and into the car! I thought we'd get buried alive! But we made it out." The duo suddenly had everything they had wished for. As Joseph Murrells notes in his *Book Of Golden Discs*, *Look At Us* alone put "the husband-and-wife team into the big money class—around $3,000,000 gross for 1965. In 1964, their income was $3,000."

CHAPTER 3
Catch The Wind

Sonny had big plans for Cher as a solo artist and to run her career parallel with that of the duo. In the midst of all the Caesar & Cleo/Sonny & Cher contract shenanigans at Reprise and Atlantic, he got her to sign a solo deal with Liberty Records' Imperial imprint in late 1964.

Cher's first single, after the Bonnie Jo Mason debacle, was 'Dream Baby,' which was written and produced by Sonny and came out in November 1964, credited to 'Cherilyn.' Arguably Bono's second most obvious homage to Phil Spector (after 'I Got You Babe'), it was a light piece of fluff that demonstrates how the world would turn during the making of *All I Really Want To Do*. Despite receiving some favorable press and local airplay, the single was not a hit. An homage to the girl-group sound, it jarred with the rest of the pop-folk material on *All I Really Want To Do*.

Undeterred by the single's failure to chart, Bono went ahead with sessions for Cher's first album, which began at Gold Star Studios in February 1965 and continued through the spring. The album was again recorded with Bono's superb team of session players led by arranger Harold Battiste and including many of the larger team with whom Bono had worked at Phil Spector sessions.

As the sessions progressed, it became apparent that Bob Dylan's 'All I Really Want To Do' should be the track to lead the album. An ironic love song about his relationship with Suze Rotolo, it had recently appeared as the opening track on his fourth album, *Another Side Of Bob Dylan*.

Cher's take on 'All I Really Want To Do' was released as a single in May 1965 and immediately went into a chart tussle with another version of the same song by The Byrds, who had just become pop sensations with their cover of another Dylan song, 'Mr Tambourine Man.' Sonny and Cher used to see The Byrds play at It's Boss, one of the prime hangouts on the mid-sixties Sunset Strip (and also, in its former incarnation as Ciro's, the place where Humphrey Bogart would drink and dine). It was here that they got to know The Byrds, and discovered their absolutely coincidental choice of the same song to release as a single.

With the experience of 'Ringo, I Love You' and 'Dream Baby' still fresh in her mind, Cher thought about "not releasing our version, because we didn't want to get creamed—the more bad singles you put out, the less DJs want to play your next song. But Sonny decided we should take the chance."

It was a chance worth taking. There were rumors of a little skullduggery on Bono's part—that he had taped some of The Byrds' club performances and then recreated them for Cher's arrangement of the song—but this was never proven. Cher would later stress that they were all friends, and that she and Bono had recorded the song with no prior knowledge of The Byrds' version.

The controversy drew attention to both records, and both climbed the charts. Although Byrds producer Terry Melcher had told Bono that The Byrds' version would "bury" theirs, Cher's raced up the chart, reaching number fifteen on *Billboard*, while The Byrds stalled at number forty. (In the UK, The Byrds won out: their version hit number four, while Cher's merely reached number nine.)

"We loved the Cher version," Roger McGuinn told the LA music paper *KRLA Beat*. "We just love the song, period. We didn't want a hassle. So we just turned our record over."

"We don't know where the row started," Cher added in the same article. "We know the Byrds dig us and we certainly dig them. There's room at the top for everyone." It was another pop storm in a teacup, but one that did neither side any damage.

Cher would become an ardent performer of Dylan's material throughout the rest of the decade. Although some would suggest that he was less than happy with her version of 'All I Really Want To Do,' she herself suggests otherwise. In her autobiography, she recalls being in a New York studio later the same year when "the freight elevator came up, and its wood-slat doors opened, [and] out stepped Bob Dylan. It was the first time we'd met. He told me he liked what I'd done with 'All I Really Want To Do,' which made me feel like floating away … I Just sat there with my jaw hanging open. Bob Fucking Dylan."

All I Really Want To Do is an honest, sincere, personal album with an individual flair that's not necessarily present on *Look At Us*. There are three songs by Bono, as well as a cut-and-paste of the best writing of the day, decidedly folk in its approach. The title track is supported by two more Bob Dylan tunes: a spirited 'Blowin' In The Wind' and a sweet 'Don't Think Twice, It's Alright.' The album also features recordings of Jackie DeShannon's 'Come Stay With Me' and Pete Seegar's 'The Bells Of Rhymney.' There is something strange and disconcerting hearing Cher sing Welsh place-names such as Merthyr, Blaenau, and Swansea, yet she carries it off with aplomb.

All I Really Want To Do would sound contemporary, too, to British ears. It contains Cher's version of Chris Andrews' 'Girl Don't Come,' a recent number one hit for Sandie Shaw, as well as Ray Davies' delicate Kinks masterpiece 'I Go To Sleep' (later a hit for The Pretenders). There's also her cover of 'Needles And Pins,' the song that Sonny co-wrote with Jack Nitzsche for Jackie DeShannon in 1963, and which The Searchers had since taken to the top of the UK charts. The album almost had a 'greatest hits' feel to it.

The other original on the album, 'See See Rider,' saw Bono—here co-writing with managers Brian Stone and Charlie Greene—update the old Ma Reiney blues standard. On this, the album's only truly up-tempo track, Cher sounds convincing as she sputters outs mildly angst-ridden lyrics about her and Sonny's recent barring from the Hilton Hotel in London ("I'm going to the Hilton, but I know I won't get in"), although the next line suggests that they would still be the Hilton's friend. With Dylan-like harmonica blaring away, the song is proof of Cher's ability to rock out—something that would not always be apparent from the songs she sang in the later sixties.

Decades after its release, *All I Really Want To Do* still sounds fresh and fun. Although Cher sounds tentative at times, she has conviction and passion. It may not make any great all-time best-of lists, but it is a pleasing, diverting, listen, and undoubtedly Cher's finest solo album of the sixties. Allmusic.com is spot-on with its suggestion that "Cher isn't the most subtle singer, but she sounds young and full of life on these tracks, like she really believes in what she is singing." This, coupled with the superb playing skills of musicians such as Battiste, Mike Post, Jeff Kaplan, and Barney Kessell, made it a more than credible release. One of the album's defining sounds is the harpsichord work of Michel Rubini and Bill Marx. The arrangements are fastidious, if somewhat overwrought at times—just like Bono's old tutor, Phil Spector.

All I Really Want To Do was released on October 16 1965 with a Robert A. Young photograph of a smiling Cher on the cover. With *Look At Us* already flying high in both the US and UK charts, this new album joined it in the top twenty on both sides of the Atlantic. A series of happy coincides made it look as if there had been a master plan to make the duo overnight superstars.

It was, of course, Sonny Bono who compiled the album's liner notes. "Usually, when you write liner notes for the back of an album, everyone tries to get someone else to say how great the artist is," he wrote. "In this case, the artist is my wife, and naturally I think she is great, but that is not what I wanted to say to you. I want to say that she feels like I do, that we owe a lot of things to you, and she is going to try and say them in this album for you more than for us. We both love you."

This love was apparent, as was the fact that the Sonny & Cher brand was gathering considerable strength. Their image and choice of material ensured that, be it good or bad, everyone had an opinion on them.

C

The first full-length product to be released after Sonny & Cher hit the big time was Cher's second album for Imperial, *The Sonny Side Of Cher*, released in February 1966. Since releasing *Look At Us* and *All I Really Want To Do*, the duo had toured the USA and the UK and cut enough material for another raft of releases.

Mainly utilizing Gold Star studios and their established team of musicians, the first fruits of these sessions was Cher's single 'Where Do You Go.' It was another Bono classic, marking him out as one of the best kitchen-sink dramatists of the sixties. While others were dealing with love, politics, and cosmic issues, Bono focused on matters that were right under many Americans noses. The song tackles loneliness and despair, alienation from parents, and the false hope of religion. Its very ordinariness and skewed domesticity marked it out as a cut above a lot of the other material around at that point. In fact, it was probably *too* sophisticated, as it only reached number twenty-five in the US charts.

The Sonny Side Of Cher itself was almost an identikit of Cher's first album—in this case, just two Bono originals and ten covers. This time, there's more of a show-tune/easy-listening bias than the strict-folk pop diet of *All I Really Want To Do*. Once again, it's the sound of Cher being guided totally by Bono.

Taking his lead from 'Sing C'est La Vie' on *Look At Us*, Bono crafted a style for Cher that would become her calling card for the next decade. The album opens with the ornate, overwrought, and just a little fussy baroque balladry of 'Bang Bang (My Baby Shot Me Down).' It's a marvelous psychodrama that conflates playground antics with the hurts of later life—and Cher's best vocal performance to date.

It would also prove to be one of Bono's most durable writing credits, with Nancy Sinatra, Petula Clark, and Stevie Wonder all covering the song in 1966. Vanilla Fudge did a grandiose, orchestrated heavy-metal version of the song in 1967, while The Bonzo Dog Band performed a skittish take on it in 1968. 'Bang Bang (My Baby Shot Me Down)' reached number two in the US charts—Cher's highest-charting solo hit until 'Gypsys Tramps & Thieves'—and captured her perfectly at her girl-woman best.

The rest of *The Sonny Side Of Cher* is moderately schizophrenic, better suited to taking her into a Las Vegas lounge than off to Woodstock. 'Our Day Will Come' is a frantic bossa nova; 'Ol' Man River' is simply overdone.

The album came complete with all the puff of a sixties liner note written by Richard Oliver. "This album has feeling," he declares; "its songs are special. Special not only because they are sung by Cher. She hopes there is something special here for you. You are special to her, and this is her way of telling you." This may have been the standard flimflam of the sixties LP, but it did underline the personal relationship that many fans felt they had with Cher—to the point where she actually received a death threat from one over-exuberant follower.

On April 2 1966, Sonny & Cher performed one of the biggest shows of their career to date when they headlined a benefit concert for the Braille Institute Of America, organized in conjunction with radio station KHJ at the Hollywood Bowl. It boasted an impressive line-up, a snapshot of current West Coast mainstream (with a special guest performance from Donovan). Sharing the bill were The Mamas & The Papas, The Righteous Brothers, Otis Redding, Jan & Dean, The Modern Folk Quintet, The Knickerbockers, and The Turtles.

Before the show, Charlie Greene and Brian Stone received a letter saying that a fan wanted to kidnap or perhaps even shoot Cher onstage. "I had received many letters like hers from the beginning," Cher later wrote. "But this time our managers got really nervous." Taking no chances with their precious charges, Greene and Stone arranged for Sonny and Cher to arrive at the show in a Brinks armored truck. Nothing happened, but it was all very good for publicity.

"The concert went without a hitch, except that Jan & Dean acted like brats," Cher recalled. "In spite of all the minor annoyances, it was a memorable night." It was the biggest night of Cher's life to date, and she was just nineteen years old. In keeping with the era, the shows the duo played were often drowned out by screaming fans—something that both delighted and unsettled Cher. "I was terrified of the crowd," she later said. "When we were doing the rock'n'roll shows and stuff like that, you never got to finish a song. You took the money and ran like hell."

C

The year 1966 was one of consolidation and change. With *The Sonny Side Of Cher* following *Look At Us* into the charts, it was time for another Sonny & Cher album. Released in May 1966, three months after *Sonny Side* and nine months after their debut, *The Wondrous World Of Sonny & Cher* is arguably their greatest sustained work.

The duo's profile had been maintained by the hit single 'Laugh At Me,' which gave Sonny a taste of solo success in 1965. Beginning with the lines "I never thought I'd cut a record by myself / But I want to say it for Cher / I want to say it for a lot of people," 'Laugh At Me' is an autobiographical account of reactions to Sonny's haircut and look, and specifically his eviction from Martoni's restaurant in Hollywood. After they had spent a considerable amount of money at the eatery over the years, the owners requested Sonny and Cher stop frequenting it as their appearance antagonized other diners.

With its plea for tolerance—in a highly derivative 'Like A Rolling Stone'-style setting—'Laugh At Me' struck a chord. Bono's delivery is heartfelt, particularly on the refrain of "Laugh at me, and I'll cry for you." The clanking tubular bell and fantastic coda mark the song out as something of a hidden classic in the Sonny & Cher catalogue.

Bono followed up 'Laugh At Me' with a second solo single, 'The Revolution Kind,' a moderately messy Spector-influenced confection. It's a mildly endearing claim for free speech, but is at once liberal and conservative—suggesting that open views are one thing, but that they don't make you one of "the revolution kind." It was the first sign of the innate conservatism within Bono that would soon see the duo fall from favor with the US record-buying public. But it was not a patch on the best material on *The Wondrous World Of Sonny & Cher*.

Once again a mixture of covers and originals, the album opens in dramatic fashion. The duo's version of George Gershwin's 'Summertime' is one of their best recordings. Cher really does grab the overheated languor of the song, and Sonny actually delivers an impassioned vocal.

The pair revisit the girl-group scene for a fantastic romp through The Exciters' 'Tell Him,' while there are several songs with connections to Sonny's plugging days: an emotional reading of Sam Cooke's 'Bring It On Home To Me,' Don and Dewey's 'I'm Leaving It All Up To You,' and a sprightly take on Johnny Otis' 'So Fine.' There is a nod to the British scene with a dreamy cover of The Kinks' 'Set Me Free' and a beautiful version of The Zombies' 'Leave Me Be,' recast here as a soul track, with a marvelous, nonchalant vocal delivery by Sonny and Cher.

They ramp up their ever-present theatrical side on their reading of Carl Sigman, Pierre Delanoe, and Gilbert Becaud's 'What Now My Love.' This became the album's second single, reaching number fourteen in the USA and number thirteen in the UK. Written in 1961 and originally entitled 'Et Maintenant,' the song has been covered by many artists, including Ben E.

King and Herb Alpert, but Sonny & Cher's was the only one of the several versions of the song to chart highly on both sides of the Atlantic.

The three Bono originals—'But You're Mine,' 'I Look For You,' and his solo 'Laugh At Me'—all carry weight. 'But You're Mine' was the first single drawn from the album. It was something of a rewrite of 'I Got You Babe'— another song that pitches Sonny & Cher as loved-up outsiders taking on the conventions of society. It shows them as a couple of hippie kids who have a "great thing going ... that's going to keep right on growing." Fundamentally, they won't be the ones to lose the fight. The people who stop and stare and judge are missing the point: this is a couple bonded by love. 'But You're Mine' has a great sound and feel: it's light and upbeat, with an uplifting payout from its two-and-a-half minutes. The public thought so too: it reached number fifteen in the USA and number seventeen in the UK.

Gratitude seemed very much the order of the day. When *The Wondrous World Of Sonny & Cher* was released it came with a 'thank you' letter from the pair to their fans. "There are so many things to thank you for," they wrote, "so many different things, that we would have to go on forever naming them—cakes that fans have baked us, dolls that they have given us, poems, rings, or anything that they feel is close to them and that they want us to have. This is the only way we can tell you we appreciate you for your kindness."

Jerry Schaztburg's cover photo of the duo highlights their easy informality and helped to define their character. Cuban-heeled Sonny looks suitably superior in his black-and-red striped T-shirt; Cher looks relaxed and informally glamorous in her sleeveless blue top. *The Wondrous World Of Sonny & Cher* is the best recording the duo would ever release. It reached number thirty-four on the US charts and number fifteen in the UK, where it remained on the listings for seven weeks in May and June. Sonny & Cher were hot property.

C

In May 1966, with *The Wondrous World Of Sonny & Cher* riding high in the charts, Cher turned twenty. It was a busy year, with filming, touring, and recording all high priorities. There was also a change in their management:

Charlie Greene and Brian Stone, the showmen and Bono's willing accomplices, had been handsomely paid off at the start of the year, having irked Sonny somewhat as a result of their activities with their other act, Buffalo Springfield, the white-hot new band featuring Neil Young and Stephen Stills.

It all came to a head when the managerial duo got more space in an article on rock'n'roll for *Life* magazine than Sonny & Cher. "You're supposed to be behind the scenes," Sonny reportedly told them. "We're the stars!" Greene and Stone had also questioned Bono's attitude as a "hotshot producer" on the movie that he and Cher were shooting, *Good Times.*

Greene and Stone maintained some publishing royalties but all other ties to the duo were severed. They went on to concentrate on Buffalo Springfield and later had great success with Iron Butterfly. Meanwhile, Sonny brought in former Greene and Stone employee Joe DeCarlo to look after his and Cher's affairs.

On August 26 1966, Sonny & Cher played their first major UK concert at the Astoria in London's Finsbury Park, topping a bill that included Sharon Tandy, Fleur De Lys, and The VIPs. While they were in Europe, they also went to meet the Pope—an event for which Cher was persuaded to wear a dress.

Released on Imperial in October 1966, *Chér* was her third solo album in the space of 18 months. It is also one of her best. Recorded once again at Gold Star, it contains only one Bono original: 'Something In The Air,' a stately, majestic number in a slow tempo. As always, there's a pinch of autobiography: a daughter falling in love and seeking independence; twitching curtains and neighbors talking about what a nice girl she "used to be." With a jaunty, Spector-esque middle-eight that adopts a waltz tempo as Cher lists the reactions of her family, 'Something In The Air' is another song that only Sonny Bono could have written. The coda is pure girl-group glitz.

On the covers here, Cher excels. Her version of Burt Bacharach and Hal David's 'Alfie,' which was used in the US version of the Michael Caine film, is masterful, while her reading of Bobby Hebb's 'Sunny' is one of the best versions of a well-covered song. Most successful is her strident take on Carole King and Gerry Goffin's 'Will You Love Me Tomorrow,' with Bono's arrangement one of the best on record. Cher's honest vocal performance leads into a sweet and tender version of Buffy Saint Marie's 'Until It's Time For You To Go.'

On side two, Cher tackles Donovan's 'Catch The Wind,' having earlier performed with him at the Hollywood Bowl in 1966. Folk songs take hold as the album progresses. Paul Simon's 'Homeward Bound' and the obligatory Dylan cover, 'I Want You,' play the album out on a strong note. It's a pity that the duo would later mark themselves out as such conservatives—this could have been one of the finest protest albums of the era.

Sonny takes up liner note duties again. "Now, at the risk of sounding prejudiced, I must add that I am especially proud of Cher," he writes. "For each song on this album, I asked her to pour out her heart and soul—she did." With its classic cover shot of Cher cradling her face in her hands, representing millions of wistful sixties girls, *Chér* marked the end of an incredibly fertile period. The album reached number fifty-nine in the US charts and was soon certified gold.

Meanwhile, another less obvious relationship had been established. Sonny and Cher met Andy Warhol and the Factory crowd at this time, right at the height of the success of Warhol's Exploding Plastic Inevitable revue. Although she and Sonny did not exactly fit with the crowd, Cher enjoyed hanging out with Baby Jane Holzer, Edie Sedgwick, and Warhol because, she later noted, "the parties made good conversation for a year."

C

In Case You're In Love was Sonny & Cher's third album. By 1967, their format was struck: a selection of originals, a smattering of covers; a bright, sunny alternative to the growing hippie music phenomenon sweeping the country. The artwork showed them in relaxed form, by a lakeside, happy with themselves.

Produced by Bono and again recorded with Harold Battiste's crack team of players—including the likes of a young Dr John on piano, Barney Kessel on guitar, and Carol Kaye on bass—the album is a skillful shop-window of the duo's talents. Although Bono was finding it hard to continually deliver original material, his songs here are not in any way shabby.

Lead track 'The Beat Goes On' would become a huge success on both sides of the Atlantic, its enormous popularity proving that Bono could step out of the shadows of 'I Got You Babe.' The marching, loping groove is a triumph, while the singers' world-weary commentary briefly put them in step with the hippie audience.

The stop-start ethnic folk track 'Little Man' became one of the duo's greatest hits in Europe. It reached number one in Norway, Sweden, and Belgium, and it is little wonder as it sounds like something you would have heard on the Eurovision Song Contest—not unlike Sandie Shaw's fairground-influenced 'Puppet On A String.'

'Living For You' is a Sonny Bono classic that captures the surprise of love. Just the right side of hippie-dippy, it is as bright and airy as a cool breeze on a summer's day—which makes it all the more astounding that he could then come up with 'Podunk,' which explores the awful vaudeville sound that had become *de rigueur* on albums of the time. Running to just 2:53, it is like a whole album of Ringo-sung Beatles tunes or Mickey Dolenz/Davy Jones show tunes for The Monkees. That said, this ragtime influence was big business. You only have to look at Esther & Abi Ofarim's 'Cinderella Rockefeller' to see that it was anything but a bum commercial steer. Cher gets to impersonate Mae West and call her husband "big nose." All in all, the song gave much ammunition to those who hated this sort of lightweight shtick.

Those who wanted something more straightforward could enjoy Cher's passionate reading of the Leiber & Stoller classic 'Stand By Me.' Taking the song at a faster pace than the Ben E. King version, Battiste's arrangement is suitably epic. Bono finally joins in toward the end, and for once the record transcends its surroundings. Also successful is Bono's version of Tim Hardin's 'Misty Roses' and Cher's singsong take on Gayle Garnett's 'We'll Sing In The Sunshine.' Elsewhere, Bono's version of Bob Lind's 'Cheryl's Going Home'—sung over Battiste's high-powered, horn-driven arrangement—is pretty exciting.

The influence of Dylan is again over-apparent on 'Plastic Man,' the single released at the same time as the album but not included on it. Sung in Bono's best faux-Zimmerman style (and with a bridge that leans heavily on The

Beatles' 'Rain'), it is a tedious anti-drug paean that highlights the schism Sonny & Cher set about creating in their audience—a case of biting the hand that feeds on a grand scale. When the duo appeared in an anti-marijuana film around the same time, they suddenly found doors closing in their faces. "That was our death sentence," Cher later wrote. "We were out of touch with our peers, totally disconnected."

In Case You're In Love was released in March 1967 and reached number forty-five on the US charts. Three singles were drawn from the album—'The Beat Goes On,' Little Man,' and 'Living For You'—and in one sense it remains their most complete work. Cher is on good form, Sonny has stopped aping Bob Dylan to an embarrassing degree, and Battiste's arrangements are assured. It would be the last time the duo would register so high on pop's radar.

CHAPTER 4
Good Times

By now, Sonny and Cher were living the Hollywood life. On January 1 1967, they became the first pop stars to ride a float during Pasadena's New Year's Day Rose Bowl Parade. Given that Sonny wrote the majority of their hits and was a moderately astute businessman, the duo had more money than most of their pop-star peers.

The hippie style was good for business, but by the end of 1966 they had moved out of their Encino pad and into a substantial house in Bel Air, purchased from the actor Tony Curtis. When Cher was questioned about the move, she replied: "People ask why you need anything larger than twenty-two rooms. You don't need any more than a living room, kitchen, bedroom, and bathroom. But what you *want* is something else again."

Living in a house that was once owned by a film star, Sonny was galvanized by the idea of seeing the duo make more appearances on the big and small screens. He and Cher had enjoyed their appearance in *Wild On The Beach* and were delighted when asked to appear in the cult television hit *The Man From U.N.C.L.E.* after Sonny had approached the series' producer, Boris Ingster.

The Man From U.N.C.L.E. starred Robert Vaughn as American agent Napoleon Solo with British heartthrob actor David McCallum as Russian agent Iilya Kuryakin, who work together for the United Network Command For Law & Enforcement (U.N.C.L.E.). Partly devised by Ian Fleming, the show first aired in September 1964 and rode a wave of James Bond-inspired popularity. It chimed perfectly with the space-age progress and cold-war paranoia of the mid sixties and was as achingly modern as could be.

In its first season, *The Man From U.N.C.L.E.* was a huge success and spawned a great deal of imitators. By the time Sonny and Cher got their chance to appear on the series, however, this US-Bond spoof was beginning to run out of steam. Although it had started off—like the Bond films themselves—as a slightly arch take on the world of espionage, by the time of the third series it had degenerated into broad, slapstick comedy, inspired by the success of the *Batman* TV show, which had first aired in 1966.

Sonny and Cher appear in the eighty-fourth episode of the show, 'The Hot Number Affair,' which was written specifically for them by the team of Joseph and Carol Cavanaugh. Originally entitled 'The Fashion House Affair,' it was filmed over four days in January 1967 under the watchful eye of veteran Hollywood director George Waggner.

The hokum-rich plot involves Solo and Kuryakin needing to find a brightly colored garment which has a secret code woven into the pattern of the fabric. Cher plays a clothing-store model, Ramona, while Sonny plays the pattern-cutter, Jerry, who has a crush on her. Ramona cannot remember where she has put the garment.

And that is about it. Sonny & Cher do not get to sing, although 'I Got You Babe' and 'The Beat Goes On' play in the background. The duo gamely struggle with their wooden dialogue. Sonny does a fairly convincing job of the scant material he has to work with; he was accidentally punched in the face during a fight sequence with David McCallum.

'The Hot Number Affair' aired on March 10 1967, at a time when the show's popularity was plummeting. The reviews were not overly complimentary. The exhaustive *Man From U.N.C.L.E.* online database suggests that, "even by third-season standards, this episode is considered by many fans as one of the less memorable ones." This second onscreen appearance did, however, bolster Sonny's confidence in *Good Times*, the movie he had been working on for the best part of a year.

By 1967, Sonny & Cher were big business, and expectations were running high for the film. Sonny, ever the entrepreneur, believed that now was the time for them to go into movies, And when Elvis Presley's manager, Colonel Tom Parker, told Charlie Greene that motion pictures would be a good step for the duo, Sonny had the validation he needed.

Released in May 1967, *Good Times* bore the names of two future Academy Award winners: director William 'Billy' Friedkin and actress Cher. Although it showed nothing of the latent potential within, the film—seriously flawed as it is—is more than a mere curio.

Prior to working with Sonny and Cher, Friedkin had made the low-budget documentary *The People Vs. Paul Crump*, which was shown at the San Francisco Film Festival. He had subsequently signed a deal with David Wolper Productions and gained further experience directing an edition of *The Alfred Hitchcock Hour* in 1965. Full of ideas, he was one of the new breed of directors clearly on a mission to shake up Hollywood. Shortly after the release of *Good Times*, he told *Variety*: "The plotted film is on the way out and is no longer of interest to a serious director ... a new theater audience, I'm told, is under thirty and largely interested in an abstract experience. ... I defy anyone to tell me what *Blow-Up*, *Juliet Of The Spirits*, *La Guerre Est Finie*, and the Beatles film are about."

Good Times was clearly not in the league of those films, however abstract they may be. But what it did show was that Friedkin's willingness to experiment chimed perfectly with Sonny's views about turning the film industry on its head. "He had seen a couple of my documentaries and was impressed by them," Friedkin later explained. "We met and liked each other immediately. I thought he was a terrific songwriter and that he was saying things that were very close to young people. I felt we could express visually some of the things he and Cher expressed in their music."

The film is *very* sixties, mired in the knowing, modernist directing style of Richard Lester while also paying homage to the phenomenon of The Monkees. But Friedkin saw it as more than that. This, he said, would mark the start of the dance-craze/beach-party cycle of filmmaking. "It will not be like *A Hard Day's Night*. That was more like a camera exercise. You never got to know The Beatles themselves. You'll get to know Sonny and Cher as a result of this film."

Originally entitled *I Got You Babe*, then *Bang Bang*, and finally *New Times, Happy Times*, *Good Times* set out to provide a comedic insight to the zany, loved-up world of Sonny & Cher. The pair owned thirty-three percent of the film, while rights were immediately sold to television.

"A movie about a movie that was never made," in the words of biographer J. Randy Taraborrelli, *Good Times* started shooting on January 24 1966 at Sonny and Cher's home in Encino, California. Working with writer Nicholas Hyams and Friedkin, they realized that no matter how hard they tried they could not come up with a storyline. Then they began to wonder what would happen if they didn't actually have a storyline at all. The fact that Cher wanted little to do with it gave them another idea: her real life indifference to the film would be how she would come across nineties.

"It was Billy's first feature film," Cher later wrote. "He was twenty-nine years old and out of his mind with enthusiasm. He always talked with his hands up in the air—about everything. And with him and Son together, they were just too much for me! I couldn't beat them, so I had to join them."

The film took a couple of months to shoot, following about eight months of pre-planning. "It took too much of Sonny's time," Cher continued. "I got told to go to my bedroom while he and Billy Friedkin sat until two in the morning figuring out what they would do the next day." Future film director Peter Bogdanovich observed the couple at work in an article for the *Saturday Evening Post*, and described Cher wondering why they couldn't make a "Beatles movie," to which Sonny replied: "'cause I don't want a Beatles movie." They clearly had very different ideas.

In the end, the film followed the course the duo's TV show would take a few years later: a selection of unconnected sketches brought together by the plot device of the duo looking at and subsequently rejecting plots for an upcoming movie. It features a lot of Sonny but not a great deal of Cher. Sonny wishes to expand into movies; Cher wants nothing to do with the plan at first but is eventually persuaded. The script offered to them is woeful, however, so Sonny comes up with his own—providing an opportunity for the duo to play out and parody some classic Hollywood scenarios.

The style is light and superficial—Brechtian almost. These are characters showing you how they play characters, rather than jumping in and embracing the tale. We go to the Wild West to give Sonny an opportunity to be a sheriff. We go to the jungle so that he can be a tribal king. Later on, he gets to live out his dream of being a private eye.

George Sanders was chosen to play the film's villain. A quintessentially English character actor, Sanders would soon be immortalized as Sheere Khan in the Walt Disney classic *The Jungle Book*. He plays the part with all the arch ennui for which he was already well known, appearing first stately and then bored to tears by the whole thing. He was supportive of both Sonny and Cher and seemed to be enjoying dressing up. "He must have needed the money," Cher later said, "because he was too great an actor to be doing this silly role."

Although the film had a modestly sized budget, the shoot ran over, so Bono and Friedkin opted for guerilla-style filming, stealing footage when they could. It was clear that while Sonny was taking the film very seriously, Cher was merely waltzing through it.

The main theme of *Good Times* is the juxtaposition of Sonny and Cher's domestic idyll, worldview, and philosophy against that of authority: The Man. The theme of commoditization of the teenage phenomenon was not new in pop films; Cliff Richard had looked into it in 1959's *Expresso Bongo*, and The Beatles rail against old-school power in *A Hard Day's Night*. In the opening sequence of *Good Times*, exactly where they're at could not be made clearer. This is Sonny & Cher's world. We see them propped up against a tree, walking through fields; it is almost as if one of Cher's album covers has come to life. Cher wears bell-bottoms, Sonny looks bored; fringes are cut. A heavily orchestrated version of 'I Got You Babe' plays, intercut with footage of the duo's 1966 Hollywood Bowl concert, to establish them as business people of this new era. They walk, they laugh, they make music.

Throughout the following eighty-nine minutes, Cher seems largely bored and Sonny is wildly enthusiastic. Cher is too preoccupied with shopping— or simply being bored—to discuss business with the man. Sonny gets lost in an office block in a skit that's very of its time. (French director Jacques Tati did something similar around the time in *Playtime*, his parody of the impersonality of modern life.)

Eventually, Sonny turns up at Mordicus Enterprises. We first see George Sanders sitting impassively at an enormous desk, watching karate. When one man kills the other, he suggests that he'd like to hire the murderer, and then, looking at the corpse, asks one of his henchmen to "get rid of the debris." Mordicus is charming, however, and knows where money is to be made. "I do so enjoy people," he tells Sonny. "It's one of my few pleasures. That's why I take time out occasionally from my other activities to make motion pictures ... Business bores me, motion pictures excite me."

Mordicus, like so many bored businessmen with little time, becomes impatient when Sonny asks if he can have a hand in the creative process. He is then shown the promo of 'The Little Things,' which Sonny had written for the film. Sonny seems ready to dismiss his recent past. "That was just a variety show," he says.

Mordicus chucks down a script he has for the couple, clearly revived from the last time he offered it to another then-contemporary pop phenomenon. Sonny does not want to do it, and so begins his quest to come up with an alternative. When he returns to Cher, she is once again shown as something of a vacant dreamer, drawing on tables outside a pavement café, leaving Sonny to deal with the fallout.

The first of the three major sections of the film—the western skit—begins after Sonny & Cher encounter a boy on the street who fires his gun at them. Sanders turns up as Knife McBlade, the evil bandit who is pitched against Sonny's Irving Ringo, the sheriff of Broken Elbow, Nebraska. It wouldn't be so bad if Sonny's simpleton characters were slightly more believable. The sight gags of a jukebox in the western saloon and the spoof western standoffs show the kind of satire Friedkin was attempting.

Cher appears from the crowd and encourages Sonny to sing, leading us into the film's title sequence: a fabulous cancan set piece of singing and swinging that owes a considerable debt to the golden age of Hollywood. The fight sequence between Sonny and Sanders is staged beautifully, with Sonny's flared bellbottoms, and all the bullets falling out of the gun—The Man once again trying to get him. As Sonny is about to be slaughtered, he snaps back into the street with the kid and his gun.

Mordicus's hoodlums demand Sonny and Cher's presence. At his office, scriptwriter Leslie Garth (played by Lennie Weinrib) goes through *Rags To Riches*, the script he has written for them. He then effectively tells the real-life story of Sonny and Cher. Mordicus falls asleep. "The story might be great for somebody else," Sonny exclaims, "but it's something we couldn't do." It is full of knowing in-jokes. "I'm not going to be a poverty stricken—whatever-it-is I'm supposed to be," Cher sighs. Sonny comforts her: "Would I ever let them do that to us?"

Sonny is given the challenge of coming up with a new plot in ten days. Launching into an impassioned version of 'Trust Me,' he is shown to be the Svengali he is supposed to be. Then, on a film set, he and Cher then pretend to be sea captains and clowns, magicians and Snow White. It is a huge exercise in playing in the dressing up box, taking its lead from *Singin' In The Rain*'s stripping away of the magic of motion pictures.

The centerpiece of *Good Times* is the jungle sequence, filmed at the Africa USA safari park in Soledad Canyon, Los Angeles. Sonny is Jungle Morry, a parody of Tarzan. But, as in The Flintstones' Bedrock, all the sixties mod cons have been transported back to the jungle. There is an 'elephant wash' and an elevator to Sonny and Cher's tree house—a desirable crash-pad reminiscent of The Monkees' beach house. There is a lovely in-joke when Sonny turns on the television to see an uncredited Micky Dolenz playing a Tarzan parody as Jungle Gino, sending up his previous role in the children's television show *Circus Boy* and the contemporaneous popularity of The Monkees.

There is an amusing scene with chimps playing craps, while Sonny is shown playing checkers with Pizza The Monkey. Sonny speaks to his onscreen son and gives him a lecture about wearing his hair short—as ever, the gags are signposted to the point of oblivion. Sanders appears again and gets to wear another moustache as a bounty hunter who comes to steal ivory from the elephant's graveyard. Jungle Morry tries his jungle call to round up the animals to help him, but not one comes.

As a chase between Sonny and Sanders's men ensues, the viewer becomes acutely aware that they haven't seen Cher for a good five minutes. Although she has just slightly more than nothing to do in the film, you then realize you really rather miss her. Sonny ends up in quicksand, being licked by a tiger, and then we're back in modern times; it has all been a dream. As Sonny drives away on his motorbike, a wan Cher sings 'Don't Talk To Strangers, Baby' while walking through scrubland in bell-bottoms and a crop top. The song is intercut with footage of Sonny cooking Italian food and riding his bike.

In the film's final act, Sonny thinks about being a detective—and, presto, he becomes Johnny Pizzicato PI. The sequence starts a great recurring gag:

"It was 8:15, 8:20, 8:40—with a cheap watch you just can't tell." Cher bursts in as the gangster's moll, speaking hurriedly; Sonny gets her to quiet down by squashing a grapefruit in her face (a parody of James Cagney and Mae Clarke's altercation in the 1931 gangster classic *The Public Enemy*).

Cher hides in the ladies room with three other girls to escape being chased by a gangster with a huge gun. Sight gags abound, such as when a wardrobe is thrown open to reveal ten identical raincoats. Johnny Pizzicato is trailed into the nightclub, Samantha's Place, where he upsets the tray of the cigarette girl in what seems today like a rather overt, unnecessary, and somewhat demeaning moment.

Cher's performance as nightclub signer and owner Samantha, however, is truly show-stopping. She sings one of Sonny's best numbers, 'I'm Gonna Love You,' at the bottom of a spiral staircase in a blonde wig that makes her look like Dusty Springfield. There is a good, knowing joke about the age difference between the two of them after she joins Johnny in his booth. We learn that Johnny was once in the police, but that politics led to him being kicked off the force. After he has opened fire on the men trailing him, resulting in a huge body count, Cher quips: "Are you sure it was politics that got you kicked off the force?" The gangsters take him to their boss, Zarubian—none other than George Sanders. Zarubian tries to hypnotize Pizzicato, regressing him to childhood to blow up his uncle, the police commissioner. A mix-up with the devices means that Zarubian's headquarters blow up instead.

Sonny then realizes his dreams are the answer to the film. When he goes to tell Mordicus he needs more time, an extension is declined and he is informed that the duo must begin filming the next morning at 6:30, or they will have a "permanent case of laryngitis" and not be able to record or perform until their contract has been honored. Sonny offers to buy out the contract, but Mordicus refuses and says that it is simply all about making money.

Back at home, Sonny acts like a spoiled brat and repeats how little Cher knows about business before speeding off on his bike. In tears, she sings 'Just A Name.' With Cher in her green corduroy coat, it gives an opportunity to provide a resume of the film as the duo make up through the song and scene.

We return to the film studio. There is a stand off; Sonny announces that he'd rather end his career than take the man's shilling. As he storms off, scriptwriter Garth says: "We'll get the next teenage idol that comes down the pike, there's hundreds of them." Mordicus smiles, tells Garth not to be uncouth, and then smirks to himself as he throws the script into a trashcan. In admiring the young radical's spunk, maybe he has learned a thing or two about himself.

At the film's close, Sonny & Cher sing a soft, bucolic country/bossa-nova version of 'I Got You Babe,' emphasizing again the strength of the love they have for one another. As the camera pans out to silhouettes of them on the beach this brash, colorful film ends with a low-key ending. They have managed to retain the freedom of their hippie idyll, unencumbered by the constraints and restraints of the man.

C

Good Times opened in April 1967 in Austin, Texas, amid frantic scenes. The local governor proclaimed Austin would be known as Good Times for the day. Sonny and Cher went on a whistle-stop tour, playing live and promoting the film. Despite favorable reviews, the film did not catch on, but thanks to Sonny's acumen they did at least get all their production costs back.

You could tell how seriously Sonny took the project. For once, he composed all the music on the accompanying soundtrack album. 'Don't Talk To Strangers, Baby' was chosen as the lead single, but the album, released on Atco to coincide with the film, barely scraped the charts.

It has been said that the time Sonny and Cher spent making the film allowed other pop stars to take their place. While the film was being made, The Beach Boys recorded *Pet Sounds* and The Beatles made *Revolver*. The landscape of pop was changing forever.

In her autobiography, Cher summed up the situation perfectly: "Son and I had started the film when we were still really popular, but we took so long to make it, by the time it was ready to come out, Son and I were no longer popular. I was disappointed, but hadn't expected much. Son was hit much harder; he was really down for a while. He had put his heart into it."

Like all of these things, the film continued to bubble away over the years. While it is hardly a cult classic, it demands your attention in a way that something blatantly self-indulgent—like The Beatles' *Magical Mystery Tour*, which premiered later the same year—does not.

Good Times was finally released on DVD in 2004, the blurb on the cover picking out superlatives from contemporary reviews, including "happy" (*The Hollywood Reporter*), "affectionate" (*Los Angeles Times*) and "loveable" (*American Cinematique*). The *LA Herald Examiner* described the film as a "fanciful fun comedy" with "fun moments" and "a charming romance." It remains a bright shiny time capsule, and proved to be an ideal training ground for director William Friedkin, who within five years would be winning an Academy Award for *The French Connection*.

By mid 1967, however, Sonny and Cher had reached a crossroads. The albums released on Atco and Imperial were all doing OK, but it felt as if the duo had reached something of an impasse commercially. 'The Beat Goes On' had been a US top ten hit, but by the end of the year that seemed quite a while back.

Dinted somewhat by the indifference to both the film and the album *Good Times* and the schism created in their audience with the anti-drug 'Plastic Man,' Bono, in conjunction with manager DeCarlo and Ahmet Ertegun, felt that it would be a prudent time to release a career resume. And so *The Best Of Sonny & Cher* was issued in November 1967, with a cover that perfectly espouses the sixties.

Loading up with every hit bar the Reprise-owned 'Baby Don't Go,' *The Best Of* showed the wider world that there was much to enjoy from Sonny & Cher's back catalogue—and this was without any of Cher's solo material. Beginning with two relatively recent successes, 'The Beat Goes On' and 'What Now My Love,' and then following up with 'I Got You Babe,' the album's release was perfectly timed for the Thanksgiving/Christmas gift market. It also offered one new track, 'A Beautiful Story,' which became a minor hit.

The Best Of Sonny & Cher was a reminder of the duo's consummate professionalism, and the overall strength of Bono's songwriting. It placed them back in the US top thirty over Christmas, bettering the number seventy-three performance of *Good Times*. It was the last time Sonny & Cher would hit the upper reaches of the charts until 1971.

The whirlwind of success was beginning to take its toll. Cher suffered a miscarriage during 1967, and although she downplayed the pregnancy—countering all rumors by saying she had been pregnant for "twenty months now"—she was distraught to lose the baby, particularly now, at the height of her popularity.

Sonny, too, had been working at a phenomenal rate. In early November 1967 he released the solo album he had been working on with Donald Peake and Stan Ross on and off for the past year—just the thing for when the record store had sold out of its allocation of *The Best Of Sonny & Cher*.

Inner Views is a strange, cultish album, and was also the first to have a full-page ad taken out for it in the brand-new *Rolling Stone* magazine. It contains a mere five tracks, each delivered in Bono's drone-like vocals. In keeping with the times, the thirteen-minute 'I Just Sit There' alludes to drug culture and references The Beatles' 'A Day In the Life.' 'My Best Friend's Girl Is Out Of Sight' is the bright and sunny pop smash that never was, hampered by Bono's lack of vocal prowess.

'Pammie's On A Bummer,' long revered by hip DJs and later included on *The Trip*, the 2006 compilation album by British pop oddball Jarvis Cocker, is a cautionary tale of a girl who turns to prostitution and drugs. Nobody knows "where she's at," and after years of not knowing her metaphysical location, the matter has now become geographical, too.

This unusual, downbeat album was ignored by a rock audience unlikely to dally with a figure as square as Bono. It would have horrified the middle-of-the-road crowd that made up Sonny & Cher's audience; just as well, then, that nobody knew very much about it.

Sonny may have been grappling with his own demons, but he was still been able to write for and produce Cher's latest album, *With Love, Chér*. Its hit single, 'You Better Sit Down Kids,' proved that he was at his best behind the scenes.

Also released in November 1967, Cher's fourth solo album for Imperial found her not straying too far from the winning formula that she and Sonny had hit upon. It contains a smattering of Bono originals combined with a blend of the best contemporary songs and a handful of standards. In the cover photo, taken by Bono, Cher looks rather uncomfortable in white, not quite the wistful ingénue of her previous three LPs.

Produced by Bono and arranged by Harold Battiste, *With Love, Chér* is probably her best solo work of the sixties. It certainly sounds heartfelt. Of greatest note is her soulful rendition of Billy Roberts' 'Hey Joe,' a song that had reached stratospheric popularity at the start of 1967 as the debut single by The Jimi Hendrix Experience.

'Behind The Door' was the album's lead single. Written by prolific British tunesmith (and future 10cc founder) Graham Gouldman, it's a fine pop song and a musical signpost on the route to 'Gypsys Tramps & Thieves,' which at the time was still some four years away. The coda adds a direct, dramatic punch before the song reverts to its slightly sinister main theme. 'Behind The Door' reached number ninety-six on the US chart—not a stunning start for the lead single from Cher's first solo album for more than a year.

The gender-reversal melodrama 'You Better Sit Down Kids,' which tackles the rather uncommercial subject of divorce ("your mother is staying / I'm going away"), faired a great deal better. It is a really rather confusing musical tale, clearly written under the influence of Brian Wilson. In his biography of Cher, J. Randy Taraborelli calls it "one of the finest records Cher ever recorded, and certainly one of the finest productions Sonny Bono ever released ... his first truly original composition." He's absolutely right. Although a mere minnow compared with the Fab Four's whales, 'You Better Sit Down Kids' is as strange and creative in its own way as anything The Beatles produced during the fabled Summer Of Love. It reached the US top twenty in December 1967, making it Cher's last big solo hit of the sixties.

There is pathos throughout *With Love, Chér*. 'Mama (When My Dollies Have Babies)' takes on the embarrassment of a child's first questions about the facts of life and comes complete with a mawkish choir arrangement. It was as if Cher was setting herself up as Agony Aunt to her masses of teenage fans. That said, she was only just out of her teens herself. Bono's ability to combine his life's crises for his muse is something that has been subsequently underrated.

'But I Can't Love You More' is an affectionate billet-doux from Sonny to his partner—an intimate eavesdrop on the couple behind closed doors. Cher's version of Michel Legrand and Jacques Demy's 'I Will Wait For You,' from the 1964 film *The Umbrellas Of Cherbourg*, shows how masterful she could be with what was to become known as the show tune. It was as if this was the point that nations of young, confused men would realize their later sexuality.

With Love, Chér was her penultimate album for Imperial. It reached number forty-seven on the *Billboard* Hot 100 in early 1968. After one more album, Atlantic's Jerry Wexler would get his way, and Cher would join Sonny & Cher at Atco, where she would make some very different records.

If *With Love, Chér* was as groundbreaking as Cher would get in the late sixties, the follow-up, *Backstage,* smacked of a holding operation. And in many respects it was. It was around this time that Sonny Bono's songwriting mojo deserted him, leaving Cher to make an album of straight cover versions. As variable in quality as Bono's compositions might have been, his quirky (and occasionally derivative) originals gave Cher's albums a point of musical difference from her peers.

Recorded between late 1967 and early 1968 and released in July 1968, *Backstage* is a straight, credible album of other people's songs. It was produced by Bono and Harold Battiste, with the assistance of Denis Pregnolato, and set out to maintain Cher's place at the very forefront of the easy listening/folk/show tune crossover—the mini-genre Cher had perfected over the course of her previous solo albums. Although perhaps only her reading of 'The Impossible Dream' from the 1965 Broadway smash *Man Of La Mancha* comes close to true emotion, there is much here to enjoy, or at least engage with, for its curio value.

Among the standouts is a low-key bossa-nova version of 'Carnival,' the Brazilian Luiz Bonfá hit Americanized by Eddie Fisher some years previously. Doug Sahm's 'It All Adds Up Now' swings by sweetly; versions of Miriam Makeba's 'The Click Song' and 'I Wasn't Ready' by John Creaux (aka Dr John) show a willingness to experiment.

Having previously cut a successful version of 'Alfie,' Cher now sings another Bacharach & David selection, 'A House Is Not A Home.' She remains true to her folk audience with an early cover of Tim Hardin's beautiful 'Reason To Believe,' set here against breathtaking strings—an 'Eleanor Rigby'-esque backing that will seem unusual to listeners so used to Rod Stewart's version of the song. The album also includes a strangely dispassionate reading of Bob Dylan's 'Masters Of War' and an anemic attempt at The Lovin' Spoonful's 'Do You Believe In Magic,' with the original's wizardry and joie de vivre all but spirited away.

Backstage was Cher's last album for Imperial. With its pensive cover photo showing Cher in her dressing room, about to take the stage, the album is now seen—if is seen at all—as the end of an era; the album that came before *3614 Jackson Highway*. It was also roundly overlooked. Three singles were taken from the album—'The Click Song,' no doubt chosen to capitalize on the recent success of South African music in the USA; Trade Martin's 'Take Me For A Little While'; and 'Do You Believe In Magic'—but neither they nor *Backstage* itself made the charts.

Not a single track from the album was selected for the deal-fulfilling compilation album, *Cher's Golden Greats*, which came out later in the year. The public had moved on; in 1968, the US charts were full of The Doors and Simon & Garfunkel. Cher's shtick was beginning to look dated. This is a pity, since *Backstage* is a constantly rewarding album that showcases her growing vocal maturity.

CHAPTER 5

3614
Jackson Highway

The year 1969 was like a whirlwind for Sonny and Cher. By now their commercial stock had fallen, and they were deep in debt. But they had little option but to work hard, especially as they had a new baby to support: Chastity Sun, born on March 4. Within weeks of Chastity's birth, Cher would be back in the studio recording one of the most interesting albums of her career.

As Harry Young puts it in his liner notes for the Rhino reissue of the album, Sonny and Cher were "running for their lives, pursued by an erupting volcano of debt that roared like a wounded behemoth, heaved like a tortured titan, and then burst into flames as it threatened to bury their career and future prospects."

To fit into the changing times and make some money, they had launched a new, more adult-oriented act in Las Vegas. They were also searching for a new direction for Cher that was more in keeping with the times. Folk-rock was out, and as Cher later put it: "Son's straight-ahead, upbeat music started to sound simplistic and corny."

Ahmet Ertegun was delighted that Cher's Imperial contract had come to an end after five albums and a compilation. She could now finally be incorporated into the Atlantic family, where Sonny & Cher had recorded since 1965. They celebrated the union with an announcement in *Cashbox* magazine on February 1 1969.

The first release of this new phase of Cher's career was her cover of 'Yours Until Tomorrow,' a 1966 hit for Dee Dee Warwick, backed by the easy-listening schmaltz of 'The Thought Of Loving You.' But Atlantic Producer Jerry Wexler had bigger ideas for Cher. One of the most successful producers in the history of rhythm & blues—a term he coined himself in his early career as a writer for *Billboard* magazine—he had helmed records by Ray Charles, The Drifters, and Ruth Brown, and had received universal acclaim for turning Aretha Franklin into one of the most revered singers on the planet.

Buoyed by the recent success of the legendary *Dusty In Memphis* LP, on which he recast British pop's high priestess Dusty Springfield as a funky, hurting, soul troubadour, Wexler felt certain he could encourage a similar transformation in Cher, another artist with a big voice who had been grappling with inappropriate material. Wexler wanted her to work with the recently assembled crack team of southern players—keyboard player Barry Beckett, bassist David Hood, drummer Roger Hawkins, and guitarist Jimmy Johnson—who together had departed Rich Hall's FAME Studios in Muscle Shoals and set up the Muscle Shoals Sound Studio in a former funeral parlor at 3614 Jackson Highway in Sheffield, Alabama. They were joined for these sessions by Eddie Hinton, and over a handful of dates in April and May 1969 they laid down the 11 tracks that were to make up Cher's new album. Sonny's usual team of Gold Star players and his long time lieutenant, Harold Battiste—a man steeped in southern soul—were stood down, much to Battiste's chagrin.

Unfortunately, Wexler never attended the sessions. Excited about the project, he and Sonny had battled it out over who would control the record. "In case of a tie," Wexler had told Sonny before the sessions began, "I win." Wexler picked the songs: "Three by Dylan, an Aretha cover, a Stephen Stills, an Eddie Hinton (lead guitarist on the dates)—but I also picked up pneumonia and went to the hospital before the actual singing started, so [Tom] Dowd and [Arif] Mardin took over. I never made it to the control room." The resulting sessions were released as *3614 Jackson Highway*—an album named for a recording studio two months before The Beatles did the same with *Abbey Road*.

It was a brave album for Cher to make: a record that focused on the cooler, soulful aspects of her career and for once left out the more extreme aspects of her vaudeville. Sonny did not take part in the recording of the music. He is credited as a "spiritual advisor" and figures in the freewheelin' cover photograph, but that was about the extent of his involvement. He was not overly delighted. "Not only did I lose my role as producer," he later wrote, "my credibility went out the window too." Uncomfortable with being on the sidelines, he nonetheless kept his calm long enough to let a remarkable album be made.

Simply put, if *3614 Jackson Highway* had been made by a critically lauded singer, it would routinely figure in all-time best-of lists. This is not casual hyperbole. It is a revelation to hear Cher without being bathed in Sonny's syrup. This is pared down, emotional music. Had this album been released in the early nineties, it would have been called *Unplugged*; a decade later, it would have been likened to Rick Rubin's work with Johnny Cash.

The first release from *3614 Jackson Highway* was the single 'I Walk On Gilded Splinters,' written by Sonny and Cher's old cohort, Mac Rebbenack, now making a name for himself as Dr John, The Night Tripper. Its wild, abandoned, swampy sound is quite some distance from 'You Better Sit Down Kids' and the songs Cher had issued in an attempt to emulate that record's success. To hear Cher sounding like a voodoo priestess with the Muscle Shoals horns tooting away in the background feels far removed from the tubular bells and fey lyrics of the past.

The rest of the album is made up of songs that would challenge her audience, as well as a series of beautiful, close-miked vocals. Wexler's decision for Cher to record three songs from Bob Dylan's recent *Nashville Skyline* LP reinforces her position as one of the principal Dylan interpreters of the sixties, with 'Lay Baby Lay' the most poignant of the three cuts.

She took on Aretha, too, with an interesting version of 'Do Right Woman, Do Right Man' that makes plural the "day" and "night" of the chorus, before interpreting 'For What It's Worth' by Buffalo Springfield. She also sings Otis Redding's 'Sittin' On The Dock Of The Bay' and performs a fabulous, raunchy take on The Box Tops' 'Cry Like A Baby.'

The cover photograph was as beautiful and relaxed as the music contained within: the cast assembled outside the studio, all laughing and smiling, with Cher in her full Native American garb out in front. Beaming smiles are the order of the day—the newly mustachioed Sonny is to her right, with Wexler to her left. Barry Beckett, Arif Mardin, and Tom Dowd are there too. The back cover contains a handwritten message from Cher, previously so reluctant to offer opinion but now in full flow. "I want to write something that when you read it you'll say: yeh, that's really groovy," she begins, "but all I can tell you is what's in my heart, and if you can dig it then I'm happy and if you can't then I'm sorry. Music sets me free; it makes me feel all the things of life. Sometimes when I hear a groovy song it makes me want to get in my car and just drive and sing at the top of my lungs. Other times when I hear a song it makes me cry. I don't know if I'm sad or happy but it really doesn't matter. Music can take you away from the bad and bring you closer to the good in life; I really hope the music in this album brings you closer! Peace."

3614 Jackson Highway is a groovy, beautiful lost treasure that lay to rest any doubt about Cher's ability as a vocalist. It was released on June 20 1969, in the week that her new film, *Chastity*, opened. Artistically, this was a remarkable place for Cher to finish her decade. *Cashbox* found "plenty of sales potential in this highly polished set ... pay attention to this one"; for *Billboard*, it was "Cher's most interesting and therefore her most commercial package in some time." In the UK, the *New Musical Express* described the record as "a pretty good mixture," while *Melody Maker* called it "a tremendous album."

Although it was well received by critics, however, the album was a huge commercial misfire. By now, of course, listeners who wished to broaden their palette into soul and R&B could listen to Janis Joplin and Aretha Franklin, not some old folk-pop artist on the turn. And so it was that *3614 Jackson Highway* entered the US charts on August 16 1969 and climbed no higher than number 160. In the fast-paced late sixties, everyone moved on swiftly. Jerry Wexler attempted to record with another singer against type, Lulu, while Cher returned to the recording studio in October and December to cut tracks for a second Atco album that would never see the light of day.

C

Sonny, meanwhile, was becoming increasingly obsessed with filmmaking. The result: one of the most controversial moves of Cher's career. Sonny's plan was simple: Cher would become a film megastar and Sonny would be a respected player in the movie industry. After all, he'd been working with

Billy Friedkin, and had seen how the director had been tipped as the next big thing. Now it was time for Sonny to do the same.

"I was bored with music," he later wrote. "Or so I told myself. And the more I hung out with Friedkin and Coppola, the more I envied their careers, and I found myself wanting to be in the movie business. I told myself that I'd done the music trip. I needed new challenges. New frontiers."

Encouraged by Friedkin, Bono began to write the story he knew best: a thinly disguised story of his partner. Or, as he put it: "A philosophic, loving interpretation of this enigmatic, multi-talented woman who had taken hold of my heart and filled me with a drive and passion that I thought were known only by great poets and heroes of timeless epics."

The biggest mistake came when Sonny decided that he was not going to take anyone's advice. This was going to be *his* film. Ignoring the warnings of manager Joe DeCarlo, Sonny put all of his own money into it, for which he had to remortgage the mansion he and Cher lived in. "Every cent he could round up went into that picture," Bono's friend and television producer George Schlatter later recalled. "No one with any brains ever puts his own money into anything but the bureau drawer."

After William Friedkin (already involved with *The Night They Raided Minsky's*) passed on the option of directing the fledgling movie, Sonny enlisted TV commercial director Alessio de Paola. This brave strike out into the youth market would chime with the times and complete Cher's transition from folk-pop doyen to some form of counter-cultural queen, while Sonny would become one of Hollywood's go-to producers.

The trailer screamed mystery and promise. Over a shot of Cher running through the Mexico desert, her voiceover is matched by the intonations of a generic, deep-voiced announcer. "My name's Chastity ... That's not really my name, but I guess that's my name now." *Meet Chastity. She's a bummer, a loser, a copout, a dropout ... she's not just a girl: she's an experience.*

This was a dark picture for Sonny to have scripted for his wife. The story was billed as an odyssey of self-discovery. We start off with Chastity running away and being picked up by a truck driver (Elmer Valentine); although she spends a great deal of the movie being soaked or near water there is a sense that her soul is never close to being fully cleansed.

At one point, Chastity goes into a motel room with the lorry driver. "Do you mind if I get undressed?" he asks.

"I don't mind if you slit your throat," comes Chastity's petulant reply.

As Chastity makes a bed up on the floor of the hotel room, the driver asks: "Why are you running away?"

"I don't know," she replies, "and if I did, I wouldn't tell you." She knows he's only here because he wants to bed her. As she lights what appears to be a joint, her mood changes—perhaps she does want some company.

"Hey mister, how can you go to sleep so fast?" she whines. "Don't you know there is a world out there? People are dying, girls are getting raped, kids are in the backs of cars making it. How would you know, you're just a dumb slob, a married slob." Clearly, she has what would today be called commitment issues.

Cut to daylight. Chastity rolls in fields of flowers as she hits another road. Men try to pick her up but she rebuffs them all. This is a woman in control of her own destiny. She hoodwinks a man at a gas station; he pays for her gas and then she runs off with the dollars. It's an almost perfect crime: the driver heads off smiling, and Chastity gets a meal out of it.

It's a shame that a girl so pretty—and with so open a face—as Cher has to spend the whole movie in a sulk. Her monologues are drab and lifeless. When she meets Eddie (played by the English actor Stephen Whittaker), she categorizes men as octopuses or bulldogs, before wondering if this one is actually a lamb. She knows he isn't a peacock, she continues, but is sure that they all want the same thing:

"They want to pant and grunt and groan and then roll over like a dead body. Chastity, you're not being very nice, you've got to be civilized in this uncivilized world. What difference does it make what type he is? They're all the same, they're all men."

In a cafe, Eddie and Chastity order steak and eggs and stare at each other meaningfully. She explains that she got her name from a dictionary. "It said 'chastity: abstinence, sexual purity, freedom from ornamentation, simplicity,'" she drones. "I liked all that apart from 'abstinence,' as I didn't know what it meant. So I went back to the 'a's—non-indulgence and voluntary restraint of desires—and I liked that."

When Chastity asks if she can sleep with Eddie—sleep at his house without sexual activity unless she instigates it, that is—he offers what Bono no doubt thought would be a mind-blowing reply: "You're not a girl, you're a whole other thing."

Chastity arrives at Eddie's house and performs a peculiar, unfunny ritual testing of everything from drawers to appliances to faucets, to make sure that it all 'works.' While Eddie sleeps, we eventually find Chastity in the bath. She goes through a long monologue about the existence of God and hints at the futility of organized religion, which she dismisses simply by saying "it all seems silly to me, I don't want to think about it."

Where *Chastity* scrabbles for philosophical weight, the film is immediately deflated. While Eddie is sleeping, Chastity steals money from his wallet and heads for a church to ponder religious iconography. Karen Black would do something similar—and with a far greater emotional resonance—while tripping in the graveyard scene of *Easy Rider*. Here, Chastity attempts to explode the myth about confession before running out of the confessional. She steals a car and heads for the border with Mexico—a truly 'in-between' place.

Arriving in Frontera for her next adventure, Chastity returns to her monologue. "Here you are in beautiful Mexico, land of potted palms, sunshine, bullfights, Spanish fly and pot," she says. "Speaking of pot, I got a dollar for a couple of joints." This scene, with the world passing her by, is one of the best in the film. Chastity is shown pornographic pictures by a dealer (played by Danny Zapien), who thinks she is rejecting them because they may be evil. "I don't know what evil is," she says, "but if I did it wouldn't be those stupid pictures." She deduces that he is a pimp and somewhat unbelievably asks to be a prostitute.

The dealer takes Cher to a brothel—"a real Mexican cathouse"—where she picks up the inexperienced, geeky Tommy, played by former child star Tom Nolan. An excruciating scene ensues where Cher fleeces him for money and asks if he wants the "special," the "quickie," or indeed "the full works." As Tommy undresses, Chastity talks to him.

"When you get me, you're not just getting anything," she tells him, before washing his hair and then leaving.

When the brothel's madam, Diane Midnight (Barbara London), calls for Chastity, a scene of bored insouciance follows, culminating in Midnight showing her around the bordello. Men are portrayed as worthless imbeciles drooling over women in bras. Midnight inspects her women before brutally slapping one of them across the face.

"I just thought I'd throw that in," she says.

"You didn't have to," Chastity replies.

A bizarre interlude ensues with Chastity trying on clothes and the two women going on fairground rides, all piercing gazes and lingering touches. Chastity smiles for the first time and pets the animals at the fair.

"Are you having a daydream, Chastity?" Midnight asks. "You're thinking, aren't you?"

"People always think," she replies. "I can think. Once I tried not to, but I couldn't help it, thoughts kept popping into my head … sometimes I even think about my toes." However profound or indeed ironic this dialogue was intended to be, it is simply toe-curling. It is clear Chastity is seeking a mother figure. Midnight is looking for something a little earthier.

A seduction follows as Chastity, in bikini and shirt, leads Midnight upstairs. The monologue resumes: "Why is this bedroom different, Chastity? Why aren't you waiting for morning so you can hurry up and get out of here? Why do you feel so peaceful? What happened to the world outside what makes it so different this time?

"Be careful, Chas, this is a new scene. You always get mad when people do this—why are you not mad this time? She touches me like my mother did … well, Chas you made the gamut, here you are rubbing noses with a dyke."

The scene is intercut with billowing corn, trees bending in the wind, and bubbling water. A steep comedown follows: after they have had sex, Midnight becomes the worst kind of mother figure. Once again, Chastity is a little girl seeking affirmation. She breaks down in tears: "You stink, and this place stinks."

Soon Chastity is back out on the road and on her way back to Eddie's house. She has a new name for him: Andre. He wants to get to sleep; she says that men are all the same, but it appears that she wants to sleep with him.

"Andre, if I got pregnant, would you marry me?" she asks. She takes her clothes off, and we see her nude, briefly, in silhouette.

"How can I answer a question like that?" Andre replies.

When Andre promises to stay with her, we see Chastity smile again. But after he goes off to college, she is left alone in the house with echoes of her family hardship ringing in her ears. There will be no happy ending; Chastity will always be dragged back into her past demons. She scrawls the words "I love you" on the wall before adding "I *think*" in front of them. And then she is out on the road again.

The film ends with Chastity wandering, trapped in a cycle of the road. A truck driver (Jason Clarke) picks her up, and off we go again—except that this time we leave her clinging to a telegraph pole, crying incomprehensibly about her mother. We finish with a freeze fame of her kneeling in the road, a long way from 'I Got You Babe.'

C

It is still difficult to know what *Chastity* was really about. Bono further confused and annoyed his wife when he told a *Washington Post* reporter that girls of the time didn't know "whether to be a virgin or whether to go ahead and be modern. This conflict creates pressures on the girl, whatever she decodes. It has caused a large increase in frigidity and lesbianism among modern women. Today, women are as independent as men, but they don't really want to be. Every woman wants a man to take care of her and protect her. A woman will always test a man to see how far she can go, but she wants him to set the limits."

As ever, Sonny Bono was working from a deeply reactionary palette. He kept rewriting Chastity's story to fit his wife. Apart from the body-double glimpse of a breast and a nude silhouette, nudity—an ever-increasing prerequisite of the New Hollywood in the wake of *Bonnie & Clyde*—was absent from the film. Sonny also shielded Cher from any excesses of dialogue. As a result, she looks sad, surly, and not especially interested throughout. You get the sense of Sonny standing behind the camera, looking on grimly, denying his wife her freedom.

American International Pictures picked up the film, which opened on

June 24 1969 in Los Angeles before premiering in Chicago on Friday August 15. At the same time, about a thousand miles across the country, the single defining moment of the Age of Aquarius was in full swing: Woodstock. *Chastity* was just too far out of step. The film reached number fourteen on *Variety*'s box-office charts, but any appeal was shortlived.

The reviews were mixed to say the least. The *Los Angeles Herald Examiner* was bald and not atypical in its view that Cher's performance was "as ghastly as the movie. Most of her part—when she is not philosophizing—consists of pushing her glum face into the camera." And that was the whole point: although undeniably beautifully photographed, Cher is just too downbeat to sustain the entire movie. It was simply too dark, too minor.

The film was heavily promoted—unsurprisingly, given how much Sonny and Cher had riding on it. Promo packs and instructions were sent out movie theaters. Sonny made a point of saying that *Good Times* had been an "error of judgment" and a "copout"; this new film was "so adult, it's frightening. It's not a hippie-dippy teenage film. It's today and it's going to offend some people." The *New Musical Express* summed the film up as "prostitution and lesbianism as Cher takes to the road."

Vincent Canby of the *New York Times* was rather more scathing in his appraisal. "In *Good Times*, Sonny and Cher were obviously fooling, but they aren't in *Chastity*, the purposeful, rather pretty, completely banal movie that opened yesterday at neighborhood theaters. ... There may also be a movie out there, but it escapes Sonny, Cher, and Alessio de Paola, who seems to have directed *Chastity* simply by keeping Cher in focus ... *Chastity* is like a small-child's frown—solemn and innocent."

Chastity cost Sonny and Cher an unprecedented sum of money. Where Sonny had been shrewd in the past, now he seemed blinded by his desire to break into film. It wasn't that the world wasn't ready for a hippie-epic dropout movie, it was simply that Dennis Hopper and Peter Fonda's *Easy Rider* had already done it mere months earlier, capturing the viewing public in a way that *Chastity*, with its dubious and shifting but ultimately deeply conservative morals, could not.

Easy Rider set the benchmark for road movies. Although it shared a great deal of the fatalism of *Chastity*, it was made through a different lens—one held by writers who were completely onside with the counterculture. *Easy Rider* chimed with the age; *Chastity* seemed small and bitter, grasping for a new realism but missing the mark.

Cher is something of a spectral presence throughout. You can almost see glimpses of what the film could have been, but every time it falls short. In years to come, *Chastity* would become one of the most fiercely debated moments of her career. "I remember going to a preview and seeing everyone laugh at the serious parts," she recalled. "I left crying and said I'd never do another film." She allegedly pleaded with Sonny to forget about the film and pretend it never happened.

The soundtrack to *Chastity*—yet another Sonny & Cher product—was released in September 1969. Bono composed the music, while the incidental pieces—fine, swampy, Southern soul—were scored by Harold Battiste and Mac Rebbenack (whose song 'I Walk On Gilded Splinters' plays in the brothel scene). There is only one vocal performance by Cher, on 'Chastity's Song (Band Of Thieves),' which topped and tailed the movie.

Chastity consumed Sonny so much that he and Cher would name their first child—conceived during filming—after the film. Her birth finally legalized Sonny and Cher, who decided to get married. "We were going to be mother and father," Bono recalled. "We were not hippies. Basically, we were straight arrows. The right thing to do, it seemed, was to get married."

While all of this was happening, in April 1969, Sonny received an unwanted gift from the IRS: a statement to say that he and Cher owed $270,000. They would have to go out to work. *Chastity* and *3614 Jackson Highway* are definitive lines in the sand between the sixties and seventies incarnations of Cher. Within weeks of the start of the new decade, she and Sonny would be singing in supper clubs in evening gowns and tuxedos. These twin relics of the hippie age seemed a long way behind them. Sonny didn't have to pretend any more, or wear outrageous clothes. It was time to fully embrace the mainstream—and for the mainstream to embrace them.

CHAPTER 6
All I Ever Need

With a small child to support and a welter of debts, Sonny knew there was only one thing for it—he and his wife needed to go back to work. He asked Cher to give him two years to get them back to the top of the show-business tree. She was deeply skeptical but begrudgingly went along with it.

Although they were household names, Sonny and Cher could hardly get themselves arrested commercially, thanks to the artistic left-turn of *3614 Jackson Highway* and the failure of *Chastity*. They could not go back to the concert halls they had played in the mid sixties, however: they were stars, and they still demanded top billing. It was manager Joe DeCarlo who suggested the duo try their hand at playing nightclubs. "Cher and I hesitated," Bono later wrote. "We weren't nightclub performers. We thought of ourselves as rock and rollers. We sang in concert halls. We didn't have a slick act … unfortunately the nightclubs were the only option open to us."

After considering this further, however, Sonny saw a way out of their situation. Although the hours would be long and hard, the overheads were relatively low; this way, they could demonstrate close up their sincerity and talent. This would be an 'unplugged' show, where they could see the whites of the audience's eyes, except there would be no rock'n'roll: it would be smooth, rehearsed and in the grand style of light entertainment, as opposed to anything remotely countercultural.

Sonny and DeCarlo got the duo a support slot for Pat Boone at the Flamingo Hotel, Las Vegas, in July 1969. They played two shows a night, Sonny dressed in a tuxedo and Cher in a long gown (something she resisted from the off). Cher was unhappy with the direction her career was taking, but played the act onstage, often directly to Sonny, taking the gripes and jibes between a married couple and putting them over onstage to humorous effect.

After the Boone support slot they were signed to the Fairmont Hotels circuit and began roughly two years of nomadic existence, traveling across the United States and Canada. Their act would comprise a selection of current cover versions; some show tunes; and only a smattering of the records that made them famous. They kept top billing but played smaller venues such as the Cave Nightclub in Vancouver, the Elmwood Casino in Windsor Ontario, and the Twin Coaches in Monroeville, Pennsylvania.

Cher was devastated. "We'd go onstage through the casino kitchen, watching out for grease spots or a waiter with three bowls of soup," she later recalled. "On a really good night, there would be a couple of hundred people out there. On a slow night, we might sing to three tables."

In between the songs the duo began to develop a sharp comedy shtick in which everything seemed to be fair game: Sonny's height, heritage, and inability to sing; Cher's weight and the dimensions of her nose. "We began joking around with each other," Cher recalled. "We did it out of desperation and boredom, and also for the band, who would get pretty restless by one in the morning. Nobody in the house was paying any attention to us anyway. I got to do most of the zinging—about Sonny's mother, or his height, or his lousy singing. Now and then, he'd zing back about my skinny figure or big nose."

Sonny printed a sample of their material in his 1991 autobiography, *And The Beat Goes On*:

SONNY: Somebody put out a really lousy rumor about me. They said I sing like a frog. So what I'm going to do is sing one song by myself and then that way at least everyone will know the truth. You don't mind, do you, sweetheart?

CHER: Croak your little heart out, froggie. Croak it to me.

SONNY: I think I know where the rumor came from. Now I'm going to …

CHER I think I got a wart. You must be a horny toad. An Italian horny toad.

SONNY: Okay, I'm going to zip along. But keep a light on her. I don't trust her when she gets in one of these moods. I got a hunch I'm being screwed, you know?

CHER: I got a hunch you're not. In fact, I'm willing to lay odds on it.

In March 1970, after around six months of playing clubs, Sonny & Cher appeared at the Century Plaza Hotel in Los Angeles, where they performed in front of a crowd that included such noted guests as Joey Bishop and Al Martino. In June they played the Empire Ballroom of the Waldorf-Astoria Hotel in New York, where they had entertained Jackie Kennedy just a few years earlier.

By August, Sonny & Cher were starting to pack out rooms around the country. Their quick-fire repartee, now road-tested, was developing into a noteworthy act. As biographer Mark Bego later put it, they had "developed comically cartoonish versions of their own public and private personas, and they were projecting their creations onstage." While Sonny had tried, during their brief film career, to find their 'reality,' he had now created caricatures of them in real life.

CBS TV's Head Of Programming, Fred Silverman, caught the duo's show at New York's Americana Hotel and liked what he saw. He was immediately impressed with the banter between the pair, and their new tuxedo'n'gown image, and felt it would be an excellent idea if they sat in as guest hosts of Merv Griffin's primetime television show while Griffin was off at the Academy Awards in Los Angeles.

The show aired on April 20 1971 and received good ratings. Sonny & Cher were a tentative success. Silverman decided to test the water again by giving them their own vehicle. "Silverman sent us a congratulatory letter, saying that he had become a fan and expected great things from us," Bono later wrote. "I expected great things from us, too, so I was not about to get too excited."

The Sonny & Cher Comedy Hour was first broadcast on August 1 1971, on a six-week trial basis, during the traditionally dead high-summer viewing period. Singer, actor, and comedian Jimmy Durante was the duo's first guest, giving all three the opportunity to work in as many nose gags as possible. "We were pretty ragged at the start," Cher later recalled, "[but] Freddie put all his weight behind us. We were his discovery, almost like his kids in some strange way."

The Sonny & Cher Comedy Hour brought them in from the wilderness and put them right at the heart of the US mainstream. The show received positive reviews and high ratings, while its positioning in front of the US screening of the revered BBC series *The Six Wives Of Henry VIII* meant that Sonny and Cher had an hour before a major drama to entertain viewers with their brand of sketches, banter, special guests, and song. Although at this point the show operated on a modest budget, it had a talented team of writers and supporting actors, and it looked beautiful. It also began Cher's long association with dress designer Bob Mackie.

In the meantime, however, Cher needed to get her recording career back on track. After issuing a slew of records between 1964 and 1969, Sonny & Cher released no new material at all in 1970. There was just one solitary Cher single: a version of Leon Russell and Bonnie Bramlett's 'Superstar,' released by Atco as an end-of-deal one-off toward the end of the year. Originally known as 'The Groupie Song,' it was inspired by Joe Cocker, Rita Coolidge, and Leon Russell's Mad Dogs & Englishmen tour, and was first released as a single B-side by Delaney & Bonnie in 1969. Cher delivered a passionate version of the song, seemingly mourning the early demise of her popularity as much as the mystery guitarist of the lyric. It was, like the material on *3614 Jackson Highway*, extremely heartfelt. But it failed to chart.

Within a year, Cher saw The Carpenters' version of the song march to number three in the US charts. When later asked about their inspiration for the hit, Richard Carpenter recalled how, "late one evening during the period we were recording our third album, I happened to tune into *The Tonight Show*. Bette Midler, then relatively unknown, was guesting on this particular show and sang 'Superstar.' I felt the song could be a hit and was a natural for Karen."

They hadn't even heard Cher's version. It was obvious that she had fallen completely off the critical and commercial radar. But with *The Sonny & Cher Comedy Hour* raising her profile like nothing else from the past five years, all of that would change very soon.

C

As *The Sonny & Cher Comedy Hour* ended its first, tentative season in September 1971, everyone was pleased. The duo had performed well, and had worked well with a variety of guests. Sonny and Cher had found their comedic personas, and they chimed perfectly with the times.

We were like Gracie Allen and George Burns," Cher later wrote. "Son was the charming buffoon; I was the glamorous bitch." The public reacted warmly to this transformation, which proved that the crazy, folky hippies of six years ago could be tamed and brought into the mainstream. The best news was that the show had been re-commissioned, with a new series due to commence on CBS in December 1971.

Against this tentative backdrop of renewed success, it was time for Sonny and Cher to get their recording careers underway again. They had been without a deal since the Atco agreement had lapsed in 1970. A half-recorded album made at Gold Star in late 1969 was never finished or released. Sonny was furious at the way they had been treated after their early success had brought in such considerable revenue for the label. Now, however, although recording had not been top of their agenda, a fortuitous set of circumstances led to the duo getting new contracts.

Johnny Musso had been the head of Atlantic's West Coast office during their tenure there and knew Sonny from his radio promotion days. Musso had recently departed for American Decca subsidiary Kapp Records (named for its founder, David Kapp, brother of Jack Kapp, who had set up the original Decca label). The label had been subsumed into the MCA family in 1967, which was itself part of Universal.

Musso felt certain that the duo's recent dip in popularity was only temporary and wanted to sign them to his new label. Initially, people were skeptical; Sonny & Cher were no longer hit-makers. But, as their popularity began to rise again through their cabaret work and television spots, other offers were forthcoming. "They were going to sign for no advance—Sonny just wanted to have a record out," Musso recalled. "Then RCA offered them $50,000, which I matched. That's when everybody at Decca thought I was really nuts—Sonny & Cher hadn't had a hit in years."

Musso's plan was to first get Sonny & Cher back in the public spotlight with a live album and then build Cher's solo career in parallel. Duly signed, Bono resumed his traditional role as Cher's A&R, writer, and producer. However, her first single on Kapp, which was produced by Bono, did not set the world alight. In fact, it was a humungous misfire. Keen to be in-step with the times, Sonny wrote 'Classified 1A,' the tale of a wife hearing the news that her husband has been killed in the Vietnam War, sung from the perspective of the dying man. Although songs like Kenny Rogers & The First Edition's 'Ruby (Don't Take Your Love To Town)' and Edwin Starr's 'War' had been huge hits, this was still a bizarre, off-kilter choice of single, particularly in terms of it being a 'comeback.' With lyrics such as "Honey, he's gonna try and tell you in a nice way that Mrs, you're not Mrs anymore," it was downbeat, angst-ridden, and a little too close to the bone for radio programmers around the country. It was roundly ignored.

This was clearly not the way to relaunch Cher onto the marketplace. "Nobody would play it because it's about a guy dying in Vietnam," said Denis Pregnolato, who would soon replace Joe DeCarlo as the duo's manager. "I remember that Johnny Musso was very nervous, because he'd just signed them, and this was what Sonny was coming up with." In the UK, radio programmers opted for the B-side, 'Put It On Me,' but this, too, did very little business.

After the 'Classified 1A' debacle, Musso told Bono that the best way forward for Cher would be for her to work with an outside producer. Bono, still smarting from the catastrophe—as he saw it—of *3614 Jackson Highway*, was unsure, but he felt that maybe his old magic touch had at the very least temporarily deserted him. "[Musso] wanted to use Snuffy Garrett," Bono later wrote. "That was OK with me. I was bored with the studio and Snuff was an old friend who dated back to Liberty Records."

Texan Thomas Leslie 'Snuff' Garrett was just the man for the job. He was an experienced producer who had recorded with artists such as Bobby Vee and Johnny Burnette. He had indeed worked with Bono, and had been a promotions man during Cher's tenure at Liberty. In fact, he had worked Caesar & Cleo's 'Baby Don't Go' all those years ago. What Musso did rate, however, was Garrett's work as an independent producer. By 1969, Garrett had produced twenty top-ten singles, including eight for his own company, Snuff Garrett Productions, which he had set up with songwriter/performer Leon Russell. He was also a neighbor of the Bonos, living next door to them up in the Holmby Hills off Sunset Boulevard.

Garrett knew that Cher needed a big record to reconnect with the masses. She may have been a household name but she hadn't been on the US charts since 1968. "I knew exactly what I was looking for," he later recalled. "I wanted a song along the lines of 'Son Of A Preacher Man,' a story-type song." Originally intended for Aretha Franklin, 'Son Of A Preacher Man' had been a huge success for Dusty Springfield in 1968. Written by John Hurley and Ronnie Wilkins, it recounted the tale, told in the first person, of the dalliances the protagonist would have with the holy man's son when the father came to visit the family. It was a mature, knowing record; it would have been perfect for Cher.

Garrett went to Sonny and Cher's house for a summit meeting discussing their future. Cher connected with Garrett on a personal and professional level. "Oh, Snuffy was so funny and such a Texan," she recalled in 2001. "And he could do a whole album in a weekend. I'd get a vocal down and he'd go: great, that's fine ... We became good friends with Snuff and Yolanda, they were really sweet. Snuff was very proud of what he'd achieved and he was always telling you about it. He's just a good guy." Cher was comfortable in the studio, and Garrett knew he could coax some of her best material out of her: something that could emphasize the richness and depth of her distinctive voice.

Writer Bob Stone, who had written singles for Teddy & The Pandas, had heard that Cher needed new material. Garrett explained the sort of song he wanted. "He was looking for something between 'Bang Bang' and 'Son Of A Preacher Man,'" Stone recalled. "I ran home and listened to everything she'd done, and what I liked the best was done in minor keys. She's [half] Armenian, and has an ethnic quality; her voice is deep and dark and heavy. Before long I had a voice and a mock chorus." Stone came back almost immediately with a song called 'Gypsys & White Trash.' Garrett was appalled by the title but thought there was something very suitable about the material. One rewrite later, 'Gypsys Tramps & Thieves' was born. It is probably still Cher's greatest moment on record.

"I knew that was going to be a hell of a song; I couldn't wait to cut that baby." Snuff Garrett later recalled. And cut it he did. Like Bono, Garrett took his lead from Phil Spector's grandiose production style: double piano, a full rhythm section, two cellos, two violas, and eight violins. He also called on Spector's famous Wrecking Crew, the crack team of LA session musicians who played on hundreds of hits. Percussionist Amal Rich brought with him a Symlin: a piano whose strings are played by mallets, which gave the record its distinctive 'rinky-tink' opening.

"When we had the track done," Garrett continued, "Cher put her mouth on top of it. The session was quick, real quick. What a voice she had by this time! I remember thinking this woman has a voice that can cut through a cement orchestra." The detail in the arrangement is remarkable, almost taken for granted, as the listener is so rapt by the tale Cher is unfolding. Acoustic Spanish guitar underpins the chorus; assorted percussion fills propel the song along.

With Garrett employing every production trick he'd learned over the preceding decade, the record was a master class in going completely over the top. Recorded at United Western Recorders in Hollywood, it was arranged by legendary LA session man Al Capps. Engineer Lenny Roberts would later recall the session with great pleasure. It was, he said, all down to "the genius of Snuff Garrett. All productions were the same. Get the song, get the arranger, get the players, and do it as fast and cheaply as possible. 'Gypsys' was done in Western Studio B. I believe we had sixteen-track recorders at that time, but Snuff thought four tracks were enough. I think we compromised and did it on a 3M eight-track."

The swirling fairground feel of 'Gypsys' sounds as stunning today, over forty years later, as it did in 1971. It is a fantastic critique of the double standards of the moral majority—quick to condemn the gypsies who visit their town yet more than happy to visit the gypsy women at nightfall for earthier pleasures—and sung with relish by Cher as the teenager "born in the wagon of a traveling show." You can imagine her singing it around a campfire. We hear of life on the road; her deflowering by a lothario with a "smooth southern style" from a village south of Mobile on their journey to Memphis; and then the payoff, as the narrator ends up a single mother with a child of her own who has also been born in the wagon of a traveling show. All this in less than two-and-a-half minutes.

With its enthralling, well-written story, Cher's emotional vocal performance, and the fairground trickery of the arrangement, 'Gypsys Tramps & Thieves' struck a universal chord. It mattered not whether you were familiar with the situation. It was powerful and poignant. As biographer Lawrence J. Quirk later put it: "'Gypsys Tramps & Thieves' capitalized on Cher's wild gypsy, do-anything-for-a-good-time image ... her voice on the record is strong and throaty and exhibits an insolent sexuality." It was a record that recast Cher in the eyes of the public: gone was the flower child; now here was someone deeper, darker, more sophisticated. It would also provide the template for the rest of her career.

The promotional video, taken from *The Sonny & Cher Comedy Hour*, features Cher lip-syncing in an incredible Bob Mackie-designed red-and-purple maxi-dress with matching headband and hoop earrings, her head backlit by a full-moon-style spotlight, capturing the twenty-five-year-old in a classic art-deco setting. The single was released in early September 1971 and promptly began a seven-week climb up the US charts.

On November 6 1971, the gradual turnaround in Cher's fortunes changed. 'Gypsys Tramps & Thieves' hit the number one spot, replacing 'Maggie May' by Rod Stewart. It was Cher's first solo chart-topper. It was certified as a million-seller on November 19, picking up an RIAA Gold Disc Award on its becoming the biggest selling single in MCA Records' history. In the UK, it sold over 250,000 copies and reached number three on the charts.

Snuff Garrett felt it was the best record that he'd ever been involved with. "I've been in the music business all my life and it surprised the hell out of me," he recalled. "I think it surprised Sonny, too, because we laid it down, they put it out, and the next thing we knew, it was number one. When that sucker started rolling, it got up there real good. Sold somethin' like three million. Me, Cher, and Sonny, we made lots of money off that bad boy."

To follow the single, Garrett fashioned an album that would not alienate Cher's newly found middle-of-the-road audience but that still retained something of a contemporary feel. With its stunning cover image of Cher, up-close with her hair brushed forward over her face, taken by her *Vogue* cohort Richard Avedon, the album, initially known as *Cher*, was re-titled *Gypsys Tramps & Thieves* to capitalize on the success of its all-conquering lead single.

Opening track 'The Way Of Love'—a cover of the sixties song by Kathy Kirby, written by Jack Dieval and Michel Rivegauche, with English lyrics by Al Stillman—was selected as the follow-up single in early 1972 and reached a very respectable number seven in the USA. It is also an ultra-camp classic, with a lyric change in the last verse that leaves the singer's gender ambiguous—it could be sung to a woman or a gay man.

"Cher didn't even realize I had done that to the song," Garrett later noted. "Hell, it was a couple of years before she called me and said: 'Jesus Christ! Snuff, we messed up the lyrics to that song. I think it's a gay song now!'

"It wasn't a foul-up," he continued. "I knew what I was doing; I just liked the way it sounded with the lyric switch." It was exactly this sort of material that would endear Cher further to the gay community, which in later years would support her through thick and thin.

There are some fine, robust covers on the album. Cher sings 'Fire And Rain,' James Taylor's tale of depression following the suicide of a friend, with a heartfelt conviction, her voice cracking with emotion on the later choruses, giving extra emphasis to the line "I've seen sunny days that I thought would never end."

Similar passion can be heard on her version of 'He Ain't Heavy, He's My Brother.' Written by Bob Russell and Bobby Scott in the late sixties, the song had been a huge hit for The Hollies on both sides of the Atlantic; Neil Diamond had also recently covered it. Cher's was the first version by a female artist. Like a lot of the material on the album, it seemed to allude to (and fuel) the public's interest in the long-running soap opera that was the relationship between Sonny and Cher. Lines like "his welfare is my concern" and "while we're on our way to there, why not share" felt like dispatches from their life together.

Several other great songs were selected for the release: Peggy Clinger's 'I Hate To Sleep Alone' is snappy; 'Touch And Go' is the sort of perfect seventies easy-listening soul not a million miles from what Cher's friend Diana Ross was now releasing in her Berry Gordy-assisted solo career. Garrett kept within Bono's guidelines of choosing tracks that were more mini-dramas than mere songs, such as Harry Lloyd and Gloria Sklerov's 'He'll Never Know,' which is about keeping the secret that a husband's child is, in fact, someone else's. Again, Cher is cast as a woman with a shady secret "locked in her mind." Linda Laurie's 'When You Find Out Where You're Going, Let Me Know' is a sprightly, country-tinged jaunt that details a wife's conversation with a wayward partner. The album closes with 'One Honest Man,' written by Ginger Greco, in which Cher wonders whether she'll ever find a decent man to settle down with.

Gypsys Tramps & Thieves was the perfect accompaniment to Cher's refound superstar status. It had an appropriate balance of light and shade, offering a populist version of the singer-songwriter boom of the early seventies. It reached number sixteen on the US chart and was certified gold by the RIAA in April 1972.

C

To coincide with the success of *Gypsys Tramps & Thieves*, *The Sonny & Cher Comedy Hour* returned at the end of 1971. This time the budgets were higher, the list of guests exceptionally strong: The Supremes, Tony Curtis, and George Burns among them. "Whole families watched us," Cher recalled. "Our demographics were huge, from little teeny kids to old grandmothers. We loved doing the show so much, we would have paid CBS to do it." The show also proved a regular and lucrative opportunity to promote the album.

By the end of the year, with the success of the single, the album, and the series, and with Sonny & Cher's live album also in the top ten, the blend of hard work, determination, and talent had paid off. They were back at the top of their game. In his autobiography, Bono recounts the tale of how they were amazed at the size of the audience that had gathered to see them at a racing stadium in the Midwest. Thinking someone else must have been added to the bill, they asked the promoter who everyone was here to see. They were stunned when they were told that the crowd was there just for them.

Cher was aghast at this new level of recognition. It was no longer just pop fans who were aware of her but people of all ages. During a break from recording the *Comedy Hour* one day, she stepped out to Los Angeles department store Saks, where she became acutely aware of everyone staring at her. "It was the first time I'd been out where I could feel that the fame of TV was different than that of records," she later wrote. "When you were one of the top-ten-rated shows on television, millions of people were watching you every week. I wasn't complaining. I was just a little shocked. The fame was all encompassing. It could just swallow you up."

Alongside Cher's solo success, Kapp needed a new single and studio album from Sonny & Cher to further capitalize on their recent success. The duo had recorded a version of Paul Anka's 'Real People' as their Kapp debut earlier in 1971, but it came out and subsequently disappeared with little fanfare. Johnny Musso again enlisted Snuff Garrett, who had already worked wonders for Cher with his adroit choice of 'Gypsys Tramps & Thieves' as her comeback single. Musso was aware of the song 'All I Ever Need Is You,' written by Eddie Reeves and Jimmy Holiday, from the version sung by Ray Charles on *The Volcanic Action Of My Soul*. He thought it would be perfect for Sonny & Cher as a means to update their message of love and togetherness—a contemporary, country-influenced take on 'I Got You Babe.' It was clear that, with the current interest in the duo, whatever single they released (unless it was something like 'Classified 1A') would be a sizeable smash hit.

Musso heard that Reeves was thinking of cutting his song himself, but managed to persuade him to let Sonny & Cher record it instead. "I played Sonny the song one afternoon," he recalled. "That night we recorded it, and the next day we had an acetate copy to KHJ. Within twenty-four hours from the time I played it for Snuffy, it was on the air." Los Angeles-based radio station KHJ had been instrumental in breaking 'I Got You Babe' six years earlier, when Bono had convinced Ahmet Ertegun to flip 'It's Gonna Rain' for its soon-to-be all-conquering A-side. Now the station was working its magic again.

'All I Ever Need Is You' was released in October 1971 and went to number seven in the US Hot 100, as well as number eight in the UK. It also topped the *Billboard* Easy Listening chart, and was adopted as the opening theme song for *The Sonny & Cher Comedy Hour*.

The accompanying album, also entitled *All I Ever Need Is You*, was another masterful Snuff Garrett production. Working closely with Bono,

Garrett again assembled the cream of LA's session players and selected ten songs that he felt would showcase the duo's strengths.

Most notable was a Bono original that equaled some of his very best compositions. 'A Cowboy's Work Is Never Done' is a bouncing novelty song that has the same excessive Romany stylings as 'Gypsys Tramps & Thieves.' Opening with David Hungate's wailing, wah-wah-driven guitar, it settles into a lazy oompah-beat with the duo singing in unison. As the orchestration builds, Cher takes a verse and a bridge before Sonny returns for a wistful reflection on the innocence of childhood games and the sadness of growing older—a recurring theme in Bono's work that harks back to the child with the gun in *Good Times*. The single reached number eight in the USA in 1972 and was later used in the film adaptation of Elmore Leonard's *Be Cool*.

The rest of the album is generally upbeat (wistful reflection having been saved for Cher's solo material). It contains a number of contemporary cover versions: The Fortunes' 'Here Comes That Rainy Day Feeling' harks back to Sonny & Cher's mid-sixties work; a cover of UK session act The Brotherhood Of Man's 'United We Stand' helped break the song in the USA, where it became a key song for the gay rights movement. There's also a new reading of Sonny's old song 'Somebody' and an affecting Bono solo version of Cher's hit 'You Better Sit Down Kids.'

The album's cover, meanwhile, demonstrated that the duo had still not completely abandoned their hippie affiliations. They are shown in the greenhouse of their home, wearing denim—a direct contrast to the tux and gown of *Live*—and posing among their band's flight cases. The whole package clicked. *All I Ever Need Is You* reached number fourteen in the USA and sold over 500,000 copies. It was further validation for Bono that his master plan was working.

Sonny & Cher were once again hot news. Very quickly, to Sonny's delight, their earning capacity shot through the roof. Sonny then signed then a deal with Lee Guber and Shelly Gross to appear at music fairs across the country, which would bring in a minimum of a million dollars. Soon, all that debt would be far behind them.

Meanwhile, Johnny Musso had a plan of his own to capitalize on the TV success of *The Sonny & Cher Comedy Hour*. The duo's live turn had, after two years in the clubs and hotels, become a smooth, professional roadshow; an album of that show would connect perfectly with the wider public. Moreover, it would be relatively inexpensive to make. At a time when their peers were recording their live albums at Winterland or Filmore East, here Sonny & Cher were captured in the less sexy but eminently more respectable West Side Room of the Century Plaza Hotel, Los Angeles.

Produced by road manager Denis Pregnolato—soon to be promoted to manager—and engineered by Angel Balestier, *Sonny & Cher Live* is probably one of the best encapsulations of a live show on record. Musso got permission from Ahmet Ertegun for the duo to record some of the old hits—a blessing freely given as Ertegun would never forget how important a milestone 'I Got You Babe' had been for Atlantic back in 1965.

So this was the new Sonny & Cher. With wisecracks intact, the album features four of their sixties classics ('Laugh At Me,' 'I Got You Babe,' 'What Now My Love,' and 'The Beat Goes On') alongside three Beatles covers ('Hey Jude,' 'Got To Get You Into My Life,' and 'Something') and four of the contemporary songs that were currently in their set (including 'More Today Than Yesterday' by The Spiral Staircase). In his review of the album for allmusic.com, Joe Viglione notes that the duo's backing band "sounds like a coiled spring ready to pounce, and Cher shows why she is the diva/icon that she is."

The quality of the band, directed by Al Pelligrini, is there for all to hear. It contained some of the cream of the LA session scene: David Hungate and Dean Parks on guitar, Michel Rubini on piano, Dave McDaniel on bass, Matt Betton on drums, and Dahrell Norris on percussion. They work completely in tandem with Sonny and Cher—happy to extend out numbers such as 'The Beat Goes On.' With all the repartee and interludes, that track extends to nine minutes but keeps all of the original's bite and razzmatazz.

They do a keen approximation of the tumultuous sound of 'I Got You Babe' and add a poignancy to 'Laugh At Me,' on which Sonny talks about his ordeals of six years earlier like they were from some old history book. But as biographer Mark Bego would later note, "Sonny was now singing with determination, as though it was now a vow that he would somehow pull Sonny and Cher out of the financial mess they had gotten themselves into."

Cher's solo performance of 'Danny Boy' shows what a passionate singer she could be. She had originally recorded the song in December 1969, at Gold Star, for the aborted follow-up to *3614 Jackson Highway*; since then, the song had become a show-stopping feature of the Sonny & Cher live set. Singing with appropriate pathos but never straying too far into mawkishness, she carries off the Irish melody and recasts it almost as a modern hymn—all this live from a hotel stage. (In a review of the duo's show in New Orleans a year previously, *Billboard* described 'Danny Boy' as "electrifying" and "masterfully arranged, staged, and sung.")

Released on September 3 1971, *Sonny & Cher Live* put the duo back into the US top forty, reaching number thirty-five in December. The front cover photograph underlined the Sonny & Cher of the seventies: Sonny in his tuxedo, frilly shirt and bowtie; Cher looking stunning in her gown. As Musso would later note, the recording is fairly rough and ready at times. "It wasn't well recorded, and we cut it all in one night, but it was a real fast gold album," he said. "Our first pressing was 25,000 copies, which sold out immediately. The name Sonny & Cher was still magic."

The rock fraternity mocked, of course. Former Halfnelson drummer John Mendelsohn filed an ironic review of the album for *Rolling Stone*. "Sonny and Cher may no longer be the king and queen of folk-rock," he wrote, "but the bag they're into now has plenty to offer the rock buff who's resisted becoming prejudiced by the couple's shoddy treatment by the underground press. Miss their *Live* album at your own risk." This wasn't music for the counterculture: it was for Middle America, where it would be bought alongside records by Andy Williams and Tom Jones.

CHAPTER 7

Mama Was A Rock & Roll Singer

T he year 1972 began in spectacular fashion for Sonny & Cher. Cher was back on the album and singles charts; *Sonny & Cher Live* was in the US top forty; 'All I Ever Need Is You,' the theme from their high-rating television series, was on its way to the top ten.

Foxy Lady capitalized on this success, and is probably Cher's best work of the seventies. Complete with a sleek production by Snuff Garrett—and a soft-focus, Sonny-shot, tightly cropped, full-face photograph on the cover— it marked Cher out as a mature balladeer.

Recording sessions for what was to become *Foxy Lady* began at Larabee Sound in Hollywood in April 1972, with Sonny and Denis Pregnolato keen to repeat the success of *Gypsys Tramps & Thieves.* Engineered by Lenny Roberts, with arrangements by Michel Rubini, Marty Paich, Gene Page, and Al Capps, *Foxy Lady* is a widescreen album that showcases Cher's vocal prowess married with a near-perfect selection of material. The title was taken from Jimi Hendrix's single of the same name, proving that being a foxy lady wasn't just for rock chicks but also for respectable adult singers.

The album's opening track, lead single, and showstopper is 'Living In A House Divided,' a sophisticated ballad about a marital breakdown written by Tom Bahler. It was a brave and prescient choice of song, but one that failed to register as highly as 'Gypsys Tramps & Thieves' and 'The Way Of Love,' reaching only number twenty-two in the USA and not charting at all in the UK. Lyrics such as "look at us, the king and queen of emptiness / living inside our castle of loneliness" would soon feel a little too close to home.

Perhaps the general public wanted Cher to sing only of marital bliss now that she and Sonny were visible again. But Snuff Garrett, for one, was disappointed by the record's relative failure. "I really worked my ass off on that record," he said. "I thought it would be much bigger for Cher than it was. It missed the boat somewhere."

Nonetheless, the song has a fine AOR sound and a great brass arrangement, casting Cher somewhere between The Carpenters and Bread. Bodie Chandler's 'It Might As Well Stay Monday (From Now On)' is another deeply affecting song about a woman who has lost her love. Cher dips into the catalog of Garrett's old writing partner Leon Russell for a second time with her version of 'Song For You,' recorded so definitively by Donny Hathaway the previous year. Just as was the case with 'Superstar,' The Carpenters would soon recorded a more popular hit version of the song, although Cher captures a sincerity and sweet desperation that is not obvious in The Carpenters' rendition.

'Down Down Down,' written by Ester Jack, is a triumph-against-adversity number with a bluesy edge, delicately arranged by Sonny's old Spector cohort Gene Page, who would soon be arranging Barry White's sweet soul symphonies, and who here gives Cher full vocal reign. Ginger Greco's 'Don't Ever Try To Close A Rose' is perhaps the album's only real misstep; although it is another pathos-rich ballad, it seems rather forced.

The second side of the album opens with a reworked version of Sonny's 'The First Time,' which Cher had originally recorded in September 1969 for Atlantic. It is given a slightly slower, more orchestral treatment here than on the original take, which had been earmarked for single release in October 1969. The original recording received good notices from the US trade papers: *Variety* described it as "an arresting contemporary ballad handled in a sensitive style," while *Billboard* called it a "strong, commercial ballad and one of Cher's top vocal workouts to date." (The magazine's prediction that the song could "easily prove a leftfield smash" was not to be, however.) The *Foxy Lady* reworking highlights just what a fabulous little song Bono had written in the first place, and he was right to reinstate it for the wider listening public. Even Garrett and Bono's replacement of the original's soul with a great deal of bombast cannot take away from the fact that this is an extremely well written song.

Al Stillman and John Simon's 'Let Me Down Easy'—which, as Mark Bego would later note, offers the first glimpse of the "Cher vibrato"—is followed by Bob Stone's sensitive and emotional 'If I Knew Then.' It may be no match for his 'Gypsys Tramps & Thieves' but it is certainly of a similar quality, and is delivered with conviction by Cher. 'Don't Hide Your Love,' written by Neil Sedaka and Howard Greenfield, is a durable composition, recorded at a time when Sedaka was at his lowest ebb in the States. It is a fine, country-tinged, radio-friendly song, complete with wailing guitar by Dean Parks. Released as the album's second single in September 1972, it reached number forty-six on *Billboard*.

The album's only earthy, swampy, up-tempo number is saved until the end, as *Foxy Lady* closes with Hoyt Axton's 'Never Been To Spain,' a recent hit for Three Dog Night. It is arguably Cher's finest vocal performance on record; as she truly lets rip toward the end, you can hear all of her rock-singer potential. Although her voice is sometimes lost amid the fussy, ornate songs that seemed to be her stock-in trade during the early seventies, *Foxy Lady* shows that there was still sufficient grit in her repertoire.

The album was released in July 1972 and reached number forty-three on the US charts. It was generally well received by critics, but performed relatively modestly in comparison with Cher's other recent releases, despite heavy promotion on the new season of *The Sonny & Cher Comedy Hour*, which premiered on CBS in September 1972. One of the key reasons it failed to scale the heights was simply that the Cher brand had been stretched pretty thinly across the past year. Two Sonny & Cher albums (*Sonny & Cher Live* and *All I Ever Need Is You*), a Cher album (*Gypsys Tramps & Thieves*), and reissues of all of their Atco and Liberty material had rather flooded the marketplace. *Foxy Lady* is also quite low-key and mid-paced, its drama all delivered at a similar downbeat tempo in contrast to the relative jolliness of *All I Ever Need Is You.*

All had not been well down at the studio during the making of the record. Tensions between Sonny Bono and Snuff Garrett were first exposed and then flourished during the making of the album. Spurred on by the duo's newly regained success, Bono became far more active in the studio once more, co-producing three tracks on the album ('Song For You,' 'The First Time,' and 'Don't Hide Your Love'). However, he and Garrett were destined to be diametrically opposed on virtually everything, while Bono was also beginning to act out his superstar status. Within his own organization, he was now known as El Primo; if members of his team were in favor, Sonny would give them ranks with stripes for years of service, and jackets with names on them such as Primadere and Primadette (Cher's was Prima Donna).

At the end of 1972, Bono fired Snuff Garrett. They had already had a number of disagreements, such as when Sonny rejected the song 'The Night The Lights Went Out In Georgia' because of concerns that it might offend listeners in the American South. Garrett later took the song to US TV star Vickie Lawrence, for whom it became a number one hit. (True, it was similar to 'Gypsys Tramps & Thieves,' but it would probably have been another smash for Cher, even if its subject matter—murder, lynching, and police corruption—may have proven rather too controversial for her career at the time.)

Now, as Kapp Records was subsumed into MCA Records, Bono took the opportunity to take over production of Cher's music. Garrett and his wife Yolanda had been on tour with Sonny & Cher at Sonny's expense. They were in Florida, miles from home; Yolanda was missing her daughter and Garrett was acutely aware that he had other work to do. When Garrett told Bono that they would be leaving for home, Bono threw an enormous fit, telling Garrett that Cher needed Yolanda with her. Bono gave Garrett an ultimatum, which Garrett gladly ignored.

As J. Randy Taraborelli recounts in his biography of Cher, Sonny told Garrett that if he were to leave the hotel, he would never work with Cher again. "That's your fucking loss, Sonny," Garrett replied, "not mine." Success had gone to Sonny's head. Within a few months, it would not just be the producer leaving.

C

Soon after the release of *Foxy Lady*, Liberty Records, now part of United Artists, stretched back and repackaged selections from Cher's first five solo albums for her new audience. Before *Bittersweet White Light* took a little of the glitter out of her stellar comeback, these two *Superpak* releases caught Cher at the peak of her popularity, while Atlantic's *The Two Of Us* did a similar job of collecting a significant chunk of Sonny & Cher's sixties output. By the end of 1972, any fan who came to the duo through their television show would be well served with their past work.

In the early seventies, back catalogue releases were suddenly big business, with labels realizing that there was a demand for older material to be made available again. The *Superpak* series was a new line from the United Artists catalogue division, which took material from Liberty's vaults and repackaged it as double albums. Double albums had increased in popularity since the release of Bob Dylan's *Blonde On Blonde*, The Beatles' 'White Album,' and *Electric Ladyland* by Jimi Hendrix; now, they were seen as the ultimate bauble in the new, sophisticated long-playing musical landscape.

Other artists to receive the *Superpak* treatment at the time included Canned Heat, The Ventures, and James Bond composer John Barry. Cher's popularity was such that her two attractively priced double-albums of previously issued material both reached the US top 100 and gained greater success than her previous compilation, *Cher's Golden Greats*, which had only reached number 195 in 1968.

What was most interesting about Cher's first *Superpak* release was its cover photograph: a close-up shot by Sonny that features ... well, just her nose, mainly, surrounded by a dark border. The sensitive profile shot made the record look—as was no doubt the intendion—like the work of a Laura Nyro or a Carole King, as opposed to the mass-media light entertainer Cher had become.

Superpak Volume One draws on material from Cher's five Liberty albums, which had captured the bohemian girl with her lack of finesse, singing her heart out over folk-rock confections. It was the perfect time to reflect on just how well crafted those albums were. Bono's selection of material, Harold Battiste's arrangements, and Cher's vocals somehow now felt rather in-step with the times.

Her early career seemed like it had been light years ago. Had she not enjoyed such a flowering of success in the early seventies, this sensitive, folky side would not now have been offered for reappraisal. It demonstrated a certain naïveté—something not immediately apparent in the material that she had recently delivered on television or on record. It also showed that the Cher of 'Gypsys Tramps & Thieves' was not a million miles away from the plaintive chanteuse of 'Bang Bang (My Baby Shot Me Down).'

Superpak Volume One reached number ninety-three in the USA—no mean feat for a two-disc set of previously released material. Buoyed by the success of this first repackage, United Artists repeated the formula later in the year with a second Superpak, which gathers together the remaining material from her first five solo discs.

This time the cover was unmistakably Cher. With her makeup not unlike that of a cartoon drawing of a doll, she is shown in a stunning bolero-style gown and beret, looking directly at the camera. Once again, the formula was relatively successful, with the album peaking at number ninety-five.

Meanwhile, given the sustained success of *The Sonny & Cher Comedy Hour*, it was time for Atco to remind American audiences that there was a story before the duo's television show and tuxedo'd universality. Whereas the *Superpak* series had at least mixed up the tracks from Cher's five Liberty albums, *The Two Of Us* was a hasty and unimaginative assemblage of *Look At Us* and *In Case You're In Love*.

Possibly the most poignant critique of the album came from *Creem*'s Gene Sculatti, who had clearly thought long and hard about what to say. His review placed Sonny correctly in the milieu of "setting preteen fashions with the supercool Cher" and "churning out highly imaginative AM folk-rock bulk alongside P.F. Sloan, Barry McGuire, and The Turtles, even making the covers of *Time*, *Newsweek*, and *Hit Parader* next to Bob Dylan. "So he must've mattered," Sculatti wrote. "In the minds of lots of kids, he probably was equally as important as Dylan and Lennon. And if his rock'n'roll life is ended, Sonny Bono at least had the good taste to remove his rotting corpse from plain view, which is far more than can be said for either the tambourine man or the Intellectual Beatle. Most of the hits, and some lesser-known dandies, are here: 'I Got You Babe,' 'The Beat Goes

On,' 'You Don't Love Me,' 'The Letter,' 'Little Man.' Just what you always wanted: relevant history and fun. "

It must have been heartwarming for Bono to finally be given this level of respect. *The Two Of Us* made number 122 on the US album charts, and did at least feature a current photograph of TV's most ubiquitous couple.

C

At the end of 1972, it became apparent for the first time that Sonny and Cher's marriage would not last. Cher had begun an affair with Bill Hamm, the young guitarist in the duo's touring band; Sonny would later paint a graphic picture of the breakdown in his book, *And The Beat Goes On*, describing how Cher asked him to leave their hotel suite in Las Vegas so she could spend the night with Hamm. Sonny, aggrieved, took up with Hamm's girlfriend.

As 1972 had been their most successful year as a professional couple, however, they decided that the only way to continue would be to give the impression—to the general public—that absolutely nothing had happened. Whatsoever. That said, from this point on Sonny would only be involved in two further studio records involving Cher: *Momma Was A Rock'n'Roll Singer* and *Bittersweet White Light*.

One of the highlights of *The Sonny & Cher Comedy Hour* was Cher's often-impassioned solo spot, where she would sing standards from the twenties, thirties, and forties. Sonny felt it would be a good idea to record an album of Cher singing these songs, seemingly indirectly inspired by Diana Ross's *Lady Sings The Blues*. And so *Bittersweet White Light* reflects the contemporary trend for raiding the Great American Songbook, taking standards from 1918 to 1953 and showing just how masterfully Cher could command her material.

Taking its name from the solo spotlight beneath which Cher often delivered her ballads, *Bittersweet Bright Light* is a near-perfect capture of the overindulgence and expense of the LA session scene of the mid seventies. Heavyweight players such as regulars Dean Parks and David Paich were joined by drummer Jeff Porcaro and keyboard player Joe Sample from the Crusaders and were directed by Bono to make an immense sound. Take

George Gershwin's legendary 'How Long Has This Been Going On,' here arranged to within an inch of its life. Starting like a progressive-rock ballad with floating synthesizers, it then moves into an excursion in swooning big band excess, with Cher affecting something of a ragtime voice that almost knocks the whole song off-kilter. The same extravagance can be heard on her version of Gershwin's 'The Man That Got Away.'

Cher biographer Mark Bego would later encapsulate the album perfectly, describing it as "heavily overproduced" and noting that "on some of the songs—especially 'By Myself'—Cher's singing style is so completely over-the-top that it devours the subtle ballads." It almost sounds like an act of self-sabotage against Sonny's latest idea. It is as if Cher is singing through a vaudeville megaphone as she adds in several bonus syllables to every lyric sung.

The record reaches its nadir on the Al Jolson medley. Adding to her repertoire of songs that mention 'Sonny' in the lyrics or title, she mauls 'Sonny Boy' before amping up the schmaltz on 'My Mammy' before closing—with the orchestra about to explode—with 'Rock-A-Bye Your Baby With A Dixie Melody.'

This was not what Cher's new middle-of-the-road soft-rock audience, wooed by the mature balladry of *Gypsys Tramps & Thieves* and *Foxy Lady*, were expecting. Moreover, *Lady Sings The Blues* had already filled the niche for this kind of record in many people's collections. *Bittersweet White Light* stalled at number 160 on the *Billboard* album chart, while the single 'Am I Blue' reached only number 111. Cher's new record company, MCA, which had taken over Kapp, made it clear that it wanted Snuff Garrett back in the production chair to get the Cher machine back on track.

C

On February 27 1973, Sonny and Cher were among the presenters at the 45th Academy Awards, handing the award for Best Original Song to Al Kasha and Joel Hirschorn for 'The Morning After' from *The Poseidon Adventure*. *The Sonny & Cher Comedy Hour* had moved to a primetime slot on Wednesday nights, and was frequently in the top ten Neilsen ratings. But all was not well in their marriage.

By now, they were openly seeing other people while holding together their popular image for the cameras. They were living—as the lead track for *Foxy Lady* had so presciently forecast—in a house divided, with Cher in one wing and Sonny in another, separate lives under the same roof. But in the public eye, it was still business as usual.

Mama Was A Rock And Roll Singer—Papa Used To Write All Her Songs was to be their last ever studio album. The front cover shows them in their bedroom, with Cher looking serenely from the bed, resting against a stuffed lion, and Sonny sitting stern and cross-legged on the floor. Cher looks like a lioness; Sonny, sitting between a rag doll and a porcelain figurine, looks small and aggrieved.

Although supposedly intended to suggest the 'mama' and 'papa' of the title, the illustration makes it look more as though Sonny is simply another of Cher's toys. The back cover is little better. It shows the couple laying down, interlinked, but what should have been a loving image instead seems cold and distant.

Produced by Denis Pregnolato and Michel Rubini, the album finds the singing duo working again with the cream of the LA session players, who are listed in detail on the back jacket. David Hungate is back on bass, Jeff Pocaro on drums, David Paich on keyboards, with extra guitar support from players such as current LA studio wunderkind Larry Carlton, and Joe Sample and Michael Omartian on keyboards.

It begins with a good, solid version of Albert Hammond's 'It Never Rains In Southern California,' with Dean Parks taking a nice country & western guitar solo. Sonny actually sounds engaged with the material as he and Cher sing alternate verses. 'I Believe In You,' written by Pregnolato, Michel Rubini, and Don Dune, is the single that never was; taken at slightly too fast a tempo, it is a song of love and believing, not unlike the duo's one-off single from 1972, 'When You Say Love,' which bore a resemblance to a popular Budweiser beer commercial.

Continuing their flair for adapting recent and contemporary material, they covered Johnny Nash's US number one hit 'I Can See Clearly Now,' demonstrating once again how they could turn any material into glittering, competent, easy-listening pop. It is a big, brash, joyous sound with massed horns. Tony Macaulay and Geoff Stevens's pop anthem 'Rhythm Of Your Heart Beat' follows. It's a heartfelt duet, although the lyrics—"Then we'll turn to each other and say love last forever ... until the end of our lives, we'll be together"—have a bitter poignancy.

Sonny's only original composition on the album is the title track, of which he was clearly very proud. Running to almost ten minutes, it was constructed as their magnum opus, with Cher belting it out in a loud, shouty blues-rock style. The overblown overture reduces into a boozy bar-room ballad, with Sonny singing pointedly to Cher: "You're rocking everybody in town / But you're jacking me around / Foxy lady shine it on, I hope you miss me when I'm gone / cos foxy lady, gone is where I'm gonna be." Later on, he concludes: "Damn you girl, you messed up the world that you had."

Sonny was doing what he knew best: turning real-life situations into pop lyrics. There is certainly an edge to his vocal. After three minutes of ever-building noise, the song returns with a reggae-influenced play-out, complete with dub-inflected horns; we are then treated to four minutes of a 'Hey Jude'-like refrain, the same phrase repeated over and over as Parks ladles on ever more rock guitar. It is a brave, bold song, yet still not as good as Sonny would have liked it to be. An edited version of it was released as a single in April 1973, when it stumbled blindly to number seventy-seven on the US charts.

The album's second side opens with a solo track by Cher. 'By Love I Mean' was written by Hod David, Will Jacobs, and Marc Allen Trujillo and features a lovely, impassioned vocal by Cher. Neil Diamond's 'Brother Love's Travelling Salvation Show' has her masterfully struggling with the lyrics in one channel while Sonny shouts his way through the first verses in the other. It is extremely off-putting. By the chorus, however, the song has become an accomplished encapsulation of the duo's strange harmonies.

'You Know Darn Well'—another dip into the songbook of British composer Tony Macauley—is a lovely piece of fluff well suited to the pathos of the situation that America's leading couple found themselves in. Bob Stone's 'The Greatest Show On Earth,' however, is the true meat of the album, covering in micro-detail the break-up of a marriage. Even listening now, in the twenty-first century, it comes with something of a chill, since we—unlike contemporary listeners—are only too familiar with what was going on in Sonny and Cher's lives.

In the song, a husband hands his wedding ring back to his wife, who now has a new lover; the "greatest show on earth" is his reaction to this rejection. We listen to his attempts at reconciliation before the woman walks away from the restaurant table—a metaphor for the dashed hopes of a collapsing marriage. With its swaggering brass and razzmatazz setting, this is arguably one of the most raw, painful records you'll ever hear. It feels much longer than its three-and-a half minutes. Still, one cannot forget that, with their chart albums, high-ranking television show, and the industry that had sprung up around them, Sonny & Cher were indeed the greatest show on earth at the time.

Throughout the album there is an underlying funk to the arrangements, heard most typically on the closing version of The Doobie Brothers' 'Listen To The Music.' It is, again, more 'show business' than the original—or indeed the mighty cover by The Isley Brothers—but it is an optimistic, upbeat reading of the tune that fits in perfectly with the surface sheen of the duo's television performances.

Although no one knew it at the time, *Mama Was A Rock And Roll Singer—Papa Used To Write All Her Songs* would be Sonny & Cher's last studio album. It reached number 132 in the charts, offering further proof that—on record at least—the duo's star was not shining as brightly as it once had.

C

As the year progressed, Cher needed another solo pop hit to put her back on track after the moderately disastrous *Bittersweet White Light*. Acutely aware of the breakdown in the couple's relationship, manager Denis Pregnolato approached Sonny's still relatively recent nemesis, producer Snuff Garrett, and asked him to work with Cher again.

Garrett's initial reaction was clear: an absolute and unequivocal no. But then he recalled how much he had enjoyed working on 'Gypsys Tramps & Thieves.' Garrett, who had subsequently been working with Vicki Lawrence and Liza Minnelli, appreciated the way Cher could learn a song on the spot and, if it connected with her, record it with the minimum of fuss. It was only Sonny he couldn't bear to work with again.

"I said, yeah, I'd work with her again," Garrett later recalled. "But only if Sonny isn't in the studio ... no, correction, only if he's not in the *area*. I didn't want him around check-marking every song and being El Primo. Those became the terms when Cher and I got back together." Resolutely off the scene, Sonny would soon be watching on as Cher rose up the charts again. It was a clear slap in the face for the man who had guided her to superstardom.

Garrett knew he had just the song for Cher. In fact, it had been languishing in his archive for some time. Lyricist Mary Dean had brought 'Half-Breed' to Garrett a while ago, having written it specifically for Cher; Garrett's arranger, Al Capps, added the music. It was an anguished tale of a girl with a Cherokee mother and white father, drawing (supposedly) on Cher's roots—which, chart-wise, had tended to provide her most popular hits. "I said from the lyrics it's a smash for Cher and for nobody else," Garrett told *Rolling Stone* in 1973. "To me, nobody else could do that song but Cher—that was Cher's story. So I held the song and then it worked out that we got Cher back, but the song sat in my desk for about three, four months."

'Half-Breed' is a fantastic take on racism—and not conventional white-against-African-American racism. It tells the story of a woman who is half white and half Cherokee—the protagonist is called an Indian squaw, yet accepted by neither Native Americans nor white people—and draws on the fact that Cher had been mistaken for a Native American for years.

With its driving beat—a cross between British glam-rock and war chant, allegedly based on the advertising jingle for a Pontiac dealership in Dallas— the sound was irresistible; Cher sung it like she meant it, shorn of all the affectations and mannerisms that had dogged *Bittersweet White Light*. Garrett marshaled his players—much the same line-up as had appeared on Cher's previous albums—to play to their strengths, while managing to contain any musical flights of fancy. The result was a fine 2:43 minute slice of on-point pop.

'Half-Breed' was another marvelously hand-tailored number for Cher. Although it was on the one hand a simple—and in some ways exploitative—tale that drew on Cher's supposed upbringing, it chimed with the times. There was at the time a growing understanding of Native American issues, which had been put on the public agenda by actress Sascheen Littlefeather, who dressed as an Apache Indian to reject Marlon Brando's Best Actor award at the same Academy Awards ceremony Cher and Sonny had recently attended. Littlefeather stated that Brando's rejection of the award was due to "the treatment of American Indians today by the film industry." The song also chimed with the occupation of Wounded Knee in South Dakota by the American Indian Movement (AIM), which had begun in February 1973. (Smokey Robinson would deliver a far more right-on, impassioned take on the subject later the same year with 'Just My Soul Responding.')

Cher felt that the song was exploitative, but it mattered not. Recorded quickly in just a few hours, it gave her another smash, reaching the top of the US charts in late October 1973 in between Grand Funk Railroad's 'We're An American Band' and The Rolling Stones' 'Angie.' The promotional video, taken from an episode of *The Sonny & Cher Comedy Hour*, marks the start of the point where Cher went right over the top. Emerging from burning flames and totem poles, she is shown wearing a stunning headdress bedecked with feathers and the skimpiest of bra tops and skirts, tailored by Bob Mackie, showing plenty of midriff. As the camera pans out, we see that she is sitting on a horse, from which she delivers the rest of the song.

The accompanying album plays to all of Cher's strengths by moving away from the rigid ballad tempo of *Foxy Lady* and the out-and-out schmaltz of *Bittersweet White Light*. Released on October 27 1973, *Half-Breed* captured her as a fabulous pop interpreter, and in many ways can be seen as the true follow-up to *Gypsys Tramps & Thieves* (which likewise had featured hardly any involvement from Sonny).

Garrett selected covers that suited Cher's voice. Her version of The Bee Gees' 'How Can You Mend A Broken Heart?' may not rival Al Green's superior version, but it certainly shows how well she could work with the right material. She also delves twice into the Paul McCartney songbook, covering his 1973 number one hit 'My Love' and the *Let It Be* tour de force 'The Long And Winding Road.'

Cher's paramour of the time, David Paich, contributed 'David's Song.' The album closes with 'Chastity's Sun,' which Cher had partially rewritten from Seals & Crofts' 'Ruby Jean And Billie Lee.' The original was a tender paean to the songwriters' wives; with several key lyric changes, Cher turned it into a tender, touching tribute to her daughter.

Another achingly poignant song came from Gloria Sklerov and Harry Lloyd, who had written 'He'll Never Know' for *Gypsys Tramps & Thieves.* Like 'The Greatest Show On Earth,' 'Two People Clinging To A Thread' is a little too close for comfort. It details the gradual breakdown of a marriage and talks about a couple who had once rushed to love each other but now make small talk when the lights are dimmed.

The other classic story-song on the album was written by Garrett's old friend John Durrill. Durrill had been in The Five Americans and The Ventures, and here contributes the singsong 'Carousel Man,' which brings Cher back to the fairgrounds of 'Gypsys Tramps & Thieves.' Released as a promotional single in late 1973, it secured further airplay for the album, helping it on its way to 500,000 sales.

Half-Breed proved a huge success. It put Cher back in the US top forty, reaching number twenty-eight. "Cher is no Streisand," Jaan Uhelszki wrote in his review of the album for *Creem* magazine, "but you gotta admit *Half-Breed* fills in the car music gap. This time around she sings about no sex, crossed lovers, and empty beds with all the lament of a daytime soap opera. Next she's a sweet sinner who's growing up too soon. Turn around and she's crooning a lullaby about her little daughter. Although Cher may be as predictable as a road map and her music is hot off the line, she knows how to make a good song click. Besides having a good frame, she's got great chemistry. High octane and potent." With Garrett back in the driving seat, it was exactly the right record for Cher to release, and it came at exactly the right moment.

Meanwhile, Sonny & Cher returned to the safe ground of their stage show for a final live album, *Live In Las Vegas Volume 2*, which appeared in early 1974. Produced by Denis Pregnolato, it once again shows off the slick machine that was Sonny & Cher live. A double album, it captures all the glory of their live show, including an impassioned reading of Stevie Wonder's 'You And I' (from *Talking Book*), and a medley of 'You Better Sit Down Kids' and 'A Cowboy's Work Is Never Done.'

Although the Sonny & Cher brand would roll on for another few years it was all coming to an end for them as a couple. The death knell for their marriage was sounded when Cher slept with Bill Hamm, the guitarist from their house band. It was the flagrant manner in which she did it—in their hotel room in Vegas—that stuck in Sonny's craw. By now, she was also having affairs with keyboard player David Paich and Elton John's lyricist Bernie Taupin. Sonny, in turn, had started a relationship with Connie Foreman. He and Cher did not have long left together.

CHAPTER 8
The Hard Way

In October 1973, Cher left Sonny for good. Around the same time came the first serious threat to his authority. After a year of dalliances, this time it was the real thing: Cher was setting up with Brooklyn-born, LA-dwelling music mogul David Geffen.

Geffen was the dazzling music-brain who had launched Asylum Records in 1971. A protégé of both Phil Spector and Ahmet Ertegun, he had managed Crosby Stills & Nash and was now working with the Eagles. He was, as Cher biographer J. Randy Taraborelli would later note, like Sonny in many respects. They were "both fiercely competitive businessmen whose consuming passion for the entertainment industry has made them very wealthy. One mountain is never enough; after it's been scaled, each begins creating new possibilities for the future. Excess is never enough; they are aggressively eccentric; the word more takes on new meaning with them."

Cher first met Geffen at a Bette Midler gig at the Troubadour in Los Angeles. They met again at a Neil Young gig at the Roxy in September 1973 and quickly became lovers. Cher had been vaguely aware of Geffen from when they had met at Gold Star Studios back in the sixties, when he worked for Phil Spector. When she saw his huge residence in Hollywood (formerly owned by Julie Andrews), she thought he was merely a promotions man who had struck it lucky. She didn't realize he had set up Asylum Records and was now responsible for the Eagles' stellar popularity in the USA. She was also surprised one night to find Joni Mitchell strolling through the house. Geffen didn't bat an eyelid. "She's recording an album," he told her, "and she's living with me." Geffen opened Cher's eyes to the cool LA scene. Gone were the Lauren Bacalls and Tony Curtises; in came the Neil Youngs and David Crosbys. Cher was at last in a milieu that suited her own age.

Geffen was a shrewd businessman with a point to prove. He was sincere in his affections for Cher, and when he began to delve into her finances he soon found huge inequalities in the numbers—stacked resolutely in Sonny's favor. When Sonny first heard Cher talking about somebody called David, he thought she meant to David Paich. "Unknown to me," Sonny later wrote, "lurking in the weeds, there was another David—David Geffen."

Sonny initially wrote off Geffen as a low-level threat but soon found out that this man was every inch his rival. That initial underestimation, he later recalled, was "one of my great misjudgments. Before long I knew exactly the kind of guy David Geffen was—a brilliant, calculating, extremely shrewd man who would do whatever he had to do, no matter what the cost—moneywise or human—to achieve his goal … to me, he was a ruthless cutthroat." Soon, Chastity was brought into the marital dispute, with Geffen intervening in Sonny's visiting rights to his beloved daughter.

Sonny and Cher's marital rift became public on February 1974. During the recording of the final shows for the fourth season of *The Sonny & Cher Comedy Hour*, Bono filed for a legal separation from Cher at Los Angeles Superior Court, citing "irreconcilable differences." Later that same month, Cher hosted a surprise birthday party for Geffen at the Beverly Wilshire Hotel, at which Cher and Bob Dylan—who had recently signed to Geffen's Asylum label—duetted on a version of 'All I Really Want To Do.'

It quickly became public knowledge that the wheels had been falling off the marital wagon for some considerable time. Although professionally the couple kept the show just about on the road, now the gloves were off—and there were still episodes of the final season of *The Sonny & Cher Comedy Hour* to shoot. Cher informed Sonny she wanted out of the TV deal with CBS. But after filming the final show, the duo still had to honor a performance commitment at the Houston Astrodome. They arrived separately, with separate entourages, and met only on the stage.

Bono captured the sorry finale to a decade of hard work with bitter poignancy in his autobiography. "We were playing the largest indoor venue in America," he wrote. "But we could barely manage a civil hello, let alone look at each other when we got onstage."

The surreal nature of the event was made even more bizarre by the fact they were performing in a place where, just hours earlier, a rodeo competition had been held. "The odor of cow and horse dung wafted up," Bono continued. "The whole place smelled like shit. It was an appropriate metaphor for what Cher and I had become."

On February 27 1974, Cher responded to Sonny's initial demand for a separation by suing him for divorce and suggesting that he had been holding her in "involuntary servitude." The case would play out in public over the next year. Fans who had grown up with Sonny and Cher as hippie role models and then laughed at them as they became respectable would look on avidly as claims and counterclaims were spelled out in low-rent news magazines. "Stardom made Sonny a huge womanizer," Cher recalled in 2010. "One woman, or even five, was not enough for him. I found all this out afterward. I asked him: how did you manage the logistics? I was trusting and faithful with him. The truth is, I'm not so sure we should've ever been husband and wife."

Against this fraught backdrop, Johnny Musso at MCA implored upon Snuff Garrett to produce another Cher album. Garrett was more than happy to oblige. Collaborating once again with Al Capps, he worked quickly, assembling another strong selection of material to capitalize on Cher's current notoriety.

Dark Lady's beautiful, Richard Avedon-shot cover photograph of Cher in a stunning black evening gown, with a black cat on her shoulder, cast her as a mature woman emanating mystery. Gone was the waif; gone was the girl who looked like she had spent too long in the dressing-up box. Here was a simple, sophisticated, sensual woman.

After the success of 'Carousel Man' from *Half-Breed*, Garrett asked John Durill to contribute to the album. Durill wrote three of the album's showstoppers, including the title track, which went on to top the US singles chart at the end of March 1974. Durill wrote the song and then departed for a tour of Japan with The Ventures. Garrett was unhappy with the third verse—he wanted the singer to shoot the lady of the title and the boyfriend who was cheating with her—so Durill amended the lyrics via a series of telegrams and long-distance telephone calls.

A fortuneteller speaks of the protagonist's man being unfaithful. When the singer realizes she recognizes the smell of the dark lady's perfume from somewhere else, she returns to find the woman with her man and kills them both. It is a superb story-song, with all the requisite pathos of 'Gypsys Tramps & Thieves.' Although Cher was allegedly not over-enamored of it, 'Dark Lady' was another big, stupid production with all the requisite bells and whistles, the session players seemingly having an absolute whale of a time. There were two promotional videos: one taken from *The Sonny & Cher Comedy Hour*, with Cher in front of her now trademark spotlight wearing a stunning, oversized veil studded with multi-colored crystals, and a cartoon version, with Cher portrayed as the dark lady of the title, handing out her card as Madame Fifi of Story Street, New Orleans.

Elsewhere on the album, Durill contributed the reflective 'Dixie Girl' and 'I Saw A Man And He Danced With His Wife,' another tale of adultery and woe. *Dark Lady* opens with Alan O'Day's classic 'Train Of Thought,' marking out the sort of intelligent soft rock that Cher longed to sing. O'Day, who had recently written 'Angie Baby' for Helen Reddy, here offers an upbeat, adult song detailing the demise of a failing relationship. Over a driving Fender Rhodes piano, Cher delivers one of her huskiest vocal performances, while Capps and Garrett employ the string section to its fullest effect.

'Train Of Thought' proved very popular, and made a worthy follow-up to 'Dark Lady.' Released in June 1974, it reached number twenty-seven on *Billboard*'s Hot 100, while also showing its rock credentials by making it into the Adult Contemporary top ten. Other highlights included a romp through Fontella Bass's 'Rescue Me,' a tribute to Cher's friend Bette Midler on 'Miss Subway Of 1952,' and a heartfelt, reflective version of Irving Berlin's 'What'll I Do.' *Billboard* described *Half-Breed* as the album that "could finally ... establish Cher as a major album artist as well as a sure single-seller, TV, and club star." Unfortunately, however, it only made number sixty-nine on the US album chart.

With its rich and varied material, *Dark Lady* would be Cher's final album for MCA. Her contract was up for renewal, and David Geffen felt that the newly independent Cher needed to break out and make an adult rock album. As 1974 progressed, she had momentarily lost a husband, a television show, and a recording contract. In return, she had gained something she had never quite experienced before: her freedom.

C

Cher's divorce from Sonny was finalized on June 26 1975. It was impossible to believe the duo were finally through as a couple after a decade together in the media's glare.

As much as she needed her freedom, Cher also needed to divorce Sonny to move away from the disastrous, restrictive contract she had been placed under by Bono's Cher Enterprises. Sonny's final counterargument in court that Cher was an unfit mother was clearly untrue, and all parties knew it.

As the duo left the court, Sonny grabbed Cher, kissed her full on the lips, and started laughing. Cher followed suit. "I wanted to be mad with him," she later wrote. "I *was* mad with him. But I couldn't stay mad at him; there was this stupid thing between us that I couldn't cut, something in that strange, gray Sonny & Cher zone." Sonny would never be completely out of her life until his death in a tragic skiing accident in 1998. Even to this day, images of Sonny appear nineties at Cher's concerts in Las Vegas.

For an artist with such a high profile, Cher made three misfires in pretty rapid succession in the mid seventies. After she had released the contract-fulfilling *Greatest Hits* album on MCA in December 1974, she was free to relaunch her career elsewhere. The grand plan was simple: sign to Warner Bros and reunite with Phil Spector, the producer who started it all for her, to cut an album.

It was not a good idea. Spector was fresh from the *Rock'n'Roll* debacle with John Lennon, who was then in the midst of his notorious 'lost weekend.' The episode resulted in Spector kidnapping the master tapes for the album from Lennon, while he had subsequently been hurt in a head-on collision in his Rolls Royce on Melrose Avenue in Los Angeles. By spring 1974, however, he was ready to fulfill his contractual obligation to Warners with his recently founded Warner-Philles Records.

Spector decided to try to recreate the old magic with Cher and returned to Gold Star Studios with a cast of thousands to cut the song 'A Woman's

Story,' later described by Spector biographer Mick Brown as "a dark lamentation in which a prostitute looks back over her life." It was as bizarre and wayward a debut release for a new label as 'Classified 1A' had been three years earlier. Sounding not unlike George Harrison's 'Hear Me Lord' from *All Things Must Pass*, the song has a funky swing and an impressive if over-zealous female chorus but is executed at a dead slow pace.

Cher also recorded the old Ronettes stomper 'Baby, I Love You,' but Spector seemed hell-bent on extinguishing any of the song's *joie de vivre*. Clocking in at over five minutes—with an intrusive heartbeat-style bass drum to the fore, even when it breaks into the chorus—the song sounds as if it is being played at the wrong speed. As Mick Brown notes, Spector "had elected to render one song after another as a monolithic plod."

The sessions broke down when David Geffen, Spector's old studio hand, arrived to see Cher and began handing out advice. Spector promptly punched him to the ground. Although the sessions continued, they were doomed to failure. Cher sang one song, a cover of Martha & The Vandellas' 'A Love Like Yours (Don't Come Knocking Everyday),' with Harry Nilsson, another man who was grappling with his demons. It was allegedly recorded earlier, at one of Spector's John Lennon sessions, and is typical of the Spector sound of the period, with overlaid saxophones slowly honking all signs of life out of the melody. Nilsson simply sounds otherworldly. The single appeared as a promo, but Cher intervened and halted the official release.

With the Spector experiment best quickly forgotten, Cher needed to record an album that continued her growth into an adult artist. After all, she was now alone, and her peers were more Carly Simon than Karen Carpenter. David Geffen suggested another musical avatar, Jimmy Webb, oversee the sessions.

Recorded throughout 1974 and early '75 at Sunset Sound Recorders, *Stars* was a great attempt at making a grown-up LA album. Webb selected songs by heavyweight writers such as Neil Young ('Mr Soul'), Eric Clapton ('Bell Bottom Blues'), and Janis Ian ('Stars'). Lead single 'These Days,' written by Jackson Browne, was a long way from her experiments with Phil Spector. An affecting piano ballad, it sets Cher against subtle strings and finds her emoting in a manner reminiscent of Barbara Streisand at the beginning of the song. Elsewhere, a version of Boudleaux Bryant's 'Love Hurts' provided Cher with one of her signature numbers, and would prove a sizeable hit when she revisited it in 1991.

Cher was optimistic for *Stars*, a grown-up album on which she is fully in charge. It's an understated, sweet, unadorned record. *Billboard* called it "a mix of MOR type cuts, bluesy rock, progressive country, and more standard rock" with "excellent musicianship throughout from a number of prominent players." Released in May 1975 to coincide with the launch of her new TV vehicle, *The Cher Show*, the album did not, however, make much of a splash, reaching a meager number 153 in the USA.

Julian Mendelsohn offered a deeply cynical take in his review for *Phonograph Record*. "All in all," he wrote, "*Stars* is certain to enrapture and delight Cher's hundreds of thousands of avid fans. If Sonny's forthcoming solo double-album (which he's currently recording in Muscle Shoals with members of Amon Düül, Focus, the Grateful Dead, and The Heywoods) is anywhere near this hot, 1975 may yet emerge as something better than the Year Barry White Ran Amuck."

Mendelsohn's review is typical of the sort of criticism that Cher would came up against—and that drew her closer to her fans, who complain to this day that *Stars* has never been released on CD. (It is still languishing in the Warner Bros vault.) Warners were as disappointed as Cher by the album's poor performance. It was a good if not great album that recast Cher as a sensitive interpreter of well-written contemporary rock ballads. But the public, who were in the slow process of falling out of love with her, thought otherwise.

C

In the mid seventies, Cher was the epitome of middle-of-the-road entertainment. Gregg Allman was the Southern rock bad-boy. Their union is still one of the most disbelievingly discussed in all of popular music.

Although Allman briefly gave Cher the sort of rock star credibility that she craved—and a beautiful son—he also gave her a disastrous marriage, rife with splits, reconciliations, and all of the requisite drama. They made for the most unusual couple.

Gregg Allman was—and still is, for that matter—the very embodiment of the Southern rocker. Primarily a keyboardist, he was the leader, vocalist, guitarist, and Hammond player for The Allman Brothers Band, a well-loved blues-rock ensemble who enjoyed enormous popularity in the early seventies. Born in December 1947, in Nashville, he originally played with his brother Duane in Hour Glass before that band evolved into The Allman Brothers.

By the early seventies, The Allman Brothers Band had done a remarkable thing. They were enjoying chart success with a string of well-crafted singles, yet retained the respect of serious music fans with their full-length albums. Their double LP *Live At The Fillmore East* was released in 1971. It was everything *Sonny & Cher Live*—released the same year—was not. Here was a group reveling in the blues and extending their songs, often to more than thirty minutes.

The Allman Brothers were just the sort of hard-rocking, hard-living players to whom Sonny & Cher were diametrically opposed. They were troubled, to say the least. Lead guitarist Duane Allman was killed in a tragic motorcycle accident on October 29 1971, while bass guitarist Berry Oakley died in similar circumstances just over a year later on November 11 1972. Drugs, drink, and women all played an integral part of the band's life on the road.

Cher met Allman at the Troubadour in Los Angeles in 1974, while she was still seeing David Geffen. Although a tentative first date turned out to be a disaster—with some reports suggesting Allman passed out in a plate of Chinese food, and that Cher was less-than-impressed with his attempts at pawing and fumbling in the car afterward—the pair met again, and it was clear that Cher was smitten. There is little doubt that, initially, the relationship was largely driven by physical urges. Cher hadn't met a man quite like this particular Southern gentleman. Allman had also already been married twice, and was, according to biographer Lawrence J. Quirk, "a bull in the bedroom."

Cher had never known anything like it. She was his Chooch; he was her Gui Gui. She was absolutely besotted. "Anybody with two eyes could have seen that we were a disaster waiting to happen," she later admitted. "I had to have known it was the wrong thing to do, but there was something about

Gregory. He was handsome and wild. He was rock'n'roll—the definitive bad boy: he was also tender and sensitive."

Cher had also never met a man with so great a capacity for drink and drugs. She thought she could change him. Aside from the odd puff of marijuana, Cher had remained drug-free even though many around her on the LA scene would frequently partake. She had seen the debilitating effects: she was at the Troubadour on the night of the Average White Band show when what was originally thought to be cocaine was passed around. It was actually heroin, and people began passing out at the after-show party. Cher, sober and responsible, was able to save the life of AWB guitarist Alan Gorrie; drummer Robbie Macintosh died the next day. Cher was briefly embroiled in the ensuing controversy.

It was during this time that Gregg Allman became further estranged from his band-mates. Although he had been running a parallel solo career since 1973, setting up with Cher seemed alien to sections of his fan base, and to the other band-members. His alienation was exacerbated when he committed the cardinal sin of testifying against his dealer, tour manager and bodyguard John 'Scooter' Herring, after Allman was arrested for possession of cocaine. Herring was convicted of five drug offences and sentenced to a total of seventy-five years in prison.

The band saw Allman's testimony as an act of betrayal. There were tales of a wider plot. The band-members were ardent supporters of Governor Jimmy Carter's presidential bid and had played a benefit for him in November 1975. Far right opponents suggested, fancifully, that the governor was involved in a bid with Coca-Cola to spread cocaine across America. It was better to find a scapegoat and deal with this problem immediately.

"There is no way we can work with Gregg again, ever," lead guitarist Dickie Betts told *Rolling Stone*. The Allmans split up; Cher, who had supported Allman through the trial, was indirectly blamed. "Gregg makes a great villain because he's taken drugs," she later wrote. "They acted as if he had turned his road manager into a drug dealer, when it was the other way around."

Cher and Greg Allman were married on June 30 1975 in attorney

Mickey Rudin's suite at Caesars Palace, Las Vegas, four days after the settlement of her divorce from Sonny. Former manager Joe DeCarlo was the best man; Cher's sister Georganne was maid of honor. The ceremony was witnessed by ten friends and family members.

Nine days after the wedding, Cher filed for divorce. It had all been a hasty mistake. It was clear she was still a lost little girl, unsure of the right thing to do, and it was clear that Allman had some deeply serious issues: not just drug dependence but also deep and unresolved grief for his beloved elder brother Duane and former band-mate Oakley.

Sonny looked on wryly. "From what I heard, their love affair had all the ups and downs of an elevator ride," he later wrote. "Red-hot one minute and nonexistent the next. The public saw it as a strange mix, but to anyone who knew Cher it made perfect sense. Nothing attracted Cher like a mean, tough and potentially dangerous rock and roller." One thing was for sure: Sonny liked Allman a whole lot better than David Geffen.

Cher returned to Allman and did all she could to help; on August 1, she dropped the divorce petition. "I think I married Gregory because I was so tired of having someone tell me what to do that I chose someone who couldn't even tell himself what to do and couldn't try to be dominant over me," she later recalled. Her relationship with Allman was volatile, and the press absolutely lapped it up, with paparazzi photographers ready to take as many shots of the beauty and the beast as possible.

Allman had known fame and respect—and myriad groupies—but he had never witnessed anything like the press he now received having become Mr Cher. And, of course, the media wanted to capture Allman looking as out-of-it as possible to show what this demon was doing to good ol' Cher. "Photographers brought in a picture of me looking like I was really stoned, like I was really in the chips," Allman later explained in an unaired interview with a New Orleans television station. "They soup up these Nikons and catch me blinking my eyes. I couldn't understand how people made a living talking about other people."

Gregg and Cher would split up and reconcile several more times during their three years as man and wife. She tried to get Allman clean, but underestimated what a drug like heroin can do to a person. Allman would pledge to give it all up; Cher would believe him; he would relapse; and so the cycle would repeat itself. "Drugs and alcohol really messed up our marriage," he later admitted. "Now that those problems have been taken care of, it's a whole new ballgame ... I'd be dead now, if it wasn't for Cher. That's almost definite." When Allman kicked heroin, he became an alcoholic.

C

While her relationship with Allman was unfolding, and alongside her variable recordings in this period, Cher returned to an area in which she knew she could excel. In 1975, a new hour-long television extravaganza, *The Cher Show*, aimed to put Cher and her music center-stage—this time, without the general buffoonery of Sonny Bono holding her back. But in the aftermath and recriminations surrounding the demise of *The Sonny & Cher Comedy Hour*, it was actually Sonny who had made it back to television first. *The Sonny Comedy Revue* ran for one season on ABC, making its debut on September 22 1974. It featured a lot of the same performers as *The Sonny & Cher Comedy Hour*, and Sonny struggled manfully for thirteen episodes before the show was pulled amid falling ratings. It could never work. There was no Cher.

The Cher Show had a much more auspicious start. It aired as a one-off special on February 12 1975, and was followed quickly by the first of a weekly series, starting on February 16. Directed by ex-*Comedy Hour* producer Art Fisher and initially overseen by David Geffen, the show still had room for Cher's slapstick comedy but focused primarily on her singing—and, of course, her stunning Bob Mackie-designed gowns. The special featured appearances by Elton John, Bette Midler, and Flip Wilson. The show was then commissioned for two seasons, with subsequent guests including Ray Charles, Kermit The Frog, Raquel Welch, Tatum O'Neal, and Dinah Shore. It gained favorable notices, with Cecil Smith of the *Los Angeles Times* offering "three cheers for Cher and her new CBS variety show ... Sonny without Cher was a disaster. Cher without Sonny, on the other hand, could be the best thing that's happened to weekly television this season."

The Cher Show will always be slightly more than a footnote in her career thanks to an appearance by David Bowie on the November 23 1975 broadcast. Making his US network TV debut, Bowie performed his current single, 'Fame,' before duetting with Cher on a superlative track from his album *Young Americans*, 'Can You Hear Me?' The couple then sang a selection of recent and current hits to the studio orchestra's accompaniment: 'Song Sung Blue,' 'One,' 'Da Doo Ron Ron,' 'Wedding Bell Blues,' 'Maybe Baby,' 'Day Tripper,' 'Blue Moon,' 'Only You,' 'Temptation,' 'Ain't No Sunshine,' and 'Young Blood.' It was fairly excruciating watching two very thin, fundamentally introverted superstars trying to come across as showbiz buddies. Bowie would later recall that Cher was initially frosty but "warmed up when we sang together. I was probably this crazed anorexic figure walking in, and I'm sure she didn't know what to make of me."

The Cher Show ran until January 4 1976. Cher had become increasingly frustrated with the involvement of censors checking and double-checking her look and her material. "It was the strangest thing," she later wrote. "When I was married and doing *The Sonny & Cher Comedy Hour*, I could get away with all kinds of double-entendre stuff, and nobody took it seriously. But after my divorce, all that changed."

The censors commented on the skimpiness of her dresses as well as anything that could possibly be interpreted as smutty. Although the show had initially enjoyed great ratings, it found itself up against the season's big hit, *The Six Million Dollar Man* on ABC. Cher sensed that it was a good time to quit. "I made the decision after I'd done four Cher shows last fall," she said at the time. "Nothing to do with the ratings."

"Doing a show alone was more than I could handle," she later added. "I had to be into everything, from helping on scripts to picking the music. And they had me doing a monologue. That's not like me, to be out there alone making with the jokes."

Soon, she wouldn't be alone in front of the television camera. Despite all the splits and acrimony, there was only one person she could turn to: Sonny Bono. And so, in late 1975, she called him and asked him to come back and join her on television. With David Geffen no longer on the scene, Cher and Denis Pregnolato had ironed out the various contractual difficulties in order to make the reunion possible.

The Sonny & Cher Show began the first of its two seasons in February

1976. The material was spikier, informed by their personal situation, yet this thinly disguised bitterness was arguably less attractive than the sparring married couple of old. This was no glimpse into a couple's life: over the past twenty-four months, the American public had come to know the most intimate of behind-the-scenes details.

The first episode begins with Sonny and Cher bursting onto the stage to Buddy Holly's 'That'll Be The Day.' It's as much of a confessional as the primetime television format would allow. When Sonny looks across at Cher to sing "you say you're gonna leave / you know it's a lie," he has the most ironic expression on his face.

The regulars, stupidity, and fun were all present and correct, including the much-loved characters of Albert and Laverne. "This makes me feel like a kid," Albert (Sonny) says as they sit at a bar in one skit. "I've felt like a kid for years," Laverne (Cher) replies, "but I always seem to end up with old codgers."

The Sonny & Cher Show highlights just how well the duo could work together. Later in the series, Sonny pipes up: "We have nine days to go, it'll be the first Tuesday in November ... it's Election Day." He is clearly referencing their divorce, but then goes on to talk about Jimmy Carter going back to his peanut farm. The skits are never less than amusing, especially the disaster-movie spoof *The Towering Poseidon Quake Port Hinden Jaws Follies '78*. Among the guests were Donny and Marie Osmond, to whom Sonny drawls: "Sonny and Cher and Donny and Marie. We are people in search of a last name."

As if to underline their popularity, Sonny and Cher were the first celebrities to be made into twelve-and-a-half-inch dolls by the Mego Corporation, which had made its name with figurines of Marvel and DC comic-book characters. Housed in little red boxes with see-through plastic fronts, the dolls would become highly collectable; the Cher doll came complete with a stunning range of miniaturized Bob Mackie gowns. Characters from *Wonder Woman* and *Charlie's Angels* would soon follow; Sonny & Cher were in a very exclusive club indeed.

C

With Cher devoting time to rehearsing the new Sonny & Cher TV show, Allman felt abandoned, alone in their mansion. She was spending more time with her ex-husband, he said, than she was with him. Bored away from the road, without the band that had made him famous, and having sufficient time to feed his addictions, it was now his turn to file for divorce. But it was not yet to be. Cher realized she was pregnant; she and Allman celebrated their volatile union by having a child together.

It was a difficult pregnancy. Mindful of the miscarriages she had suffered in the sixties, Cher took extra care. During a brief vacation with Chastity in Hawaii, she felt premature labor pains. Gregg flew from Macon, Georgia, to be by her side, and the couple reconciled. The family spent five blissful weeks in a villa in Oahu. A boy, Elijah Blue, was born on July 10 1976, shortly after the return to television of *The Sonny & Cher Show*. Elijah, Allman later noted, was "the last prophet to die, and a real rascal. And Blue [came] from blues."

A couple of months later, in October 1976, Cher released a follow-up to *Stars*, *I'd Rather Believe In You*. It did absolutely nothing commercially. With her life story being played out on television—reuniting with Sonny, getting married to and having a child with Allman—Cher the singer seemed way down the list of priorities.

It wasn't for want of trying. *I'd Rather Believe In You* sounds lovely, and has a stunning cover illustration by Norman Seeff, but it just didn't click. The title track, penned by producer Michael Omartian, is a gentle rock ballad; 'Silver Wings & Golden Rings' an affecting country narrative. 'Long Distance Love Affair,' a white soul stomper with more than a touch of the Buckingham–Nicks Fleetwood Mac, was issued as the album's lead single. It sank without trace. The album's true shining moment is a spirited, aggressive version of Eddie Floyd's 'Knock On Wood,' cut three years before Amii Stewart's disco version. With swaggering brass and high-in-the-mix guitar from Jay Graydon, it showed just how capable Cher could be with appropriate material.

For the next year, while Cher released albums, reared her children, and performed in cabaret and on the television with Sonny, the American press watched and waited for the next episode in the life of Mr and Mrs Allman.

Who would leave whom next? It was a comic's dream, and few could resist a swipe at the pop singer and her wayward Southern lover. Cher and Gregg were invited to Jimmy Carter's inauguration dinner on Thursday January 20 1977. Cher, a lifelong Democrat, later recalled: "I would have never thought that I would be having dinner with the president—and on his first night in office."

To further capitalize on the Sonny & Cher reunion, Warner Bros urged the duo to get back into the studio. Duly released in early 1977, their final single together sank without a trace. It was notable only for being their first (and last) foray into disco. Both sides were written by Bono: The A-side, 'You're Not Right For Me,' plays on the psychodrama of their relationship; 'Wrong Number' is an amiable show tune.

Although the early episodes proved very popular, *The Sonny & Cher Show* gradually began to fall down the ratings. By the summer of 1977, hampered by a nomadic timeslot, the show had fallen out of the top thirty ratings for the first time in its run, and was promptly canceled. Audiences had loved them when they were the nation's sweethearts; now, with Cher very publicly married to another man, and having just given birth to his child, any spark between her and Sonny would have looked like adultery. The last episode aired on August 29 1977, and with that, the Sonny & Cher show came to a close.

Cher's new life, as volatile as it was, seemed a million miles away from her cozy primetime existence with Sonny. In any case, Cher was wrapped up in the promotion of her album with Gregg, *Two The Hard Way*, recorded after he had cleaned up with a spell at the Silver Hills Foundation in Connecticut. She also had another solo album to promote as well. Warner Bros released *Cherished* in September 1977 and would prove to be Cher's final solo album for the label. Taking no chances, Warners reunited Cher with the winning team of Al Capps and Snuff Garrett and moved her back to Larrabee Sound Studios in North Hollywood. John Durrill and Gloria Sklerov were back on the writing team. Durill contributed some sensitive, appropriate material, including 'Thunderstorm,' 'Dixie,' and 'Love The Devil Out Of Ya,' a sweet song of reconciliation about a woman who would do anything to protect her lover. 'Warpaint And Soft Feathers' revisits 'Half-

Breed' territory in its doomed tale of love between a Cherokee and an Apache, set against scraping violins and chiming lead guitar.

'Pirate' was a suitably dramatic choice of lead single. It's a propulsive, string-heavy rewrite of 'Gypsys Tramps & Thieves,' with a gutsy vocal, seagull effects, and high-seas accordion wheezing away throughout. The main problem was that Cher wasn't all that interested. "Cher wasn't into this album at all," Garrett later recalled. "She was beginning to want to sing rock'n'roll ... she complained about the songs we chose."

No matter how her releases were adorned, what had worked in the early seventies was now simply not registering with the public at large. 'Pirate' scraped into the *Billboard* Hot 100, which was more than could be said for its parent album. In the new era of *Hotel California*, *Rumours*, and disco, Cher's dramatic narratives of love and loss seemed somehow out of step. Cher the soap opera had overtaken Cher the popular entertainer.

And Cher the soap opera had its prime exhibit with *Two The Hard Way*. Credited to 'Allman And Woman' it simply came out at the wrong time. It was ignored by Cher's fan base and made Allman a laughing stock with his. This was an era of smooth rock in the USA and punk rock in the UK. Warner Bros pleaded with Cher to put her name on the sleeve, but she resisted. "My publicist said I couldn't possibly have a record without my name on it," she said at the time, "so I fired the publicist."

Two The Hard Way was an old-fashioned rock'n'soul album that might well have worked by taking the respective artists to each other's fans. Instead, it was roundly ignored. In a different time, the album could have been a huge success. It was produced by Allman, who enlisted some heavyweight friends to come along and make the sessions go with a hugely professional swing: Willie Weeks was on bass, Bobbye Hall on percussion, Timothy B. Schmidt on vocals, and Jim Horn on saxophone. This gave the sound a hugely polished radio-friendly edge.

In an ironic nod to the past, the album contains a respectful cover version of Smokey Robinson's 'You Really Got A Hold On Me'—just as Sonny & Cher's debut album, *Look At Us*, had twelve years earlier. Perhaps Allman And Woman saw this as the start of a long-term recording proposition.

There is much to enjoy: Sandford–Townshend's 'In For The Night' is uptight and swampy, while Michael Smotherman's 'Can You Fool' is a sweet and tender ballad that features prominently Allman's Rhodes piano. (The line "you can take all the medicine you need to figure out who you are" seems especially prescient.) 'I Love Makin' Love To You' is a superb slice of FM-friendly soul, as if pop duo Captain & Tennille had recorded at Muscle Shoals.

The album closes with an impassioned cover of Lieber & Stoller's 'Love Me,' made famous by the recently departed Elvis Presley. It was intended both as a tribute to Presley and a catalogue of Cher and Allman's marital traumas. The album artwork, which shows the couple entwined, looking at the camera as if they had been caught unawares *in flagrante delicto*, caused a good deal of controversy, although as biographer Lawrence J. Quirk would later note, it is as hilarious as it is sexy, with Cher "the sophisticated hooker" and Allman "the good ol' boy who never changes his underwear." The album itself is much better than you might think it would be; viewed through the most romantic of lenses, it is a passion play for a doomed romance. The more either party pleads and confirms their love, the less likely love becomes. The most interesting thing is actually hearing Cher sing with a proper vocalist. It has long been unavailable to buy, and has never been reissued on CD. Vinyl copies change hands for around $100 on eBay.

What was amazing was that promotion for the album continued throughout autumn, with a small yet ambitious European tour. After a couple of trial gigs in Japan and Germany, The Gregg Allman Band and Cher departed for Europe in November 1977. It was rumored that the pair spent $100,000 of their own money on the tour because Warner Bros did not believe in the album.

The show opened in Brussels, where UPI reporter Ruth Gruber would note: "Their performance onstage, backed by an eight-piece band, still has rough edges, but both singers are enjoying the experiment. The act is a mixture of hard-driving Allman Brothers classics, with Gregg singing solo, and soft country-western-blues-type duet arrangements. Cher, known in the past for her exotic costume changes, dressed simply in tight, faded jeans, a see-through tank top, and a cowboy hat in keeping with the downhome qualify of the music. But she dominated the show with her powerful voice, her dancing, and her exceptional stage presence."

The stage show featured solo Allman, solo Cher, and duets between the pair. It was as strange an enterprise as you'd think it would be. Allman later told *Us* magazine that the audience was, to put it mildly, weird. "She had the people in the upper age bracket, who came wearing corsages, with eight-to-eleven-year-old children. Then there were the Allman Brothers people, the backpackers. Her audience would never think of yelling out to people onstage. But mine was always giving a lot of hell, calling out songs. It got to her."

While they were in the UK, Allman, Cher, and their six-piece band performed 'Love Me' and 'Move Me' on the cult BBC television show *The Old Grey Whistle Test*. By December 3, however, Cher had left the tour and headed back for the States. It was all too much for her. Allman was drinking again. "I realized it was never going to be any different," she later noted. "And finally I became bored. That sounds capricious of me, or whatever, but I knew I was the one who was trying to put the strength back into him. I would just leave him and go back, leave him and go back. Finally, I just said: fuck it." Both the marriage and the professional union were over. Cher filed for divorce again.

Gregg Allman and Cher's divorce was finalized on January 6 1979. They had been living separately since early 1978, and it had been a strange interlude even by Cher's standards. "I wouldn't have gone through it all except that nobody ever made me feel as happy as Gregg did," Cher reflected. "God, he's wonderful. I just don't understand why he can't see it. He's the kindest, most gentle, loving husband and father. But then he forgets everything and it all goes right to shit."

For Sonny, the relationship was always doomed simply because Allman could only ever be a junior partner to Cher's overarching success and worldwide familiarity. "He had to compete with Cher egotistically, because she was a hot television property," he later wrote. "He seemed to me to be a very nice guy, but confused; a great musician too, which doesn't mean anything if you're strung out. He was very nice to Chastity, and that's what really mattered."

"It took a lot of growing up real fast," Allman told a US television reporter in 1982. He spoke with tremendous affection about Cher, revealing his utter surprise and amazement at how he became public property as soon as his relationship with her went public. "The reason that we split up, I think, was more her surroundings, where she was in Beverly Hills, Hollywood—I couldn't take it, I couldn't live that way, I couldn't do it. I had to come back south; it's where I belong. I think if she'd come with me it might have worked. I knew that was where her roots were and I respected that."

Gregg Allman would subsequently reunite with The Allman Brothers Band and continue to play with them in between pursuing a successful solo career. Cher needed to reconsider her options, but she loved her dalliance with rock'n'roll and knew that it must continue. She and Gregg kept in intermittent contact over Elijah. "Elijah's never been close to his father," Cher said in 1992. "He sees him, but he doesn't really know him. It's a sad thing because I think Gregory would have got an awful lot out of Elijah, but it just wasn't meant to be."

Portrait of a young Cher, Los Angeles, California, 1963.

LEFT: Cher rehearses with Jerry Wexler at Muscle Shoals Recording Studios in Sheffield, Alabama, 1969.
ABOVE: Sonny and Cher in *Chastity*.
RIGHT: Sonny, Cher, and Chastity on *The Sonny & Cher Comedy Hour*, 1971.

ABOVE: Sonny & Cher leave the set at the end of their
Comedy Hour, 1976.
RIGHT: Cher on stage at the Resorts International Hotel,
Atlantic City, New Jersey, 1979.

LEFT: Cher and co-star Nicolas Cage in *Moonstruck*, 1987.
BELOW: Backstage at the premiere of *Come Back To The Five & Dime, Jimmy Dean, Jimmy Dean*, with Elijah and Chastity, 1982.

LEFT: Cher in New York City, 1988.
BELOW: Cher and Darlene Love rehearse for the Heart Of Stone tour at the Fox Theater, Atlanta, Georgia, 1989.

CHER

THIS PAGE: The Love Hurts tour arrives in London, England, 1992; promotional stills for the *Believe* album and Cher At The Colosseum. OPPOSITE PAGE: The Living Proof tour hits the MEN Arena, Manchester, England, 2004.

Cher and Christina Aguilera at the *Burlesque* premiere, Los
Angeles, California, 2010.

Take Me Home

With the Gregg Allman interlude safely behind her, Cher decided that the only way forward was to work hard and reinstate her position in the hearts of the American public.

In 1978, she took to the stage again. "I was a working single parent with two children and loads of debt," she recalled. Although the new show was fairly modest, it put Cher back in the supper-club environment, as opposed to the universities she had been playing with Allman. To overcome her nerves she hit upon the idea of coming out initially as Laverne, the character she had created on *The Sonny & Cher Show*. With the ice broken, she launched into her set, which would more or less remain the same until she formed the rock band Black Rose in the early eighties.

After making these tentative moves back into the world of live performance, it was time for Cher to get a deal again. For once, the label she chose was just as grandiose as she was.

Casablanca can be seen as the apotheosis of the excesses of the record industry in the seventies. It was set up by larger-than-life executive Neil Bogart, who had cut his teeth working at Buddah Records in the late sixties. Everything about the label was overstated. After a shaky start, cartoon-rock outfit Kiss began rampaging around American stadiums racking up the dollars, thereby providing a decent financial bedrock for Bogart's dreams to be fulfilled. The release of Donna Summer's 'I Feel Love' in 1977 marked another turning point for the label. This strange, off-kilter, futuristic sound at once defined the future. A worldwide number one hit, it gave Bogart ever more extravagant dreams and visions.

As Cher celebrated her independence by becoming ever more wayward, it seemed only a matter of time before she and Bogart would hook up artistically. Disco thrilled her; she was exactly the core consumer of the populist art form in its post-*Saturday Night Fever* popularity. She was opulent, ready to party, and had lots of friends to hang out with. She had also been photographed extensively at New York's Studio 54, the club at the center of the disco scene.

Cher's involvement with Casablanca came as a result of her romance with Kiss bassist Gene Simmons, which preoccupied gossip columnists for most of 1978. How the pair met was like manna from heaven for journalists. Cher went to a fundraising party for democratic Californian governor Jerry Brown, where she was asked if she'd be interested in meeting Simmons. She thought she was about to meet the legendary Hollywood actress, after whom Kiss's Simmons had renamed himself in affectionate parody.

Although Cher and the rocker didn't initially see eye-to-eye, romance soon blossomed. Simmons may have been an excessive womanizer, but he did not drink, smoke, or take drugs. He was all rock and little roll. After Gregg Allman's excessive lifestyle, this was perfect for Cher. She could enjoy the rock lifestyle but not have to lose her man to the secretive world of addiction.

What Simmons did do, however, was the sex. He had a voracious appetite for women and famously boasted that in 1974 alone he had bedded 365 virgins. Cher admired his intelligence and his stability. And in a strange family twist, her sister started dating Kiss's Paul Stanley.

On September 18 1978, to highlight the excess of Casablanca and the popularity of Kiss, all four band-members released solo albums on the same day. Cher appears on Simmons's 'Living In Sin,' a paean to the groupie scene and a kind of slower dry run for her duet with Meat Loaf on 'Dead Ringer (For Love)' in 1981.

It was through this album that Cher met Neil Bogart. She was charmed by his charisma and highly receptive to his offer for her to join the Casablanca roster. She signed to the label in March 1978, becoming label-mates with Kiss, Donna Summer, The Village People, and a host of machine-driven European disco acts.

Bogart felt that one of the best things to do with his new signing was to get her back before the camera and announce to America that this was very much business as usual. The first step was a one-off ABC-TV broadcast, *Cher ... Special*, which aired in April 1978 and was one of the ten highest-rated shows of the week. With special guest appearances by Dolly Parton, The Tubes, and Rod Stewart, *Cher … Special* demonstrated that all was ostensibly well in Cher world. It was bright and shiny, with a great deal of costume changes—just how the public wanted to see Cher. She did a fifteen-minute take on *West Side Story*, in which she played all the parts; there was a set piece entitled 'The Musical Battle To Save Cher's Soul,' where she duetted with Dolly Parton on a wild, spiritual medley, with Parton playing God in a spaceship, taking Cher to heaven. Cher then had to fight The Devil, played by The Tubes, whose theatrical new wave had made them the toast of Los Angeles, and who here sang their recent hit 'Mondo Bondage.' *Cher … Special* had high production values and high-octane camp. It was a million miles away from the Southern swamp-rockers with whom Cher had until recently been fraternizing. It was just how the public wanted to see her.

Although Cher wanted to make a rock'n'roll album, Bogart felt that it was time for her to go disco. After all, she would hardly be alone in doing so: artists as diverse as The Rolling Stones, Mike Oldfield, and even Kiss had dabbled with the form. Yet Cher knew that now that she was rolling with a new rock crowd, any moves toward disco would be frowned upon. After all, she'd tried Southern soul twice—*3614 Jackson Highway* and *Two The Hard Way*—and that hadn't worked; she'd tried ballads from the Great American Songbook (*Bittersweet White Light*), and that hadn't worked either. If she went disco, it would be interpreted as Cher diving onto another bandwagon to resuscitate her career. Couldn't she just be the rocker she was at heart?

Bogart would hear nothing of it. He had his vision, and Cher was very much part of it. Cher had recorded some material for a prospective album with Barry Manilow producer (and former voice of The Archies) Ron Dante, but Bogart thought it was too similar in style to her recent Warners flops. He enlisted producer Bob Esty and his writing partner Michele Aller instead. Esty had produced both Donna Summer and Barbara Streisand, so was very familiar with working with beautiful, demanding singers who expected the best but worked quickly and professionally in return.

"Neil wanted Cher to fit into the Casablanca image," Esty later recalled. "The Casablanca image [meant] either disco or KISS. He wanted her to have a hit like [Donna Summer's] 'Last Dance.' So Michele and I were asked to write a song in the style of 'Last Dance,' which she could sing. At the time—like everyone else—I was thinking: Cher? Disco?"

Esty began to construct the album and enlisted writers to tell Cher's story in song—not a million miles from what Sonny had done in the sixties. He corralled the very best session musicians to back his idea of how Cher should sound: 'Wah-Wah' Watson on guitar, Jai Winding on piano, and Ed Watkins on bass, with Stan Farber, Jon Joyce, and David Lasley providing redoubtable backing chorus vocals.

Released on January 25 1979, *Take Me Home* is one of the best of the many superstar excursions into disco. With lyrics that retain the best of Cher's narrative songs, it avoids the pitfalls of encouraging people to dance or to go down to the disco. In many respects it is as if one of Cher's early-seventies Snuff Garrett albums has been taken for a night out on the town. It is impossible to hear it without smiling. Although it has all the musical tics and clichés of the era—Syndrums, sultry saxophones, scraping staccato strings—it also has Cher, who adds a touch of class and superiority to the material. As much as she resented recording the album, she performs the material with great sincerity. At best it is joyous, frothy, and fun. At worst, it sounds like the theme to a TV soap opera.

The album is divided into a disco side and a more conventional rock side. The title track is where the action is, reintroducing Cher to the American public in all its seven-minute glory and proving her biggest hit since 1974's 'Dark Lady.' With this superb, strident piece of sexual come-on set to a propulsive, joyous beat, Esty and Aller had found something that suited the Cher of 1979 and encouraged her to sing in a different style. Esty worked Cher into taking and retaking vocals—something that initially caused tension between them, but something that Cher would ultimately appreciate. If it had worked for Donna Summer and Barbra Streisand, it could work for her too.

"I thought she would be a lot funnier than she was," Esty later said. "And livelier too. She's very moody, and that's the most difficult thing with her. She's not the easiest person to spend the afternoon with. She's like Barbra in the respect that unless you get into a conversational role with her, you could be in a lot of trouble."

Listeners loved the track and Cher soon found herself back inside the *Billboard* top ten, playing the disco queen. The transformation was stunning, and almost as quick as her switch from bell-bottomed hippie to be-gowned TV institution a decade earlier. Here was Cher, still in her skimpy outfits, joining the ranks of the disco divas—and on Casablanca, no less.

Any previous private reservations about disco went temporarily out of the window. "I never thought I would want to go disco," she said at the time. "People keep saying: there's no such thing as disco! It's like saying the world is flat! It's here … people should know it. It's terrific! It's great music to dance to. I think that danceable music is what tells everybody what's *in*."

The video for 'Take Me Out' has Cher draping herself over eight male-model mannequins in a sequence that harks back to the twenties, America's last golden age of dance. The mannequins slowly come to life, and before you know it Cher, in her gold sequins, is being twirled and sashayed by her suitors. The clip ends with her appearing in her 'normal' clothes and dancing with a stagehand. For Cher, it was clear that dancing was not simply something she did before the camera: it was her life.

Take Me Home wasn't all about the title track, however. Although a common trait of the disco scene was to pad an album around an extended version of the single, Cher's was a well-balanced set with plenty more than mere two-dimensional disco. 'Wasn't It Good' is a strident slice of camp disco with Ernie Watts's saxophone providing a smooth LA disco sheen, and Cher congratulating herself and her partner on the union they had enjoyed after he had taken her home. 'Say The Word,' written by Esty and Aller, is a fine CHIC takeoff, with Ed Watkins's bass adding a slippery urban feel to the groove. The song builds to an irresistible chorus in which Cher plays the dependable lover willing to fight against any adversity by her lover's side the minute he calls for her.

With its throbbing Syndrums and sundry electronic bangs and crashes, 'Happy The Day We Met' brings the disco side of the album to a rather more generic close. Side two opener 'Git Down (Guitar Groupie)' then allows her the opportunity to rock out. The compromise was fair enough. Reuniting Cher with her old studio cohorts David Hungate, Jeff Porcaro, and Steve Lukather, it features a wailing guitar solo from Jerry Doucette and a vocal cameo from Gene Simmons. According to songwriters Esty and Aller, it was the only song on the album that Cher *really* liked.

'Love And Pain (Pain In My Heart)' is possibly the most interesting track on the album. Written by Richard T. Bear and recorded during the Ron Dante sessions, it is a direct precursor of the power ballads that Cher would make her stock-in-trade in the late eighties and early nineties. With a swelling chorus and bombastic instrumentation, Cher tries out her showcase vibrato on this overwrought yet undeniably heartfelt tale. It may sound as if adrift from another album—which indeed it was—but served as a useful reminder to her new audience of her amazing vocal capabilities.

Tom Snow's 'Let This Be A Lesson To You' is an exercise in jaunty gospel, while 'It's Too Late To Love Me' is another high-production-values excursion in heartbreak. Written by Gene Dobbins, Jay Wilson, and Rory Bourke, it had been recommended to Cher by Dolly Parton. The other sweet moment comes at the end of the album in the form of another Ron Dante production, the tender ballad 'My Song (Too Far Gone).' With simple orchestration and vocals over an acoustic accompaniment, it offered an intimate deconstruction of Cher's relationship with Gregg Allman. With lyrics supplied by Cher herself, it was the sort of mature ballad that she thrived on, giving a rare glimpse into her inner workings, in the same way as had *Half-Breed*'s 'Chastity's Sun.'

Bogart's hunch was right. The world was more than ready to watch Cher turn disco. With 'Take Me Home,' Casablanca had crafted another song up there with Cher's classic early-seventies triumvirate of 'Gypsys Tramps & Thieves,' 'Half-Breed,' and 'Dark Lady.' It was the last of Cher's classic seventies records.

In his liner notes to *Inside The Casbah: The Casablanca Records Story*, Brian Chin describes *Take Me Home* as the label's *coup de grace*. It was the ultimate in excess, the final hurrah before the wheels began to spin off the disco bandwagon. Cher's effortless grace and smoky vocals are suited perfectly to the material. And it succeeded because nobody tried to turn her into Donna Summer or The Bee Gees: she was still resolutely Cher, singing her tales of love, hope, and heartbreak, even if the method of carriage had changed. More than the various attempts by the likes of Phil Spector,

Michael Omartian, Jimmy Webb, Gregg Allman, and Snuff Garrett to rekindle her hit potential, here Cher sounds exactly as she should having been updated for the late seventies.

Take Me Home also had a jaw-dropping cover shot—one that seemed to synthesize all of Cher's excessive fashion statements of the previous fifteen years into a single, over-the-top creation. Photographed by Barry Levine, it shows her in a startling winged headdress with gold cones covering her recently surgically enhanced breasts. Heavily made up, she has the appearance of a sci-fi/fantasy diva like no other, regal and commanding like a contemporary Greek goddess. This was how the public wanted to see Cher. The album propelled her back into the US top forty.

Esty was in awe of his new charge. "The best thing about her is [that] when she puts on 'Cher'—as anybody who is a real star knows how to do—she becomes bigger than life," he later recalled. "She's so charismatic, she was a big hit at the Billboard Disco Convention. It was a great moment for me."

Casablanca paid for another TV special to support the release and showcase this new, larger-than-life Cher. *Cher … And Other Fantasies* aired on NBC on March 7 1979. The faded denims were no more: this was an hour-long extravaganza that brought the album to life, with guest-star turns from Lucille Ball, Shelley Winters, Andy Kaufman, and Elliott Gould. The press response was mixed but the viewing figures were excellent. With a blend of music that went from show-stopping standards to the present day, it demonstrated that Cher was very much the queen of the prime-time television extravaganza.

The success of *Take Me Home* meant that Casablanca wanted a quick follow-up. Producer Bob Esty envisioned an album that would tell the story of Cher's life, with the working title *Mirror Image*. To that end, there would be a song about Cher's love of roller-skating ('Hell On Wheels') and another about her concerns about the current oil crisis and its impact on gas prices ('Holy Smoke'). Esty imagined what it must be to see yourself in the papers every day ('Mirror Image'); and paid a generous tribute to Cher's favorite pastime, ('Shoppin").

The original concept was to have the front cover of the album capture her public persona, with the reverse to show her in the same pose but surrounded by tabloid headlines. The concept began to go awry, however, when Cher brought in songs that she wanted on form part of the project, as well as alternate ideas for the cover art.

After the excess of the *Take Me Home* cover, it was time to go a little further. *Prisoner*—as the album was now entitled—took matters so far over the top that it is hard to deduce whether there was any irony involved whatsoever. Photographed by Harry Langdon, Cher is shown in a fantasy setting, almost entirely naked and chained to a pillar. Perhaps this was an ironic commentary on her role as a prisoner of The Man, her record company, or a genre of music with which she was not overly thrilled. Or maybe she was there, chained, waiting for a man to use her. Suffice it to say, *Prisoner* did not win many plaudits from the women's movement.

The album contained five songs written by Esty and Aller and three other numbers specifically written for Cher. Of these, 'Prisoner,' written by David Paich and David Williams, is an extremely enjoyable opener; more radio-friendly dance tune than an-out-and out trip to the discothèque, it owes something to Donna Summer's 'Bad Girls.' Cynthia Weil and Tom Snow contributed 'Holdin' Out For Love,' which was recorded with a small band and has the sort of machine-driven faux-soul sound that would soon be topping the charts in the form of records by artists like Hall & Oates. 'Holdin' Out For Love,' by Billy Falcon, shows where Cher really wanted to be. It's a speedy, effective piece of rock'n'roll, with chopping guitars and a shred-metal solo by Steve Lukather. It was resolutely *not* disco.

The rest of the album offers a return to recent territory. 'Shoppin'' is an enjoyable bit of fluff on which Cher wails like a siren about her desire for consumption over a shuffling ragtime-inflected beat. She seems happy to send herself up, especially when she sings that "while everyone else around is smokin', tokin', cokin' / I'll be shoppin'." Luther Vandross—doyen of the session-vocalist scene at the time—appears on the chorus.

Elsewhere, 'Mirror Image' conveys all the power and pathos of a woman reeling from bad press, while 'Holy Smoke' is another marriage of rock and disco that owes something to Isaac Hayes's 'Theme From Shaft.' It is interesting to hear Cher dealing with current affairs—atomic energy, stagflation, and the environment—over such a grinding beat.

Lead single 'Hell On Wheels' pays generous tribute to the roller-disco phenomenon that had, well, rolled in at the tail end of disco. As Alan Jones and Jussi Kantonen note in their book *Saturday Night Forever*, "the former Mrs Sonny Bono was so enamored of the craze she not only added the track 'Hell On Wheels' to her *Prisoner* dance album in 1979, she also opened up one of the most popular roller-discos in West Hollywood—Flippers at La Cienaga and Santa Monica Boulevard." The song also appeared as the lead track in the Linda Blair cash-in movie *Roller Boogie (It's Love On Wheels)*. A great disco-rock hybrid with a pulsing beat, it captured the moment perfectly; people really believed this stuff.

The video for 'Hell On Wheels'—the first Cher made specifically for the purpose—was quite remarkable. It shows her in pink zebra-stripe leotard and tights, wearing her roller boots, and dancing in the street, surrounded by what appear to be exclusively gay men—all of them dressed as Village People stereotypes—looking at her out of car and truck windows, clearly ready for some form of action. The clip also features Cher's two stage dancers and singers: Kenny Sasha, who appears as Bette Midler, and JC Gaynor, who plays Diana Ross. Cher leads them on a merry skate through a desert town, with trucks, wagons, and cars left in her wake. It is bizarre, to say the least, and defiantly of-the-moment. Yet there is an endearing charm about it. And you cannot deny Cher's enthusiasm for the concept.

Unfortunately, the single halted at number fifty-nine on the *Billboard* Hot 100. The disco craze had peaked in the national psyche with the Disco Demolition at Chicago's Comiskey Park in July 1979, and Cher was widely seen as another disco *arriviste*, taking away a lucrative share of the market from white, mainstream, traditional rock. The party was over, too, for Neil Bogart, who was leaving Casablanca. The label had been subsumed into the Polygram stable, and the video, for all its finery and oddness, didn't really get shown. "She was ahead of the craze by years," Bob Esty later noted. "They had a video but no one knew what the hell to do with it, so they showed it to the secretaries in the office."

The roller-disco craze was extremely shortlived because, as Alan Jones and Jussi Kantonen would later note, "very few other records aimed specifically at the exploding market were as good as 'Hell On Wheels.'"

Prisoner was released on October 22 1979. It failed to chart. The public had enjoyed Cher-does-disco once, but once was enough.

There was one last piece of disco business for Cher. In late 1979 she contributed a song to *Foxes*, a Casablanca movie production released in February 1980. Directed by Adrian Lyne and starring Jodie Foster and Cherrie Currie, *Foxes* was a coming-of-age film set in the San Fernando Valley. Cher's contribution to the soundtrack marked the first (and to date only) time that she worked with producer Giorgio Moroder, the man who made Donna Summer famous with 'I Feel Love,' and who is seen by many as the avatar of synthesized disco. With lyrics by Cher, 'Bad Love' is a fine, muscular piece of LA Disco that owes rather a lot to Moroder and Summer's 'Hot Stuff.'

Although Cher's albums for Casablanca were somewhat confused, they mapped out a territory that maintained her new role as a strong, independent woman. In 1979, she legally changed her name simply to Cher. She would no longer be a Mrs Bono or Mrs Allman, or even a Miss LaPiere. From now on, to mark her new independence, she was JPC—Just Plain Cher.

C

Cher's all-singing, all-dancing spectacle A Celebration At Caesars Palace brought a fitting end to a variable decade. And for her, it brought the decade right back to where it had started: playing to affluent middle-class audiences in Las Vegas.

In the intervening decade, Cher had topped the US charts three times as a solo artist and had clearly earned her place as one of the world's most dynamic and gifted performers. Yet she still lacked the rock-star cool possessed by many of her lesser-talented peers. For now, however, she parked her rock'n'roll dreams and concentrated on her day job of providing spectacle and razzamatazz.

With dancers and drag queens in tow, Cher's residency at Caesars Palace on Las Vegas's fabled strip pointed the way to the later excesses of her live extravaganzas. She played eight dates at the hotel in August 1979 and then a further seven from November 16–22. The hotel resort held some negative connotations—it was in a suite here, just over four years earlier, that she had married Gregg Allman. But that was all behind her now; here was Cher the entertainer, the toast of America.

Inspired by her recent TV specials, A Celebration At Caesars Palace was put together by Cher with veteran producer Joe Layton and boasted a stunning array of gowns by Bob Mackie. Gary Scott served as musical director, while the backing singers included *Take Me Home* lyricist Michelle Aller, Warren Ham (formerly of the touring line-up of Bread and soon to join Cher in Black Rose), and Petsye Power, with Gary Ferguson on drums and Ron 'Rocket' Ritchotte on guitar.

At the time, Caesars Palace was probably the most renowned and prestigious cabaret venue in the world. Although the resort hotel had first opened in 1962, it had been rebuilt and renovated for a reopening in 1977. "Nothing else compared to Caesars—it was the biggest club in the country," Cher recalled. "I saw Frank Sinatra there the night before I opened, and it was hard to believe I was about to go up on that stage."

The opulence of the surroundings matched the excess of her recent material—and Cher certainly understood how to put on a show. Her audiences were high-rolling businessmen, gamblers offering a night out to long-suffering partners, and tourists, some of whom had saved for an once-in-a-lifetime vacation. These people were paying top dollar and were resolutely not going to watch a show of low-key introversion and despair. Cher's Celebration was a mixture of cabaret, disco, and rock'n'roll, featuring no fewer than twelve costume changes, five dancers (Wayne Bascomb, Damita Jo Freeman, Warren Lucas, Mykal Perea, and Randy Wander), a slide show, a 'mammoth magenta slipper,' and a mechanical bull.

This was Cher at her high-camp zenith. It was at Caesars that she introduced the world to her two principal drag queens, J.C. Gaynor and Kenny Sasha. She did some comedy business, where she talked offstage to Diana Ross and Bette Midler on tape; the real Diana and Bette would reply, then out would burst Gaynor, singing 'Ain't No Mountain High Enough' (and, later, the CHIC-produced masterpiece 'I'm Coming Out'). Sasha would then join them to sing 'Boogie Woogie Bugle Boy' as Bette Midler before all three duetted on 'Friends.'

Such was the skill of the drag artists' performances that the audience would wonder where Midler and Ross had gone. "People weren't used to drag queens in those days, and they actually thought they were seeing Diana Ross, Bette Midler, and Cher onstage," Cher later wrote. "They never knew what was going on. Even when I introduced J.C. and Kenny at the end of the show, they didn't get much applause, because the audience had no idea what they'd done in the show. People just didn't get it." (A third drag queen, Russell Elliot, played Cher herself during the interval.)

The Caesars show was a variation of the *Take Me Home* concert tour, which had begun in July 1979. What was amazing was Cher's lack of reliance on any of her signature material. The set opened with a Pointer Sisters cover, 'Could I Be Dreaming,' before running through songs from the newly released films *Fame* and *Urban Cowboy*. 'Take It To The Limit' by the Eagles and 'Signed, Sealed, Delivered' by Stevie Wonder were also included. It was high show business but also great fun—and one of the loudest shows in Las Vegas history. In September 1980, The American Federation Of Musicians filed a complaint with the State Department Of Occupational Safety & Health, stating that the show frequently exceeded the ninety-decibel safety limit. Cher cooperated with the agency, and an initial fine of $480 was reduced to $180.

The show would run in seasons at Caesars Palace until August 1982 in between further dates out on the road. Although critics were sniffy, dismissing the entire spectacle, it attracted rave word-of-mouth reviews and demonstrated the extent to which Cher's audience adored her. While she was performing, 'Hell On Wheels' made number fifty-nine on the *Billboard* Hot 100. It would be the last time Cher made the singles charts for eight years. But with a spectacle like this taking place, she was not to be hemmed in by mere chart positions and statistics.

Cher was not thrilled with the prospect of performing the same show over and over but knew it would provide some form of financial stability. It funded her newly purchased home as well as her ongoing dalliances with rock music. "Las Vegas is my gig," she told *Rolling Stone* at the time. "That's how I pay my rent and my kids' school. It's not my favorite thing to do. It's like a play: there are lines, and it's the same every night. It's not like walking onstage with a band, where I can wear what I want and say what I want."

In Vegas, Cher definitely could not do that. She also found that the tough two-shows-a-night regime gradually wore her down. "It was nice except it was so hard," she recalled in 2008. "That is something I don't miss at all. There was such a long lag between the first show and the second show, it just killed me."

The seventies had been an incredible decade for Cher, full of highs and lows. She had topped the US charts on three separate occasions, been divorced twice, seen her baby girl grow into a child, married and had a beautiful son with Gregg Allman, and starred in top-rated television shows with and without Sonny. Yet standing surveying her packed houses in Las Vegas, she knew that something was missing. She wanted to act—something she had been trying to do since the mid seventies. With *Chastity* now a distant memory, and having demonstrated her skills by holding down a weekly job performing skits to twenty-three million people, she decided that taking acting seriously would be the next step in her career.

PART 2

1980–2012

BY EDDI FIEGEL

CHAPTER 10

A Rock Singer
Is Born

By 1980, most people thought they had more or less got the measure of Cher. She was the one-time hippie chick who had become the queen of Las Vegas: the diva to die for, resplendent in an ever-changing series of Bob Mackie gowns, dripping in rhinestones. But Cher was once again about to surprise her public. Over the next two years, she would begin to reinvent herself, embracing a tougher, raunchier persona and an equally gutsy new musical approach. It was an incarnation that would eventually have a momentous impact on her career.

Although Cher had had solo hits in both the sixties and seventies, she still liked the idea of recording with someone else—particularly if it happened to be someone with whom she was romantically involved. She now had a new man in her life, virtuoso rock guitarist Les Dudek, and it seemed obvious that they should work together at some stage. Revered today by some as one of the great unsung heroes of blues-rock guitar, the tall, dark, long-haired, and mustachioed Dudek was at the time between groups, having previously played with The Steve Miller Band, Boz Scaggs, and The Allman Brothers.

Cher seemed to be genuinely happy with Dudek and his relaxed lifestyle. "Les is the person I've had more fun with than anybody I ever knew," she told Us magazine. "He has a wonderful sense of humor. He's really carefree and not very materialistic at all. We just have a good time—riding motorcycles and doing nothing."

Perhaps inevitably, Cher's thoughts soon turned to music. But if she was going to record with Dudek, she was determined that this time things were going to work differently in every way from her past collaborations.

Although television appearances and Vegas shows had become an intrinsic part of her career, Cher would later acknowledge that she felt they were becoming "repetitive and boring." Rock music, on the other hand, was a genre she felt she had not yet fully explored.

Both *Take Me Home* and *Prisoner* have moments where Cher veers toward rock territory; now, however, she wanted to let her hair down and have a little more fun as a performer. "[Rock'n'roll is] a very free-flowing and unpredictable medium," she explained at the time, "and that's what makes it so much fun."

The plan was for her to sing while Dudek played guitar. But rather than having one leader, this new project was to be a democracy, with everyone involved having equal say. This was a band, not a partnership. "I just decided I wanted to become part of a real rock'n'roll band," she explained. "[This] isn't *my* band. I'm just the group's singer—it's as simple as that. I know that a lot of people think [it's] pretty bizarre that I've joined a band like this, but it's something that I've been wanting to do for a long time."

Soon the band began playing clubs around Los Angeles under the name Black Rose. Alongside Cher and Dudek were Mike Finnegan on keyboards, Ron 'Rocket' Ritchotte on guitar, Trey Thompson on bass, Gary Ferguson on drums, and Warren Ham, a sax player and vocalist who had previously played with David Gates & Bread. The idea was that they would try to make a name for themselves in just the same way as would any new band, without relying on Cher's celebrity status to open any doors.

The next obvious step seemed to be to record an album, for which producer James Newton Howard was drafted in. Howard had provided string arrangements for Elton John's 'Don't Go Breaking My Heart' and 'Sorry Seems To Be The Hardest Word,' and had toured as a keyboard player with Crosby Stills & Nash. (He would later become more widely known as a film composer, writing scores for films like *Pretty Woman*, *My Best Friend's Wedding*, and *The Sixth Sense*.)

The album's opening track, 'Never Should Have Started,' was written by one of Cher's former beaus, David Paich of the rock band Toto, and sounds exactly as you'd expect if you imagine Cher singing Joan Jett-style—or even Toto-style—rock'n'roll, complete with heavy-metal guitar solos and all-male backing vocals. Not to mention some typically eighties synth sounds thrown in for good measure.

With the exception of the heavy rocking 'You Know It'—written by Dudek and sung as a duet between the guitarist and Cher—most of the other numbers on the album are also covers, such as a similarly hard-rocking version of Carole Bayer Sager's 'Take It From The Boys' and the gutsy 'Julie,' written by Bernie Taupin (Elton John's long-term lyricist) and fellow Brit hit-writer Mike Chapman.

Cher was delighted with the results. "I'm very pleased with the album," she said at the time. "And I must admit, I don't think my voice has ever sounded better. My voice has always been strong. In fact, I always thought it might be a little too brash for the type of material I did. Now, though, I need every bit of volume I can get just to be heard over the music that the guys put out. I've always been more used to having an orchestra there to help me along. In rock'n'roll it's just every man for himself."

It may have been every man for himself but Cher was still thrilled to be part of a combo in which she had at least as much say as everyone else. "In this band we all share equal footing," she continued, "which is something I really like. I think that if people will just open up and give us a chance, we can convince even the true skeptics that we can rock and roll with the best of 'em."

Black Rose was released on August 21 1980. The front cover features a comic-strip-style illustration of a woman's ankle in high heels with a 'black rose' tattoo; the back contains a group shot of the band. Nowhere on the cover does it mention Cher's name. However, the band did make several TV appearances to promote the album, including *The Tonight Show Starring Johnny Carson*, *Midnight Special*, and *The Merv Griffin Show*. They also did a short East Coast tour, performing in Pennsylvania, New York's Central Park, the Garden State Arts Center in New Jersey, and in Holmdel Township, where they opened for Daryl Hall and John Oates.

For live performances, Cher wore leather outfits designed by Bob Mackie and had her hair heavily backcombed into a pseudo-punk, rock-chick style mane. Nevertheless, neither the glam-punk clothes nor the hair seemed entirely convincing to anybody and the live shows did little to boost record sales. Consequently, the album did not even chart, while the reviews were lukewarm at best, with critics questioning Cher's credibility as a rock singer and comparing her unfavorably to hipper new wave acts of the time, such as Blondie.

Part of the problem seemed to be that, in her enthusiasm for *Black Rose* to be judged on its own musical merits—rather than in terms of her celebrity—Cher seemed perhaps to have acted rather too subtly. The result was that many Cher fans were not even aware she had made an album, let alone released one.

As far as Cher was concerned, this didn't matter. "To think that Cher even gave a second thought to how her public would react to Black Rose is silly," said Bob Esty, who had recently co-written her hit 'Take Me Home.' "She sang rock'n'roll because she had a passion for it. To me, that's what art is all about: passion. Maybe it wasn't a smart move, but it was courageous art."

Given the album's lack of success, those around Cher began to question the wisdom of pursuing Black Rose. But Cher remained steadfast. When she had first signed to Casablanca Records and told label president Neil Bogart that she wanted to sing rock'n'roll, he had tried to discourage her, telling her it wasn't her forte. "Do *this* ['Take Me Home'] first," he had said, "and let me try to get you back in the music scene."

"I did it and it was successful," Cher later recalled, "so I went along, but it wasn't what I wanted. This is."

Rumors later surfaced that Cher and the group had recorded enough material for a second album, but that it had been shelved after the failure of their first effort. One of the songs she and Dudek wrote for the record, 'Don't Trust That Woman,' was subsequently recorded by Dudek himself, and later by Elton John. Cher and Elton were old friends, and she had at one point been keen for Black Rose to support him on tour, but the British star was apparently less enthusiastic. Cher's new act seemed doomed to failure on all fronts.

Cher's relationship with Dudek also seemed to be heading toward a crisis point. Dudek was reportedly keen to get married, while Cher was—perhaps understandably, given her earlier experience—more hesitant. With their romance now in question, and Black Rose failing to achieve critical or commercial success, it soon became obvious that it was time, once again, for Cher to move on.

C

Despite Black Rose's lack of success, Cher's dreams of rock stardom were not necessarily lost. Sometimes the unpredictable magic element in the hit equation can come from the most unexpected quarters, and this was indeed what was to happen for Cher—this time courtesy of Meat Loaf.

In the late seventies, Meat Loaf (aka Michael Lee Aday) had achieved huge success with the album and single *Bat Out Of Hell*. By the time of his second album, *Dead Ringer For Love*, he was a major international star. Duets at the time were fashionable: Michael Jackson had recently recorded 'Rock With You' alongside Diana Ross, and would soon sing 'The Girl Is Mine' with Paul McCartney, while Jennifer Warnes and Joe Cocker had had a major hit with 'Up Where We Belong' from the film *An Officer And A Gentleman*. It did not seem too unusual therefore for Meat Loaf to approach Cher to duet with him on his new album's title track.

'Dead Ringer For Love' was originally written by producer and lyricist Jim Steinman, with Tony Hendra and Sean Kelly, for the shortlived US comedy series *Delta House*, a small-screen adaptation of the cult film *National Lampoons Animal House*. Steinman then reworked the melody into what would turn out to be one of Meat Loaf's all-time biggest hits. Released as a single, 'Dead Ringer For Love' went to number five in the UK charts in February 1982.

As much as the song itself was clearly a hit, so too was the accompanying video. At this point in the early eighties, with MTV in its infancy, the notion of the rock or pop video as feature film in miniature was just starting to gain credence. Promo videos were also beginning to be seen as a major part of the marketing campaign for any release.

Having duetted with Meat Loaf on the single, it seemed only natural that Cher should also co-star with him in the video, which casts her as a raunchy, gum-chewing rock chick—not in fact dissimilar to her recent Black Rose outing—in a thigh-skimming leather mini-skirt, high heels, and a Bob Mackie-designed leather jacket.

The pair's eyes meet across a crowded bar and, amid much swagger and knowing looks, they proceed to sing to each other. It is almost an old-fashioned courtship tale—albeit in rock'n'roll garb—as they declare to each other that "you're everything I'm dreaming of / I don't know who you are but you're a real dead ringer for love." The clip closes as they walk off, arm in arm, presumably to get to know each other a little better.

C

Inspired by the experience of recording with Meat Loaf, by the end of 1981 Cher was more than ready to get back into the studio herself and reassert herself as a solo artist. Her contract with Casablanca had expired, and after talking to various labels she eventually signed a new deal with Columbia Records. Now it was just a question of finding some good new material and the right producer.

In terms of style, Cher had to decide what would work best for her—and what would yield a hit. The edgier new-wave sound of the likes of Blondie and Talking Heads was very much still in vogue, as was the AOR rock of America and Toto, but equally successful were the softer pop-rock hybrids of artists like Cliff Richard and Cher's friend Olivia Newton-John.

In 1981, Newton-John had sold over two million copies of her global hit 'Physical,' and it occurred to Cher that maybe the man who had produced that song might also work well for her. "I've been spending quite a bit of time finding the right label and the right producer for my next album," she said at the time. "I needed to find a producer who was consistent, album after album. Then I thought: I really love what John Farrar does with Livvy [Newton-John] and I adore all of Livvy's albums. Somebody said he doesn't record anybody but Olivia. So I got him to come over, we talked, and it's set now. I'm looking forward to seeing what John wants to do. What he is going to write is going to be how he sees me: he's going to do his interpretation of 'Cher' and that should be *very* interesting."

Farrar and Cher duly began work on the track that would eventually lend the album its title, 'I Paralyze,' a mid-tempo song with a light power-ballad feel. Its composer, Australian-born hit songwriter Steve Kipner, also wrote 'Physical,' and would later go on to write numerous global hits over the coming decades, including Chicago's 'Hard Habit To Break' and 'Genie In A Bottle' by Christina Aguilera.

The song had originally been recorded but then rejected by Newton-John herself for her *Physical* album, so Farrar suggested Cher try it. There were even rumors that Farrar used the original backing track he'd recorded with Newton-John and simply overdubbed Cher's vocal on top of it—and indeed, listening to the track, it certainly sounds possible.

'I Paralyze' would end up being the only track Farrar produced for Cher. The rest of the album was subsequently produced by David Wolfert, who had worked with Dusty Springfield in the late seventies and would go on to write 'I Believe In You And Me' for Whitney Houston as well as songs for Barbara Streisand and Dolly Parton.

The rest of the songs on *I Paralyze* cover a mix of styles, although they're all given an AOR soft-rock production, complete with a barrage of now rather dated-sounding synths. Three tracks—'The Book Of Love,' 'Walk With Me,' and 'When Love Is Gone'—were written by Desmond Child, who would shortly thereafter go on to have global success as the co-writer of the nascent Bon Jovi's super-hits 'You Give Love A Bad Name' and 'Livin' On A Prayer.' He would also pen some of Cher's subsequent solo hits.

The soft-rock style continues with a cover of British rockers The Babys' 'Back On My Feet Again' and the marginally more catchy 'Rudy,' which became a particular favorite of Cher's. "That was a good one," she later recalled. "I remember liking 'Rudy' a lot. I had a lot of fun recording it. Like 'Turn Back Time,' this is the kind of song that pulls you up."

In the months between finishing the album and its release in May 1982, Cher would have moved on to other new projects which would turn out to be the beginning of an entirely new career for her. This meant that she had no time to promote *I Paralyze*, and neither the album nor the two singles drawn from it—'I Paralyze' and 'Rudy'—charted.

Although generally considered to be one of Cher's lesser musical moments, *I Paralyze* still has a small coterie of admirers among Cher devotees and fans of eighties AOR rock. It can also, with the benefit of hindsight, be seen as the beginning of a new phase in Cher's career—one that was to be highly significant. This particular album may not have yielded any hits, but the soft-rock style and formula would eventually bring her unimagined success. In the meantime, however, there were other, equally exciting career developments ahead.

CHAPTER 11
Getting My Act Together

Having had little success with either Black Rose or *I Paralyze*, Cher once again returned to Las Vegas. She needed to bring in some more substantial earnings to pay for the palatial Egyptian-style home she had built in Los Angeles. She also had her children's school fees to pay—not to mention what some might describe as an epic shopping habit and a luxurious lifestyle complete with extensive staff. But that didn't necessarily mean that performing at a cabaret venue—albeit the world's most lavish—was what she wanted to be doing. She increasingly found the meticulously pre-planned and rigidly structured nature of the Vegas shows constricting. Every line and every joke—as well as the costume changes and dance moves—were rehearsed down to the nanosecond. There was no room for spontaneity or ad-libbing. That's just not what Vegas is about. Audiences expect a slick, highly polished, and super-professional show; anything remotely alternative or rough around the edges is simply not part of the deal.

Consequently, she began to find the repetitive nature of the shows wearing and reasoned that if she was going to be saying rehearsed lines every night she might as well be playing a serious role. Indeed, while Cher had been experimenting with different musical styles and looking for a sound that she could fully embrace, she had still never entirely given up on her teenage dreams of acting. Acting had of course been Cher's original ambition before she had ever considered becoming a singer.

"As far back as I can remember, acting was what I always wanted to do," she later recalled. "When I met Sonny I always wanted to be an actress. I never even thought about being a singer, it just didn't occur to me that you could make a living being a singer!" But while her break into the music industry had been relatively simple and smooth thanks to Sonny, the fulfillment of her acting ambitions was to prove anything but easy. Cher had started acting classes at sixteen and now began to think that the time might be right to attempt to break into acting again. She had tried several times over the previous few years but it had never quite worked out. It wasn't for lack of contacts. Her friends included Angelica Huston, Jack Nicholson, and Warren Beatty, and she had been to see various directors and producers, both in Hollywood and on the East Coast, asking them to just give her a chance. Each time, however, the answer was the same. "I couldn't get arrested," she later recalled.

Because of her success in television and music, some of the people she saw thought of her primarily as a TV personality and singer—and not 'serious' enough to be an actress. Others told her she was "too old, too tall, or too ethnic." Unsurprisingly, Cher found this lack of vision and faith in her disappointing and frustrating. She had been famous for most of her adult life, but always as a 'celebrity.' Now she wanted to be taken seriously, and to earn respect and admiration for being good at what she did. Serendipitously, two separate events would soon give her the inspiration she needed to give acting one last try.

The first was a chance visit by Francis Ford Coppola to Las Vegas. Coppola happened to see Cher's show and was so impressed with her timing and delivery that he came to see her backstage afterward. "You're so good," he told her. "Why aren't you doing movies?" Sadly, he wasn't there to offer her a part, but simply getting this kind of encouragement from the director of *The Godfather* and *Apocalypse Now* gave Cher new confidence.

The other event was the sudden change in direction for Cher's friend, the country-rock singer Linda Ronstadt. During the summer of 1980, Ronstadt landed a role in hip New York stage producer Joe Papp's Broadway production of the Gilbert & Sullivan operetta *The Pirates Of Penzance*. She was an overnight sensation, suddenly feted as a new acting and theater talent.

This was precisely the kind of career change Cher wanted for herself. Seeing it happen to Ronstadt made her even more determined. After all, if Linda Ronstadt could make the transition, why shouldn't Cher? Nonetheless, she knew that trying to break into acting at thirty-five—an age at which even established actresses found that parts would begin to dry up—was always going to be an uphill struggle. If she was going to try it, she could obviously not afford to waste any further time. Actress Shelley Winters had once told her that if she wanted to be taken seriously as an actress she would need to go to New York, so that was what Cher decided to do.

Her first call was to Joe Papp, in the hope of getting a role, as Ronstadt had, in one of his Public Theater productions. However, Papp was, initially at least, not encouraging. "How do I know you're talented?" he asked her. "There's no way I can tell from all that junk you've been doing over the years."

Despite this, Papp decided to give Cher a chance. He asked her to look over the script of a musical called *I'm Getting My Act Together And Taking It On The Road*, with the instruction that she study it and then come back and audition for him. Petrified but desperate to impress, Cher called on none other than Lee Strasberg, the legendary creator of the Actors' Studio and 'method acting' tutor to stars such as James Dean, Marlon Brando, Robert De Niro, and Al Pacino. When it came to the audition, Papp seemed to like what he saw, but he still didn't offer Cher a part. She was deeply disappointed until she arrived back in the director's office, where the receptionist gave her a message: she was to call Robert Altman immediately.

Cher was mystified as to why the director of *M*A*S*H*, *Nashville*, and *The Long Goodbye* would be calling her. He was one of the few directors she had never approached. The solution to the mystery turned out to be connected to none other than her own mother. Georgia Holt counted Altman's wife Kathryn amongst her oldest friends, and while trying to reach Cher on the phone to find out how the audition with Papp had gone, she had dialed Kathryn's number by mistake. Robert had answered the phone and Georgia ended up telling him about Cher's attempt to break into acting.

Altman suggested Cher get in touch. He was casting for his directorial debut on Broadway, a play called *Come Back To The Five & Dime, Jimmy Dean, Jimmy Dean*, and believed there was a part in it that could be perfect for her. On reading the script, Cher immediately guessed the part Altman had in mind: Joe, the transsexual. But the role that really appealed to her was Sissy, the 'small-town sexpot' with a big personality and bigger dreams who has secretly had a double mastectomy.

In the play, thirty-six-year-old salesgirl Sissy fantasizes about being whisked off to fame and fortune when a professional ice-skating company come to town to hold auditions, but her laugh-a-minute bravura masks a deep sadness and disappointment at her small-town existence and personal circumstances. Cher felt she could understand and relate to this part in a way that she didn't at all with Joe.

If the audition with Papp had been nerve-wracking, reading for Altman would prove even worse. This time, far from being alone, she had to read alongside three highly experienced actresses: Karen Black, who at this point had already starred alongside Jack Nicholson in *Easy Rider* and *Five Easy Pieces*, as well as in Altman's *Nashville*; Sandy Dennis, who had won an Oscar for her performance in *Who's Afraid Of Virginia Woolf?* and was reading for the part of a woman who still pined for James Dean some twenty years after his death; and Kathy Bates, who would later find fame for her part in the film adaptation of Stephen King's *Misery*.

Cher was hugely intimidated. The reading did not go well. In fact, Sandy Dennis later told Cher she thought it was the worst reading she had ever heard. However, Altman saw some potential in her and decided—despite the lackluster audition—to give her the part of Sissy.

"I never had any qualms about her," he later remembered. "She had a natural ability, the guts and the confidence. It gets around to her desire to do things. If Cher says she's going to do something, she will do it. She had good instincts and respect for her fellow actors. The only thing that would surprise me would be if she did something badly."

After rehearsals, Cher began three weeks of previews on Broadway in early 1982. She couldn't have been happier. She loved playing the part, became friends with Sandy Dennis, and was given a dressing room that Elizabeth Taylor had once used. She was also reveling in the New York social scene. Here, unlike in Los Angeles, she was able to meet other stage actors. She loved hanging out at hip late-night venues like Cafe Central and Elaine's with John Hurt, Christopher Reeve, and David Keith, or going out for late-night suppers downtown at the Odeon. There were plenty of other showbiz stars around, and Cher was often to be found dancing the night away with stars like Liza Minnelli at the legendary Studio 54.

But while she may have enjoyed spending time offstage with other actors, onstage she frequently felt out of her depth. Gradually it began to get easier. "I don't really know what I'm doing most of the time onstage," she explained, "and if I stop to think about it, I won't know what I'm doing at all. When we started, everyone was talking about 'preparation,' and I didn't know what that was. What I do is sort of turn my mind to 'pretend.' I thought I'd hate having to be the same character every night, but then I found it was natural. There was a lot of freedom in it."

The play formally opened on February 18 1982 at the Martin Beck Theater. Despite having had a good run during the previews, Cher was so nervous that she had a panic attack halfway through the play and almost didn't go back onstage. It was only thanks to Sandy Dennis's reassurance that she was able to finish the show.

Cher had also been terrified of the critics, and not without reason. "Forget about whether or not Mayor Koch is going to run for governor," Frank Rich began in his review for the *New York Times*. "The *truly* momentous question of the month is: can Cher act?" Rich went on to answer his own question by calling Cher's turn in the play a "cheery, ingratiating non-performance." It was hardly the kind of review Cher had been hoping for, although Rich didn't seem to like much else about the production either, describing it as a "dreary amateur night". The other critics were hardly any kinder, and audience numbers soon began to drop off. When it looked like the show was going to have to close, Altman decided to put his own money into promoting it. Eventually, through word of mouth, audiences begin to pour back in and soon the show was such a success that on some nights there was standing room only.

In the end it seemed that, although Altman had helped with the promotion budget for the show, part of the attraction for audiences was Cher herself. "I was the curiosity factor," she remembered. "They wanted to see if I *could* act. But I did bring people into the theater who'd *never* seen a play, people who didn't even know the proper decorum for live theater. They'd yell out in the middle of a line—but I could tell they *really* enjoyed it. God that made me happy! This gay club bought out the whole theater one night, and it was our best performance! They cheered, they stood to applaud, but they *listened*."

As the run progressed, Cher began ad-libbing lines of dialogue here and there, not realizing that you weren't really supposed to do that kind of thing on Broadway. Although Altman didn't seem to mind, the writer of the play, Ed Graczyk, was less than pleased. After he complained to Altman, the director felt compelled to reprimand Cher and insist that she re-memorize the script, word for word, and stick to it.

Come Back To The Five & Dime eventually ran for fifty-two performances but as soon as it closed, Altman decided that he wanted to make a film version—with exactly the same cast. This was to be a momentous decision for Cher, and one that would have an extraordinary impact on her future career.

As with the stage production, this was new ground for Cher, and she was understandably nervous when it came to the shoot. "I cried a lot while we were making the movie," she later remembered. "Bob (Altman) took so little notice of me. I really didn't know what I was doing and I was sure the camera would pick that up in my eyes. But apparently I was all right. Afterward, Bob said: 'I didn't have to talk to you. You were doing just fine.'"

When the film was released, many audiences began to see Cher differently, as did her peers in the industry. Altman's initial faith in her had paid off, as had her own determination. Not only had she played a 'serious' role on Broadway, she had also now made her first appearance in a major movie. She received a Golden Globe nomination for Best Supporting Actress, and although she did not ultimately win the award, she was now on the way to proving herself as an actress.

C

When it came to Cher's next outing on film, her past connections would once again prove invaluable. One afternoon, after a matinée performance of *Come Back To The Five & Dime* on Broadway, she received a knock on her dressing-room door. It was film director Mike Nichols, best known for *The Graduate* and *Who's Afraid Of Virginia Woolf?* Cher had been to see Nichols some eight years earlier, when he was making *The Fortune* with Jack Nicholson. Her old beau, Warren Beatty, had asked Nichols to find her a part but, as had so often been the case in the past, Nichols turned her down. "You know what?" Cher replied. "I am talented and one day you are going to be so sorry."

Several years on, of course, Cher was in a different position. She had proved herself on Broadway and gained professional credibility as an actress for the first time. Nichols was suitably contrite. "You were right," he told her. "You *are* talented." He then asked her how she felt about the idea of making a movie with him and Meryl Streep. Cher did not need to be asked twice—she said yes before he had even finished the sentence. This was exactly the kind of offer she had dreamed of.

The film Nichols was about to make was based on the true story of Karen Silkwood, a young woman who, while working at the Kerr-McGee nuclear processing plant in Oklahoma, had become dangerously contaminated with radioactive substances. Silkwood had died suddenly in suspicious circumstances in 1974 just as she was about to expose Kerr-McGee to the press for exposing workers at the plant to highly toxic levels of radiation.

Cher had not been aware of Silkwood's story prior to receiving the script from Nichols and was shocked and frightened once she started to find about more about it. She would later discover that she had in fact met Silkwood and her boyfriend Drew Stephens some years earlier when they had come backstage at a Sonny & Cher concert.

The part of Silkwood was to be played by Meryl Streep, while Cher was to take the role of Dolly Pelliker, based on Silkwood's real-life former roommate, Sherri Ellis. Nichols had told Cher straightaway that the other main thing she should know about her part was that Dolly was a lesbian. Cher had no problem with this aspect of her character—she was just keen to make sure that her portrayal didn't come across as stereotypical, and that she focused on Dolly's personality rather than her sexuality.

"I've always thought that people are people, whatever their sexual preference," she later said. "I knew I didn't want to play Dolly stomping around with a pack of Marlboros rolled up in my T-shirt sleeve."

Cher was ready to cut her hair short if necessary, but Nichols was keen for the character not to conform to clichés. "Let's not make a statement about Dolly with a butch cut," he told her. "It'll be harder for you to bring her across, but let's not help you with something obvious. Let's have you work to get everything out of her without externals."

Cher was delighted that Nichols felt this way about the character. "This is a *girl*," she said. "This is her way of life. And I don't think Dolly's gayness is the thing you remember the most about her."

She was right. In the end, thanks to the way Cher portrayed Dolly, the character is indeed memorable for much more than just her sexuality. But that doesn't mean that it all came easily to her. She may have been ready to cut her hair but what she was not prepared for was wearing grungy, baggy, unflattering clothes with no makeup.

Prior to making *Silkwood*, Cher would barely have considered leaving the house without makeup, let alone be seen in a movie without it. What's more, since she and Sonny had relaunched themselves with their television shows and Vegas engagements, glamour had become a major part of her stock-in-trade. This was therefore not at all her idea of movie stardom—and not, she suspected, her audience's idea of movie stardom, either.

To make matters worse, Cher had started to have problems with her skin, first in Las Vegas and then during the stage production of *Come Back To The Five & Dime*. She had developed an allergic reaction to the heavy pan-stick stage makeup used as standard and her face had broken out in spots and rashes. However, Nichols was adamant that Dolly should not wear any makeup whatsoever. So, while Streep and Kurt Russell (who played her boyfriend) were surrounded by hair and makeup artists, Cher was completely bypassed.

If Cher had sometimes lacked in self-confidence before, this new situation was guaranteed to dent her self-esteem still further. "The first day of the shoot," she recalled, "Kurt asked me: what are *you* supposed to be? I ran into the bathroom and cried. I'd waited my whole life to be in movies and, OK, Meryl's no glamour queen either. This isn't *French Lieutenant's Woman*, but I looked like I worked in a stable. I am so convincingly ugly. It sure is easy to tear down an image."

Desperate to try to remedy the situation somehow, Cher thought at first that she might be able to get away with wearing a little base makeup without Nichols noticing. But Nichols was sharper than that. Every day, as soon as they began filming her scenes, he would carry out what he called the white glove test, running his finger across her cheek. If the glove came up with even the merest hint of makeup, he would order her to wash her face.

Eventually, Cher began to get into the spirit of the character. Despite her initial reservations she started to enjoy the freedom it brought. For the first time in her life, she didn't have to worry about her appearance. It was strangely liberating.

Nevertheless, while Cher may not have had any qualms about the character she was playing, she was absolutely terrified at the prospect of working alongside Meryl Streep, who at this point had just starred in *The Deer Hunter* and was considered a major new star. "I *panicked*," she recalled. "I was so terrified of even *meeting* Meryl Streep, the best actress in the *world*, that I really thought I wouldn't be in the movie."

She need not have worried. Streep was welcoming from their very first meeting onward, and the pair would soon become firm friends. "The first time I came on the set," Cher recalled, "she took me by the shoulders and gave me a kiss and said: I'm so glad you're here. We got along so well."

Filming took four months, with Cher required to be on set six days a week. During the long hours of waiting around, she would often do needlepoint while Streep knitted, or they'd listen to music or joke around with Kurt Russell. On Sundays, the two of them would drive to Dallas, have lunch at a black-eyed-pea restaurant, and then go and see a movie double-bill. "We became *such* good friends so quickly," Streep recalled. "We'd talk endlessly and we found we had so much in common, both as women and as mothers."

By the time they came to the movie's most emotional scenes the two women felt very much at ease with each other, but director Mike Nichols also was adept at helping them get into the right frame of mind. Just before they were due to shoot the scene where they talk on the porch after having a fight, Nichols called them aside while the lighting rigs were being set up and told them a very sad story about the real-life Karen Silkwood and how isolated she became before she died. Both Cher and Streep were deeply moved and saddened by the story, and both had tears in their eyes when Nichols suddenly shouted "Action."

When the film was finished, Cher was anxious to see how audiences would react to her new role. She may have challenged some of their prejudices and preconceptions by appearing on Broadway and in Altman's film version of *Come Back To The Five & Dime* but, as she was to discover, there were still plenty of people who had yet to be converted.

"Before shooting, people would ask: who's in the movie besides Meryl?" the late Nora Ephron, who co-wrote the film, subsequently recalled. "We would say Cher, and they'd say: you're kidding? We went through that for months. We just told people to trust us. It was extremely high-risk casting. If it hadn't worked, it would have been devastating to the movie."

Ephron's experience was repeated when the film opened in New York. Cher later remembered hearing the audience laugh out loud when her name appeared nineties during the opening credits. "I was devastated," she recalled, "and yet I couldn't really get angry, because it was such an organic response. Everyone had that kind of reaction. It was painful beyond belief but it was interesting because at the end when my name came up everyone clapped. This is an upward climb, this is an uphill battle."

It may have been an uphill battle, but by the time critics came to review the film, it seemed like a battle that Cher was starting to win. As the *New York Times* put it: "When you take away those wild wigs, there's an honest, complex screen presence underneath." The *Times* was not alone: Cher subsequently received a Golden Globe for her performance in the film as well as an Academy Award nomination for Best Supporting Actress. She did not win the Oscar, but just the fact that she had been nominated at all was a huge step forward.

C

For someone known primarily as a singer to have made her movie debut alongside directors of the caliber of Robert Altman and Mike Nichols was highly impressive. Cher's next film role would likewise lead to her working with yet another top name director: Peter Bogdanovich.

Like Altman and Nichols, Bogdanovich was part of the wave of New Hollywood directors who had come to the fore in the late sixties and early seventies with movies like *The Last Picture Show*. The film he was currently working on was another true-life story, this time about Roy L. 'Rocky'

Dennis, a young boy whose face is disfigured by a rare disease but whose brain and body are entirely normal. The other central character in the plot was the boy's mother—in real life a feisty and beautiful woman, particularly notable for her penchant for cussing and hanging out with bikers. To Bogdanovich and producer Marty Starger, the character's mixture of ballsiness and vulnerability made Cher the perfect choice for the role.

"I felt Cher's persona—or at least the persona people think is Cher— fitted the character exactly," Bogdanovich said at the time. "The woman had to be free, outspoken, tough … but also a lot more vulnerable than she lets on, which I think is also true of Cher." In fact, screenwriter Anna Hamilton Phelan would subsequently say that she had used an eight-by-ten photo of Cher for inspiration while she was writing the script.

Cher found the script incredibly moving. She later said she had cried when she first read it, having found it "very real." She immediately said yes to the part. But if she had been nervous before making *Silkwood*, this latest venture was to be even more of a challenge. The experience and praise she had received for *Silkwood* had boosted her confidence in her acting, but this was the first time she had been given such a central role in a movie.

In order to fully prepare for her character before filming started, Cher went to meet Rusty Dennis, the mother on whom her character was based. Bogdanovich's assumption that the two women had a fair amount in common turned out to be not so far off the mark. Dennis subsequently remembered that the two women "rapped like old friends" about the script and her life. They also talked about Cher's own life, and about motherhood. "Personality-wise, Cher has an element of danger," Dennis later said. "You never know what she's going to say or do next. We share that element of danger."

Similarly, Cher warmed to Rusty and found that she was not entirely as she seemed. "She is tough," she told *People* magazine, "but she has an edge of softness about her. She laughs a lot. She's soft-spoken and very warm, with a metaphysical side to her about finding her way through life. She is also quite a beautiful woman, even though, when she speaks, you hear those biker expressions."

While Cher's initial research went well, the filming process did not run so smoothly. Whereas Cher had developed an affectionate working relationship with Mike Nichols—he would call her 'child,' while she called him 'dad'—taking direction from Bogdanovich proved much less straightforward. Rather than encourage her, he just "wasn't very nice," as Cher later put it, and took to "beating me up verbally" on a daily basis.

Cher, by her own admission, didn't like to be given too much detailed direction, particularly not the line-by-line readings Bogdanovich favored. "I don't really like being directed that much," she said. "I like having a certain amount of freedom with which to work." Her initial reaction was to confront the director and contradict him on set, telling him she thought a particular line would sound better her way. This was not what Bogdanovich wanted to hear.

"Just remember," she recalled him telling her one day, "this movie isn't about the woman, it's about a boy. I can cut you out [of the story]." Cher's reaction, as has so often been the case, was stoical. "I'm going to take that information," she remembered thinking, "and just stash it, and get real, real tough. And I did."

As well as having to cope with Bogdanovich's often less than kind approach, Cher was also experiencing some difficult times in her personal life. After a succession of brief liaisons, she had recently embarked on a relationship with a then-unknown young actor by the name of Val Kilmer, but during the early days of filming, Kilmer briefly walked out on her.

Eventually, after taking advice from co-star Eric Stoltz, who plays her son Rocky in the film, Cher found a way of dealing with Bogdanovich and keeping everyone happy. "Peter tells you *exactly* what to do," she later said, "and you listen to it and then you do what *you* want to do. And if it's as good as or better than what he expected, he'll let you do it your own way."

Bogdanovich may have been a hard taskmaster on set, but when asked about working with Cher, the director couldn't praise her highly enough. "What Cher has that immediately makes her a movie star are those extraordinarily soulful and penetrating eyes," he told *Premiere* magazine. "When you move into a close-up with her, it doesn't matter if she's saying the line right. You think: with eyes like that, how could anyone not be saying the truth."

When *Mask* was released, in March 1985, Bogdanovich was by no means the only one to be impressed with Cher. Jack Matthews of *USA Today* called it "a career performance," while Kathleen Carroll of the *New York Daily News* wrote: "In Rusty, Cher has found a part that suits her as well as a black leather mini-skirt ... Cher definitely puts her heart into this performance and the emotion shows through. And this is what makes *Mask* so appealing."

Cher herself was similarly delighted with the film, and indeed with her own performance. "When I finally saw the film, I cried all the way through it," she said. "By the very end I was sobbing and I knew no other experience would ever be so special as that had been."

Mask grossed $185,000 in its first week of release in March 1985 despite only showing in four theaters. By the time it opened at the Cannes International Film Festival in May it had made over $37 million in tickets sales. On May 20, her thirty-ninth birthday, Cher was named Best Actress at Cannes. In her acceptance speech, she described it as "the best birthday present of my life."

The success of *Mask* was to have a huge impact on her career as a movie actress. After years of trying to break into acting, she finally seemed to be making a name for herself as a serious actress. She could also now demand the kind of elevated fees commanded by the upper echelon of Hollywood actors. In her early film work, she had had to accept a radical drop in salary compared to what she was used to earning in Las Vegas or on television. She had willingly accepted this, knowing that she had yet to prove herself in the movies. By the time she came to make her next film, however, she was a big-name box-office star and could expect fees to match.

Cher was beginning to receive more and more scripts and had in fact turned down several that she didn't think were suitable, such as *Baby Boom* and *Black Widow*. But the next offer she received was a more attractive proposition in every respect: one million dollars to appear in *The Witches Of Eastwick* alongside Jack Nicholson, Susan Sarandon, and Michelle Pfeiffer.

The script was based on the novel of the same name by John Updike. It tells the story of three single women: Alexandra, a sculptress and single mother; Jane, a newly divorced music teacher; and Sukie, a journalist with six children. Their lives change when a mysterious stranger (played by Jack Nicholson) arrives in town and gradually seduces each of them in turn—and eventually turns out to be a live incarnation of the devil.

Cher had doubts about the script at first but was still very keen to work with Nicholson. The salary was also very attractive to her. Although she had not earned very much for her recent film roles, she still maintained a luxurious lifestyle, and had consequently run up significant debts. Her only problem now was with the role.

Eastwick's producers had originally thought of Cher as Jane, and had offered the role of Alexandra to Susan Sarandon. Cher, meanwhile, was adamant that Alexandra was the part she wanted. She felt that she couldn't really do Jane justice and insisted that unless the producers let her play the part she wanted she would not appear in the film at all. Eventually, they relented. But while Cher had got what she wanted, Sarandon was less than happy to return from a holiday in the Philippines only to discover that she was now playing a different character.

Eventually, the three lead actresses became firm friends and enjoyed working together, but none of them could say the same for the film's Australian director, George Miller (best known for the *Mad Max* films). "Once we started the film, we were very, very close," Cher told Swedish television presenter Jacob Dahlin. "We used each other for protection." In fact, such was their unhappiness with Miller that all three actresses walked out on the picture on separate occasions.

From the outset, Cher felt that Miller had no idea that she was now thought of as a genuinely serious actress. "The director didn't want me," she recalled. "He only knew me as part of Sonny & Cher. But the movie company put pressure on him. I said to George: I don't know where you've been; they didn't find me under a rock."

Miller, it seemed, wasn't very keen on anyone he considered to be "too famous." He hadn't wanted Jack Nicholson in the film either. His first choice was Bill Murray, who at the time had not yet become a major star. Indeed, there was so much antagonism between the director and his cast that Cher would later compare the shoot to "filming a movie on Friday the thirteenth in the middle of a hurricane."

Despite the fraught atmosphere on set, the movie was generally well received, even if most reviews singled out Nicholson as the undoubted star. Released on June 12 1987, it went on to do well at the box office and pick up Academy Award nominations for Best Original Score and Best Sound. In the UK, the film won a BAFTA for Best Special Visual Effects.

Happily for Cher, her next movie, *Suspect*, was to be a much more enjoyable experience. She once again found herself working with yet another acclaimed director, this time British filmmaker Peter Yates (best known for *Bullitt*). The film was also to prove a departure for Cher in terms of the role she played: workaholic Washington DC defense attorney Kathleen Riley, who is called upon to defend a homeless mute (played by Liam Neeson), on a murder charge. During the course of the trial—and against her better judgment—Riley risks being disbarred by getting involved with a slick member of the jury (Dennis Quaid). As well as Neeson and Quaid, the strong supporting cast also included Joe Mantegna and John Mahoney, best known later in his career for playing Kelsey Grammer's father in *Frasier*.

The part of Riley was not an obvious one for Cher. There was nothing unusual, eccentric, or glamorous about the character—but in a way that was part of the appeal. Similarly, there was very little about the role that chimed with Cher's own real-life personality or sat within her own life experience. Because of this very unfamiliarity, she was keen to do as much research as possible. She went to meet real women at the public defender's office, sat in on a murder trial, and also spent time in jails getting to know convicts. She similarly became friends with Mitch Snyder, the well-known activist for the homeless.

She rehearsed intensively, paying particular attention to the complex legal terminology she was required to use. Yates in particular was impressed with her performance. "In the interrogation scene, when she's facing Liam Neeson's character, the way that speech starts softly, builds, holds that long pause," he recalled. "A lot of people would have gone on without a pause. With Cher's Kathleen, she is fighting an emotion, and it feels more honest. That is really what people do."

Yates was also impressed with Cher's professionalism and determination when it came to learning her lines. Some years earlier, she had discovered that she was dyslexic, but although this meant it took her longer to read scripts, it had not interfered with her ability to memorize them. "She has a wonderful memory," Yates said. "I'm dyslexic, too, and I understand the enormous compensation that goes on with it. When you play in a courtroom drama, you have very long scenes. When other actors blow it, they typically blame their costume, whatever. When she blew it, she'd just scream 'come on Cher! What the hell do you think you're doing?'"

Cher was highly critical of her own performance. "It was disappointing," she said at the time. "In my effort to be really real, I was really boring. I wasn't embarrassed, but I wanted it to be *more*." She was perhaps being a little hard on herself: her performance is convincing, and overall the movie is well acted and well filmed, even if the plot is often more than a little implausible. The critics for the most part felt the same. Although Janet Maslin of the *New York Times* found Cher's performance "crisply compelling," most others felt that she had been miscast or drew attention to the inauthenticity of the plot.

The public seemed to agree. *Suspect* was not a great success at the box office. But since breaking into serious film acting with *Come Back To The Five & Dime, Jimmy Dean, Jimmy Dean* she had begun to establish herself as much more than merely a singer or showbiz personality. Through sheer determination and persistence, Cher had successfully managed to disprove those who questioned her acting ability. She was also to show that, contrary to what many might have thought, it was possible to maintain two parallel careers.

CHAPTER 12
I Found Someone

By 1987, having starred in several successful movies, Cher was being offered a much wider range of roles, and choosing the right one therefore became that much harder. The one she was about to accept, however, would become one of the defining roles of her career.

While she was working on *The Witches Of Eastwick*, Cher received a script with the title *The Bride And The Wolf*, a charming romantic comedy about a slightly dowdy, prematurely grey, Italian widow who falls in love with her fiancé's brother. The central motif throughout is the full moon which affects each of the key characters in different ways, and it was this *bella luna* that provided the movie's eventual title: *Moonstruck*.

Director Norman Jewison, well known for hit films like *The Cincinnati Kid*, the original 1968 version of *The Thomas Crown Affair*, and *Rollerball*, was adamant that he wanted Cher for the lead role of Loretta, the widow, but Cher was initially uncertain whether playing such an unglamorous part was really right for her. She was concerned, just as she had been with *Silkwood*, that it might disappoint her fans.

"As much as I liked it, it wasn't like *Mask*, which I felt I just *had* to do," she later said. "I was a little frightened because there seemed to be all kinds of possibilities and all kinds of risks here. I wondered if, at this point in my career, when there might be some people out there interested in seeing my movies, they would accept me in this role."

She was also hesitant about having to play a character with an Italian accent, and worried that she wouldn't be believable. "The reason I was so nervous was because I didn't think I could really be Italian and that people would believe it, that I would have the accent right," she recalled. "You know I have a hard time if you take on something and you can't do it exactly. I don't like it at all when you see people and they lose an accent halfway through a film."

Jewison was confident that Cher would be perfect for the role, but decided that if he wanted to convince her he should not be too pushy. If she didn't want the role, he told her, she needn't worry—he had another actress who was happy to play the part. But he wouldn't tell Cher who the other actress was.

It later emerged that Jewison was under considerable pressure to convince Cher to take the lead role. The film studio, MGM / United Artists, had only agreed to finance the $11-million picture on the condition that she accept the part. If any further proof was needed that Cher had really now become a bankable box-office star, this was surely it.

Cher eventually relented, but not without using her newfound star-power to influence the casting of Ronny Cammareri, the impassioned Italian baker that she falls for. Nicolas Cage would end up playing the part, but he was not the studio's original choice. He was by no means a major star back then, and had received mixed reviews for his recent performance in *Peggy Sue Got Married*. The producers favored Peter Gallagher, who would come to fame a couple of years later in 1989 as Andie McDowell's errant husband in Stephen Soderbergh's *Sex, Lies And Videotape*.

Although Cher thought Gallagher a good actor, she felt that Cage was at least as good. She also strongly believed he was much better suited to bringing out the crazier elements of Ronny's character. She saw some of the same mercurial qualities in Cage himself, and eventually gave the studio an ultimatum: she would only do the movie if Cage played Ronny. This time it was the studio's turn to give in.

From here onward, in contrast to both *The Witches Of Eastwick* and *Mask*, rehearsals and filming went smoothly, with Cher enjoying virtually every minute. She would later say that *Moonstruck* was the most enjoyable movie she'd ever worked on. It was, she said, "too silly—too much fun to be work. It was like getting paid lots of money to have a good time with a bunch of people you wouldn't have minded spending time with anyway."

Cher also got on terrifically well with Jewison, who likewise recognized her talent. "Her comic timing is natural and almost infallible," he told *Premiere* magazine. "I'll say so even though she nicknamed me 'the curmudgeon.'"

The fact that the movie was to be shot in New York also perfectly suited Cher. She had taken an apartment in the city, and both of her children were attending school there. This meant that she could work reasonably normal hours and still spend time with her family.

Before filming began, Jewison decided that he wanted the cast to rehearse together so that, by the time they began shooting, they would have developed a natural rapport and would be able to convincingly resemble a close-knit family. By now, Cher and Cage had been joined in the cast by Danny Aiello, who plays Cher's fiancé; Olympia Dukakis, who plays her mother; and Vincent Gardenia, who plays her father.

The five actors spent two weeks together in a studio on Lower Broadway. Often, when one of them couldn't attend, another would read their lines; by the end of the fortnight, they all knew each other's parts almost as well as their own. They had also developed exactly the kind of intimacy and naturalness with each other that Jewison had been looking for.

The rehearsals likewise helped Cher to develop a feel for the part of Loretta, allowing her to work out ideas for the character and make the role her own. "I don't know where I get these ideas," she explained, "but I usually have one for each scene, and if it's right, if it works well, it ends up carrying the whole scene ... I know that in watching movies, my own or anybody else's, it's the little ideas—the stray moments of behavior that don't seem 'acted'—that interest me the most."

Cher had been nervous about giving a convincing performance, but once rehearsals started she found it much more straightforward than she had expected. She had had experience herself of being part of a traditional Italian-American family through years of marriage to Sonny Bono, which she drew on for the film. "It kind of reminded me of Sonny's family," she recalled. "Everybody eating and talking and shouting, but you have such good times."

Some of Cher's more recent experiences proved equally relevant. After parting company with Val Kilmer, she had begun a new liaison with a handsome twenty-two-year-old Italian-American named Rob Camilletti. By sheer coincidence, Camilletti worked in a bagel bakery in Queens.

In the movie, Cher's character Loretta goes through a Cinderella-like transformation from frumpy thirty-seven-year-old widow to glamorous cover girl. Despite her earlier doubts about playing the earlier incarnation Loretta, once filming began she found that she not only enjoyed it but in fact preferred playing the character this way. "I much prefer playing her 'before' than 'after,'" she recalled. "The freedom is not interesting to me because that's something I know usually. Yet I don't think of her as being constrained exactly. My idea was to play her more as bossy and controlled."

Director Jewison played a crucial role in helping Cher to create one of her finest performances. One scene in particular stuck in her mind: the moment when Ronny persuades Loretta to go with him to see *La Bohème* at the Metropolitan Opera. Rather than filming the scene in front of a live opera, Jewison planned to shoot the opera scenes separately, believing he could get just as good a reaction from Cher and Cage by playing them the music and explaining the opera's tragic plot.

Some directors might have considered this a risky strategy, but Jewison was clearly a highly effective storyteller. "We sit down," Cher recalled, "and the music starts playing and Norman starts explaining it, and he was doing such a great job of explaining it and the music was so fabulous that the scene really worked. I couldn't help from crying. I really like the way I cry in it, too. I think it's my best work. And then, when we were finished, Norman was crying. So I figured, well, that must be pretty good."

Cher was clearly not alone in her appraisal. Released on Christmas Day 1987, the film became an immediate hit, with some critics calling it "the best work Cher has ever done." The members of the Academy Of Motion Pictures thought so too. Ever since Cher had first dreamed of becoming an actress as a young girl, she had fantasized about winning an Oscar. In 1988, it finally looked like she might achieve that dream. However, also nominated alongside Cher in the Best Actress category that year were Holly Hunter, for *Broadcast News*; Glenn Close, for *Fatal Attraction*; Sally Kirkland, for *Anna*; and Meryl Streep, for *Ironweed*. Cher couldn't help but be conscious of the fact that it was Streep who had helped her so much on *Silkwood*; it seemed ironic that they were now competing against each other.

When it came to the awards night itself, Cher was almost beside herself with nerves. To make matters worse, the Academy had saved the Best

Actress category till last. When Paul Newman finally walked onstage to present the award, and Cher was stunned when she heard him announce her as the winner.

"When I was little my mother said: I want you to *be* something," Cher told the audience in her acceptance speech. "I don't think this means I *am* somebody, but I guess I'm on my way."

She certainly was. Although in her shock at winning the award she forgot to thank some key parties—including Norman Jewison, Nicolas Cage, and the Academy itself—she did express her gratitude to her hairdresser and makeup man, as well as Meryl Streep, whom she thanked for teaching her so much about acting.

After the ceremony, Cher spent time backstage doing press interviews. At one point one of her childhood idols, Audrey Hepburn, came over and told her: "I wanted you to win." As far as Cher was concerned, life couldn't get any better.

When the photo-calls and media interviews were finally over, Cher decided to skip the star-studded after-parties and instead went home with her family to celebrate in private. There were often times when she enjoyed the Hollywood glamour, but there were also at least as many when this kind of thing was much more her style—a pizza party on her bed with her mother, her sister, her children, her assistant Deb, and her new boyfriend. For Cher, it was the perfect end to this most memorable of evenings.

"It's hard for me to explain how great I felt," she later recalled. "I know you're not supposed to act too excited about these things. But what can I say? I'm not that cool! It was one of the great nights of my life!"

C

Cher's triumph in *Moonstruck* was to coincide with one of the most successful periods of her career, not only as an actress but also as a singer. But whereas her leading role in *Moonstruck* had come about as the natural progression of her acting work over the previous few years, her return to the top of the charts was much more of a surprise.

Since her first serious film role in *Come Back To The Five & Dime, Jimmy Dean, Jimmy Dean*, Cher had focused almost entirely on her acting career. She had had to work hard to be taken seriously as an actress, but as far as her musical career was concerned she was convinced that her days as a chart-topping artist were well and truly behind her. After all, she hadn't had a hit since the 1979 disco anthem 'Take Me Home,' and her last album, *I Paralyze*, had not even charted at all.

Consequently Cher was perhaps understandably reluctant to make any attempt to revive her musical career. Why try to resuscitate something that had showed few signs of life while her fledgling new movie career seemed to be flourishing?

However, A&R man John Kalodner was certain that Cher could have another hit. Kalodner had worked for Atlantic Records in the eighties, gaining industry fame for his work with Foreigner. He was now at Geffen Records, home to the likes of Elton John, Neil Young, and Joni Mitchell (as well as being the brainchild of Cher's ex-boyfriend, David Geffen). After some heavy persuasion, Kalodner managed to convince Cher to make a new album after she finished filming *Moonstruck*. It would be the first time she had ventured into a recording studio for five years.

"It really wasn't my idea," she later explained. "There's a man at Geffen records who just kept bothering me. For two years. He kept saying you should go back into the studio, and I kept saying I really don't think I would make a good album. He said: well, I'll help you. And he did."

Cher had first encountered Kalodner, with his long blond hair and straggly beard, some years earlier at an awards ceremony she attended with Geffen. "John was sitting five or six rows in front of us," Cher later recalled. "He just kept turning around and looking at me. Finally, I said to David: who the fuck is that weird guy and why is he looking at me? David said: oh, that's John Kalodner, he works for my label ... then, all of a sudden, David says: you know, John thinks that you need to be singing again."

Aside from the question of whether she should be recording again at all, there were some close to Cher who doubted the wisdom of signing to a label run by her ex-boyfriend. But as far as Cher was concerned, that didn't seem to be a problem. When asked whether the fact that she and David had previously lived together affected their working relationship, she replied that it did—but not in any way that was a problem.

"It makes it more cut and dried," she explained. "I don't think he knows any of the artists on his label. When I first met him, Joni (Mitchell) was living with him, making *Court And Spark,* and he was always in the studio and really into it, and he was excited if Jackson (Browne) was writing something new. He was really involved. But now David doesn't *run* Geffen. We have a very strange relationship. I'm very close to him but it has nothing to do with our business. We're just close personally."

A decade earlier, of course, Cher had made a rock album with Geffen, 1975's *Stars,* but it hadn't met with much success. This album, on the other hand, would become her first platinum seller, and the first of three she would record for her new label.

The songs on the new album, which was eventually to be titled simply *Cher,* were not radically different from what her fans had heard last time around, on *I Paralyze.* There's a similar—if more commercial—selection of bombastic power ballads and eighties-style stadium-rock numbers. There would once again be several songs by hit songwriter Desmond Child, as well as new compositions by Diane Warren—who would later go on to write some of Cher's biggest hits—and an as-yet unknown writer called Michael Bolton, as well as a couple by two rather better-known friends, Jon Bon Jovi and Richie Sambora.

Instead of having one person oversee the album, the plan was to work with a number of different producers: Michael Bolton, Jon Bon Jovi, songwriter Jon Lind, Desmond Child, and Peter Asher, the LA record mogul, producer, and former performer who had found fame himself two decades earlier as half of the sixties duo Peter & Gordon).

The album's opening track is 'I Found Someone,' a belting rock anthem complete with heavy-rock guitar solos, which very much sets the tone. Michael Bolton and Mark Mangold had originally written it for eighties rocker Laura Branigan, who had had a minor hit with the song in 1986. It would now provide Cher with her first comeback hit.

Bolton had initially wanted to record the song himself, "but his record company didn't like it," Cher told the UK's Heart FM, "which was really silly. So he came [to me] to produce it and I remember it was really strange because the more I did it, the angrier he got. He kept saying he didn't understand why his record company wouldn't let him do it." Bolton clearly missed out. Cher very much made the song her own with a soaring, no-holds-barred vocal.

The album continues in similar vein with another epic power ballad, 'We All Sleep Alone,' written by Jon Bon Jovi and co-produced by Bon Jovi and Sambora. Cher later explained that the Bon Jovi collaboration had come about thanks to her existing friendship with the New Jersey rocker. "I didn't really choose him," she said. "He kind of chose me. I met Johnny when he was a janitor."

'We All Sleep Alone' bears all the hallmarks of a Bon Jovi song; more than anything else, it sounds like Cher backed by Bon Jovi—which is essentially what it is, right down to the backing vocals by Jon and Richie. Lyrically, the song is darker than 'I Found Someone.' It deals with loneliness—a subject that was not entirely alien to Cher, following her divorces from Sonny Bono and Gregg Allman. "You may have lovers wherever you roam," she sings, "but sooner or later, we all sleep alone."

Bon Jovi also contributed production and arrangement for another track on the album: Cher's re-recording of her 1966 hit 'Bang Bang (My Baby Shot Me Down).' This is 'Bang Bang' as apocalyptic rock-opera, complete with a choir full of backing vocalists and a thunderous, overblown accompaniment.

Bon Jovi was by no means the only guest star on the album. On the chorus of 'Perfection,' which was co-written by Desmond Child and Diane Warren, Cher is joined by Bonnie Tyler—already a major star following her global hit 'Total Eclipse Of The Heart'—and an old friend from the Phil Spector days, Darlene Love. Love was undergoing a career resurgence of her own at this point, having recently appeared in the first of the *Lethal Weapon* films. 'Perfection' is yet another highly charged, anthemic rock number, this time with a pounding synth bassline, as per Survivor's 'Eye Of The Tiger,' the usual heavy guitar solos, and a rabble-rousing chorus about how "nothing's perfect if love ain't right."

The album's other main guest star, Maurice White of Earth Wind & Fire, appears on the album's most atypical track, 'Skin Deep.' Unlike the rest of the songs, which helped establish Cher's own brand of eighties power rock à la Bon Jovi, Toto, and Heart, 'Skin Deep' takes her down another road entirely. It has a featherweight, synth-fuelled dance-floor production and sounds more like Madonna's 'Material Girl' than anything—albeit with the occasional rock power-chord thrown in for good measure.

Cher was delighted with the new album. Despite her initial reservations about returning to singing, she soon remembered how much satisfaction she gained from it. "Once I actually got into it, I really enjoyed it," she recalled. "It was really an exciting time for me. I loved working with Jon and Richie, and I loved getting back into the music business after so long."

Cher—her nineteenth studio outing—was released on November 10 1987 with a head-and-shoulders cover portrait by rock photographer Matthew Rolston showing Cher in black leather jacket and suitably 'big' eighties hair. She dedicated the album to the two men to whom she felt she owed her recording career. "This album is dedicated with love to Sonny Bono for the first time," she wrote, "and John (His High Kalodner) for making me do it again."

When 'I Found Someone' was released as the first single in November 1987, it went straight to number ten on the US charts. It was Cher's first major hit in more than five years; suddenly, at the age of forty-one, she was back at the top of the charts.

The single was accompanied by a video featuring live footage of Cher performing the song and looking very much the raunchy rock chick, complete with cutaway ripped fishnet body-stocking, thigh-high boots, leather biker's jacket, and a massive curly black wig. These scenes are intercut with a storyline that shows her at a disco—looking more feminine in a chainmail silver mini-dress—where she meets and begins to slow-dance and grind with her new, real-life boyfriend Rob Camilletti.

The follow-up, 'We All Sleep Alone,' was almost as big a hit, reaching number fourteen in the USA, but the album's third single, 'Skin Deep,' did not fare so well, stalling at number seventy-nine. Nevertheless, Geffen considered releasing a fourth single from the record, 'Main Man,' and got as far as filming a promo video. The song—a soft ballad that builds gently to a rocking climax—was another Desmond Child composition, originally recorded by Child himself in 1978 with his band Desmond Child & Rouge.

Cher's version re-interprets the song as yet another rousing, heavy-rocking power ballad, while the video once again features a mix of live footage of Cher singing the song—with son Elijah on guitar—intercut with romantic scenes of Cher and Rob Camilletti, her real-life main man, at home in Los Angeles. In the end, the single was never released, but the video found its way into circulation, and is now easily viewable on YouTube.

The *Cher* album was a phenomenal success, selling nearly one-and-a-half million copies in the USA and no fewer than seven million worldwide. It reached number thirty-two on the *Billboard* 200 and number twenty-six in the UK. Cher couldn't have been happier. "It was my favorite time as a singles artist," she later noted, "because I was getting to do songs that I really loved, songs that really represented me, and they were popular!"

C

With her newfound musical success, the last thing on Cher's mind was any kind of reunion with Sonny Bono. But in early 1988, she received an unusual phone-call. The producers of *Late Night With David Letterman* had apparently contacted Sonny to see if he would consider coming on their show. But they did not want Sonny alone. They wanted Cher, too. At the time, Sonny was running for Mayor in Palm Springs; the producers assured him that an appearance—especially with his ex-wife—would do wonders for his political campaign.

Prior to this, Cher had only ever made one appearance on Letterman's show, in May 1986, and the interview had caused a minor scandal. The producers had previously invited Cher on the show on numerous occasions, but she had always refused. She had no interest in the show and didn't particularly like Letterman. She was still in considerable debt at the time, however, and told the producers that she would indeed appear on the show if they paid her $30,000 bill at the upscale Morgan's Hotel in New York, where she had been living, on and off, for some months.

The deal was agreed, but on the day of the show the producer called to ask her why she had originally been so reluctant to come on the show. "Because I thought he was kind of an asshole," she said.

Later that day, Cher went into the television studio to record the show.

Letterman had been told about her earlier comment and, true to his reputation for unnerving his guests, he asked her the same question on camera. He was obviously hoping to unsettle Cher by forcing her to come up with some kind of polite excuse on the spot, and at first he seemed to be succeeding.

"I thought that I'd never want to do this show with you," Cher replied, elusively. But Letterman was clearly determined to make her squirm.

"Why now?" he asked, prodding further. "Let's explore this a little."

Cher had had enough. She didn't care if Letterman was one of the most powerful men on American television; she had never been in the habit of shirking a challenge.

"Why?" she replied. "Because I thought you were an asshole."

The producers bleeped out the offending a-word, but anyone with a basic ability to lip-read could see exactly what she had said. Letterman was clearly flabbergasted and visibly unsettled throughout the rest of show. It became one of the most notorious episodes in either star's career.

Cher was therefore understandably a little anxious about the idea of reuniting with her ex-husband for the first time in several years on live TV with a host who was likely to be wary of her at best and more likely antagonistic toward her. The producers also wanted Cher to sing. She did, after all, have the single 'I Found Someone' to promote, but it had also been six years since she last sang live in front of an audience. It had also been nine years since she had been on camera with Sonny.

Despite her concerns, Cher agreed to appear. When it came to the day, Sonny was the first to arrive at the studio, accompanied by Chastity and his new twenty-five-year-old wife, Mary, who was seven months pregnant. Cher then arrived with boyfriend Rob, her hairstylist, a couple of girlfriends, and her son Elijah.

Sonny went on first and talked politics for a short while, before Cher came on in a micro-mini black dress, fishnet stockings, stilettos, and an oversized white jacket, heavily adorned with chains. After singing 'I Found Someone,' she joined Sonny on the interview couch.

Letterman was in playful mood, it seemed, and rather than being combative he started making light-hearted jibes about Cher's tattoos and outfit before moving on to her relationship with Sonny.

"Does [being back together] bring back any kind of emotions?" he asked. "Because you guys retain an amicable kind of relationship, right?"

"I feel nothing!" Cher quipped, laughing. She then rescinded the remark slightly, explaining that she and Sonny "have a very strange relationship that no one will ever understand except us. I don't think *I* understand it even."

"I don't either!" Sonny deadpanned.

It was like *The Sonny & Cher Show* all over again. The audience loved every minute of it. Finally, Letterman asked Cher if there was any chance they'd get back together again as a couple.

"I don't think Mary would like that," Cher replied. "She's pregnant."

This might not have been the most upbeat moment of the show, but what followed hit a different note altogether. Just before they had gone on air, Chastity had told Cher that she thought the producers were going to ask Cher to sing with Sonny—and not sing just anything, of course, but sing 'I Got You Babe.'

They agreed, and as they sang the song with which they would forever be identified, you could see genuine affection and emotion in their faces. The show was a triumph: viewers tuned in in their millions, providing Letterman with one of his biggest ever ratings.

Audiences clearly still loved the idea of 'Sonny & Cher' but they also knew that Cher had moved on. Just as Sonny Bono had helped launch her into musical stardom decades earlier, John Kalodner had now helped her find her way to a new level of fame, this time on her own terms. This new sound and new look would soon bring her even further success.

CHAPTER 13
Turn Back Time

While many of her contemporaries who had first found success in the sixties struggled to fit in with the musical styles of the following decades, Cher had no such problems. On the contrary, the late eighties would in fact provide some of her most popular and enduring hits. This period would also see her return to the road, this time as bona fide rock'n'roller rather than cabaret star. But first she had a new album to record.

Following the success of the *Cher* album, John Kalodner and Geffen Records were understandably eager for Cher to return to the studio as soon as possible. Cher was similarly keen, but in the early months of 1989 she fell sick. She was suffering with a succession of sore throats, flu-like symptoms, and a severe lack of energy, which made returning to work virtually impossible. Despite seeing numerous doctors, nobody seemed able to fathom what was wrong with her. Eventually she was diagnosed as having the Epstein-Barr virus (also known as Chronic Fatigue Syndrome).

"I was constantly sick and had no energy," she recalled. "I was someone who went full-tilt boogie when others were dropping like flies. But I should have figured out another way." The virus laid her low for much of the year, but after months of frustrating illness she gradually began to feel better, and by the fall she had returned to the studio.

Given that her previous album had yielded such strong hits, it made sense to use the same songwriting and production teams again. The overall sound and feel of what became *Heart Of Stone* is very much in the style of *Cher*, with the same combination of power-belting epics, eighties synths, heavy-rock guitars, and catchy, rabble-rousing choruses. As per *Cher*, there are also further guest appearances by some of her celebrity friends, including Bonnie Tyler and Michael Bolton.

With no fewer than six songs written or co-written by Diane Warren and more still by Jon Bon Jovi, Richie Sambora, and Michael Bolton, the album contains enough power ballads to fill a string of arenas. Indeed, it opens with a Diane Warren composition that was to provide Cher with one of her biggest-ever solo hits.

'If I Could Turn Back Time' is a power ballad *par excellence*, and one that provided the ultimate showcase for Cher's voice. With its infectious chorus, the song is both a love song and a plea for forgiveness, its lyrics cleverly dealing with the universally human feeling of regret for things that can no longer be changed.

The second track, 'Just Like Jesse James,' is another Warren track, this time co-written with Desmond Child, and would become a further smash hit. It very much follows the 'Turn Back Time' formula of impassioned love ballad, this time with Cher bemoaning the fact that her lover is unreliable—or, as the song says, just like the outlaw Jesse James.

While the song would prove a hit with her audience, however, Cher herself never really liked it—partly, she said, because there were too many words for her to remember. For many years afterward she was reluctant to sing the song live, but latterly began to include it in her shows, under pressure from fans, many of whom cite it as a favorite.

The Peter Asher-produced 'Love On A Rooftop' is another Warren–Child number, first recorded by Ronnie Spector on her 1987 album *Unfinished Business*. Cher's version is clearly an unofficial homage to Ronnie's ex-husband, with its own eighties-rock version of a Wall Of Sound-type production, complete with castanets and one of the signature sounds of the eighties: chiming bells. In a more classically AOR style, it also features saxophone breaks and guitar solos by The Heartbreakers' Waddy Wachtel.

Elsewhere on the album, there were some surprises in store, including the title track, a cover of a song that had initially been a hit for British Eurovision Song Contest winners Bucks Fizz. In contrast to the UK pop combo's gentler original, Cher's version starts off slowly before gradually building to a crescendo in which Cher gives it the full rock treatment, complete with storming, stadium-rock backing vocals.

Another noticeable step away from the Warren style was the inclusion of 'After All,' featuring Chicago singer Peter Cetera. Written by another hit songwriting double-act, Tom Snow and Dean Pitchford, the track also appeared prominently in *Chances Are*, the 1989 rom-com starring Cybill Shepherd, Ryan O'Neal, and Robert Downey Jr. It's a slower, gentler ballad which, despite being produced by Peter Asher, does not have the same heavy-rock feel as the rest of the album. (Despite appearing to sing their 'duet' together, Cher and Cetera were never in the same studio.)

The other clearly identifiable imprint on *Heart Of Stone* comes from Jon Bon Jovi and Richie Sambora, who contributed several songs. Just as with their earlier collaborations, on *Cher*, the duo's contributions sound as if they could almost be Bon Jovi out-takes with Cher on guest vocals. 'Does Anybody Really Fall In Love Anymore?' is a case in point, although this particular track was actually a four-way collaboration between Bon Jovi, Sambora, Warren, and Child in what amounted to an eighties power-rock songwriting supergroup. The same could similarly be said of 'Emotional Fire,' with its 'Livin' On A Prayer'-style chorus and backing vocals by Bonnie Tyler and Michael Bolton.

Two further tracks were recorded during the *Heart Of Stone* sessions but did not ultimately make the cut. 'Don't Come Cryin' To Me' was eventually included on the Geffen compilation album *If I Could Turn Back Time: Cher's Greatest Hits*; 'Some Guys' later surfaced as the B-side on the 'Turn Back Time' single.

The finished album credits Geffen A&R man John Kalodner not once but twice. Without his encouragement, Cher felt, she would almost certainly have abandoned her singing career altogether. She also dedicated the album to Rob Camilletti, her boyfriend of nearly three years.

When the album was released, in June 1989, the artwork featured a drawing by one of Mexico's best-known artists, Octavio Ocampo, showing Cher in a white frilly dress looking like the heroine of some kind of dark, Gothic fairytale, crouched down on the ground alongside an oversized, heart-shaped boulder with large cracks in it. From a distance, the image of Cher with the rock face bore more than a passing resemblance to a human skull, and seemed to echo a famous Victorian illustration devised to create the same optical illusion. It was a look more traditionally associated with British heavy-metal groups, and was unquestionably a strange choice for an album by someone like Cher.

Almost as soon as the album was released, everyone seemed to agree that the cover was a mistake, although Cher herself had mixed feelings about it. "I think the album cover is a fiasco," she said at the time, "but I'm crazy about it. It's like one of those gigantic mistakes that got totally fucked, but when I look at it, it's so me. I think it's ugly, but I like it a lot."

The artwork seemed to have little impact on Cher's fans, and the album went on to become one of her most successful solo releases. Her record company was loath to take any further risks, however, and by the time the album had gone platinum, it had a new cover: Cher as photographed by top fashion photographer Herb Ritts, looking glamorous and forthright, eyes straight to camera and legs astride, in a tight black strappy vest and skintight black pants. Gone was the gothic lettering of old, replaced now by a more conventionally eighties-style typeface.

'After All' was released as the album's first single in North America and reached number six on the *Billboard* Hot 100, but it was 'If I Could Turn Back Time' that catapulted Cher back to the top of the charts across the world. It reached number three in the USA and number six in the UK while also hitting the top ten in numerous other countries, including Australia, Norway, The Netherlands, and Ireland.

But success rarely proved entirely straightforward for Cher. While the single was a monumental success, the accompanying promo video proved more than a little controversial. Shot at night aboard the USS Missouri, a US naval battleship, at the former Long Beach Naval Shipyard, it shows Cher and her band—including twelve-year-old Elijah and his father, Gregg Allman—performing the song to a large crowd of sailors.

It was Cher's outfit—or perhaps lack of it—that caused the furor. If some of her past outfits had been skimpy, this one took skimpy to a whole new level: a black body-stocking slivered over a virtually nonexistent bathing costume that looks more like two strips of satin gaffer tape—just enough to cover the bare essentials, and rounded off with black fishnet stockings, complete with low-slung suspenders. With only a black leather biker's jacket covering her upper torso, Cher proceeds to gyrate raunchily around the deck, straddling the ship's cannons and missiles while sailors cheer her on.

Even by the occasionally raunchy standards of the music video, this was considered way too risqué and MTV only allowed the clip to be shown after 9:00pm. It was subsequently re-edited with the addition of some newly filmed scenes to create a slightly less raunchy version.

If anyone expected Cher to be angry, they were to be disappointed. She was more than used to controversy; in this instance, she seemed not only unperturbed by the fuss surrounding the video but quite happy to go along with any censorship. "When they pulled my video from MTV, I understood it," she said. "I didn't care that they banned it. I really didn't. It might not be suitable for very young children."

She also felt little connection between herself and her more outré performing persona. "Someone once asked me how I was able to wear that revealing outfit on the new video," she said, "but it's weird because that's not really me. In my private life, I'm really shy and introverted. I can do things in my public life that I could never do in private. 'Cher' could play to 100,000 people, but I would have trouble talking to one person. They're both me, but 'Cher' is just such a different part of my personality. One's private and one's something else that I don't understand at all."

The third and fourth singles to be drawn from the album were 'Just Like Jesse James' and 'Heart Of Stone.' Both were hits, reaching number eight and number twenty respectively on the *Billboard* Hot 100. While the video for 'Just Like Jesse James' incorporated clips of earlier Cher videos intercut with excerpts from old Westerns, the 'Heart Of Stone' promo proved to be yet another source of controversy.

This time the problem was not Cher's outfit. Here, she is dressed demurely in a loose black top over dark drainpipe trousers, and sings the song alone in what appears to be an empty studio in front of two large video screens. At the start of the song, the screens show images of her early life with Sonny and then pictures of her with her children. However, as it progresses, we see a melee of reportage footage of world events and figures: Ronald Reagan, President Nixon, the Vietnam War, Jimi Hendrix, Woodstock, anti-nuclear protesters, and more.

The idea was presumably that the images on view were generally tragic and might therefore prompt audiences to wish that they had hearts of stone, but many were unconvinced. "According to Cher's new video," Jim Farber of the *New York Daily News* concluded, "the greatest American tragedies of the last twenty years were Watergate, the Vietnam War, and her marriage to Sonny Bono. The point of this clip is to picture the situations that, over the years, have made us all wish our hearts were made of stone. Of course, some of you may think it's a tad offensive for Cher to equate her love blunders with our national tragedies."

The video may not have been the most considered move of Cher's career, but that in no way hindered the success of the single or its parent album. *Heart Of Stone* would eventually sell more than eleven million copies. More than two decades on, it is still Cher's third bestselling album.

C

With the global success of 'If I Could Turn Back Time' and the subsequent singles, any doubts about Cher's currency as a singer were now long gone. Her fans were buying her records in droves so the obvious next step was for Cher to go out on the road and sing for them live. Although she had played shows in Las Vegas numerous times over the last decade and played several shows with Black Rose, it had been eight years since she had performed live on her own. Consequently she was determined to make sure her fans were not disappointed, so her manager of the time, Bill Sammeth, arranged a kind of warm-up mini-tour of the USA to get things started.

As part of her stock-in-trade was showbiz glamour, Cher wanted to make sure there was plenty of it. Instead of comprising merely of Cher singing with a backing band, the tour would offer a *show* in every sense of the word. To that end she hired top choreographer and director Kenny Ortega, best known at the time for his work on the hit film *Dirty Dancing*.

Cher and Ortega did not have a lot of time to put the show together, but Cher insisted on being involved in choosing every dancer, singer, and musician. She sat through endless auditions—including some seventy guitarists. "I wanted to look at the dancers," she later explained, "I wanted to see the musicians. I wanted to know that they would be right."

Following on from his appearance in the 'If I Could Turn Back Time' video, one of the musicians to join Cher's touring band was her thirteen-year-old son, Elijah Blue Allman, on guitar. Cher's old friend from the

Spector days, Darlene Love, also joined the entourage as a backing singer.

Cher and Ortega planned an elaborate staging involving scaffolding, runways, and giant projection screens as well as the one element which surely no Cher show could be without: show-stopping Bob Mackie costumes. There were to be no fewer than nine costume changes, with Cher's outfits ranging from scruffy, ripped jeans to sequins and furs. But rather than being the product of hours of calculated thought and planning, Cher claimed most of the costumes arose from ideas that just came to her spontaneously. "I seize moments," she explained, saying that she just looked out for pieces that she thought were either "really spunky" or "interesting" or simply "something I can pull out that's going to be really fun!"

Cher wanted to make the show 'fun' at every level. Two days before she was due to leave Los Angeles for the first date, she told Ortega: "Kenny, let's get props, let's get crazy!" And indeed they did.

The elaborate set, designed by Ortega with input from Cher, meant that for each show, engineers had to hoist 300lb beams into place, with the crew effectively having to construct the equivalent of a multistory building, often in less than ten hours. When the one-hour show eventually set out on the road, it took two days to set up and required five full container trucks, five buses, and seventy-six staff, including seven musicians, seven dancers, three back-up singers, a cook, and a personal trainer, as well as numerous stagehands and construction engineers.

Also on board was a female impersonator, Elgin Kenna. Cher had used drag queens in her earlier shows, dressed as Bette Midler or Diana Ross, but this time the impersonator was to appear as Cher herself. "This show is a sort of *Phantom Of The Opera* meets ... Metallica," she told one audience, "It's like Disney World on acid. I'm the E-ticket."

As far as Cher was concerned, putting on a show—complete with costumes, wigs, and even female impersonators—was all part of the spectacle her fans deserved. "At my house I just go 'round in old, falling-apart sweatpants and no makeup," she explained. "But ... if I charge people money to come and see me, it certainly is my obligation to give them the best show and the best version of me that I can give them and so I don't even mind doing it. It seems to me that's my job."

One of the first dates of the mini-tour was at an outdoor amphitheater in Mansfield, Massachusetts, in front of a crowd of some 16,000 fans. Having not played live for so long, Cher was understandably more than a little nervous. "Every night I'm standing on the stage," she explained, "I say: God, just you and me. We've gotta do it together, because *I* can't do it, but I know it's not a problem for you."

When the show began, the audience—some of whom had paid up to $200 for the best seats—was shown an introductory short film featuring clips through the years, beginning with Cher as a baby and running through footage of *The Sonny & Cher Comedy Hour* and her recent Academy Award acceptance speech. The screen then rose to reveal Cher dressed in ripped jeans and a fawn sequined jacket, descending on a freight elevator, flanked by her band and back-up singers.

First was 'I'm No Angel,' a song by Cher's ex-husband Gregg Allman—an unusual choice for an opening number, perhaps, but one which no doubt pleased young Elijah. It set the tone for the rest of the show, which was very much dominated by rock songs and left the audience in no doubt that Cher had moved on from her previous incarnations as hippie chick and seventies disco diva. This was Cher as Rock Queen.

Next was an impassioned cover of Eddie Money's 'Baby Hold On' before the first real crowd-pleaser, 'We All Sleep Alone.' At one show, Cher introduced the song by explaining that it had "particular meaning for me, because I just broke up with my boyfriend." She had recently split from Rob Camilletti—but, as it turned out, her days of sleeping alone were to prove shortlived. She soon began a relationship with her friend and collaborator Richie Sambora, and the Bon Jovi guitarist would subsequently make guest appearances at a few of her later tour dates.

Meanwhile, 'We All Sleep Alone' was a grand-scale production number—the first of several during the show. Cher appeared in the lace body-stocking and thigh-high boots she had worn for the video and ended the highly choreographed routine by falling into her dancers' arms. Other big numbers included 'I Found Someone' and 'Perfection,' from *Cher*. When it came to her old hits, however, Cher temporarily left the stage to screen a montage of clips from 'I Got You Babe,' 'All I Really Want To Do,' 'Gypsys,

Tramps & Thieves,' and 'Half-Breed' rather than singing the songs again herself. Her only concession to fans of her older material was a rendition of 'Bang Bang'—albeit the recently revamped rock version—which she likewise performed as a big production number with her dancers.

Rather than looking backward, Cher seemed much more interested in her latest reinvention as ballsy rock-chick supreme. Instead of her old hits, she presented the audience with hard-rocking covers of the Eagles' 'Take It To The Limit,' Bob Seger's 'Fire Down Below,' and Bruce Springsteen's 'Tougher Than The Rest.'

When it came to the costumes, however, nobody could be disappointed. As the show drew to a close, Cher reappeared in a floor-length white mink coat and a headdress that looked like a cross between a white satin spaceship and a Frisbee with a scarf tied under the chin. Cher later recalled that she hated this particular combo, saying the mink was swelteringly hot under the stage lights, but she did not have to endure it for long. When the song ended, she threw the coat aside to reveal the notoriously skimpy black body-stocking and leather jacket combo from her 'If I Could Turn Back Time' video. This, her recent major hit, provided the perfect finale, and as Cher strutted across the stage, the audience clearly loved every minute.

The initial American dates in 1989 were a huge success. Over the course of eight months from the spring of 1990, Cher headed back out on the road, taking in extensive dates across the USA (including her old haunt, Las Vegas), Europe, and even Australia. Such a schedule would have been tiring for anyone and at forty-three, Cher often felt the strain. "I'm getting too old for this," she groaned after one show. "I can barely move around onstage."

Although clearly an exaggeration, Cher had nevertheless continued to suffer with the Epstein-Barr virus, while the discovery of a lump in one of her breasts understandably caused her severe stress. However, rather than having the lump examined immediately, she decided to continue with the tour first. "I decided not to go to a doctor on the road because if there was something wrong with me, then it would hit the papers," she explained. "It was three weeks that I waited, and I was really frightened. When I got back, I went in and had a mammogram and a sonogram. I was fine; it was just a cyst. But I was so nervous about it."

Cher successfully managed to keep the health scare out of the press. None of this stopped her playing sell-out shows in thirty-five North American cities as well as standing-room-only performances in the UK and Australia. Her fans obviously loved the show but some of the critics were less convinced. According to Jon Pareles of the *New York Times*, Cher's new show was "a kind of Las Vegas mystery play with a message: trust yourself, don't give up on life or love, and eternal celebrity can be yours. 'There's a time for substance and all that,' she said, 'but it's not here and it's not now.' No one could argue with that."

Bob Harrington of the *New York Post* was more favorable. "The impersonator, doing an impeccable impression and dressed to kill, looks more like Cher than Cher," he wrote. "But it's the real article, without the glitz, that's got the glamour. She's incandescent, vibrant, and compelling, even competing with what was virtually an identical twin." Cher's fans clearly agreed, and the tour grossed over $40 million.

C

During the course of the Heart Of Stone tour, Cher had also agreed to allow a CBS TV special, *Extravaganza: Live At The Mirage*, to be filmed using live footage from the shows at The Mirage Hotel, Las Vegas, the previous year.

While playing the shows at 1,500-seat theater, Cher purposely adapted some of her stage outfits for the more conservative CBS TV audience. In place of the notorious 'If I Could Turn Back Time' body stocking, she appeared wearing a low-cut, sheer black sequined mini-dress with black calf-length boots. It was hardly the kind of outfit one would call modest, but it was still decidedly demure compared to the video outfit. The live footage, meanwhile, was intercut with clips from the promotional video, so that, ultimately, TV audiences got to see the body stocking in any case.

Another change in outfit occurred for the opening number. Instead of wearing ripped jeans for 'I'm No Angel,' she appeared sporting a more sedate pale pink pantsuit—albeit one dripping with silver sequins. This was still a Cher show, and in no way could it be called dull.

When the TV show was aired on February 4 1991, even the *New York Times* could not fail to find it entertaining. "This special captures Cher in most of her uninhibited, sometimes contradictory guises," John O'Connor wrote. "Supported by an orchestra, energetic dancers, and a trio of soul-thumping background singers, she prances and dances about the hotel's huge, high-tech stage ... looking curiously frail beneath a gargantuan black wig."

Cher's audience repartee was also a success. "Much of the material is autobiographical," the review continued. "References are made in passing to former husbands and lovers. She laughs easily with the audience about her reputation for being partial to younger men and cosmetic surgery. At times, strutting about in see-through lace tights, Cher revels in the role of friendly tart."

Produced and directed for television by Marty Callner, *Extravaganza* was subsequently released on VHS and Laserdisc with commentary from Cher. It was also issued on DVD in 2005 with further bonus features including home movies and the option to watch extra footage of songs either in rehearsals or at the Mirage.

Cher's return to the live stage had been an overriding success, whether seen live or on film. Her next ventures, in both music and film, would prove equally successful.

CHAPTER 14
Love Hurts

After a year's worth of focusing on music for *Heart Of Stone* and the ensuing tour, many artists would have taken a well-earned break. But Cher had her alternative career to think of, and the movies once again beckoned. By this point, she had achieved the relatively rare feat of success as both a singer and an actress, even winning an Academy Award. Over the next couple of years she would further develop her ability to maintain her parallel careers, but the challenge for the moment was to choose the best new role.

With nearly all of her recent movie roles, Cher had looked for parts she could identify with in some way or other. Even with *Come Back To The Five & Dime, Jimmy Dean, Jimmy Dean,* she had fought for the part that she wanted rather than the one Robert Altman had originally planned for her. But having won an Oscar, she was able to pick and choose, and her next role was to be one to which she felt a particular connection.

Cher now had the clout of a major box-office star and could command as much as four million dollars per movie. She could insist that she had input and control over her own role, as well as the rest of the cast and crew, but while this and the financial aspects of being an Oscar winner were clearly advantageous, in other ways it was a difficult position to be in. Having won an Academy Award for *Moonstruck*, she was understandably anxious that her next role should not be seen as a disappointment. She looked at numerous scripts and at one point considered taking on the character that Kathleen Turner would eventually play in *The Wars Of The Roses*. However, at the last minute, Cher decided against it, frustrated that the producers would not guarantee her the artistic control she demanded.

"I couldn't find anything that I wanted to do," she said. "I was desperately looking. There are not a lot of great scripts and there are so many women in my area. There were two years between *Mask* and *Witches [Of Eastwick]*.

I don't want that to happen again ... it's stifling to do TV for as long as I did, and I ended up hating it. I don't ever want to do that with movies, and therefore, because of my age and because I'm a woman, I'm not going to get the best script out of thirty scripts. I'm going to hope that I get the best script out of two or four scripts and I'm going to wait a long time for them."

Eventually, she came across a script she liked, written by screenwriter June Roberts and based on a novel by Patty Dunn. Set in the early sixties, *Mermaids* told the story of Mrs Flax, a glamorous, sexy single mother with two young daughters who has a series of affairs but moves town every time one breaks up. In the script, Mrs Flax meets a local shoe-store owner with whom she begins a liaison, but while their relationship develops, we also see a separate story unfold, focusing on her teenage daughter, Charlotte.

Mrs Flax—the part suggested for Cher—is not a conventional mother in any sense. She has an unorthodox approach to romance and relationships, and as the film progresses we see that she is extremely wary of emotional involvement and commitment. Her domestic routine is similarly unusual. Instead of preparing dinner for her daughters, she serves up finger food, comprising cut-up bagels or kebabs with marshmallows and maraschino cherries, colorfully presented with toothpicks and miniature American flags.

Cher warmed to the idea immediately. The transient nature of the mother and her children's existence reminded her very much of her own childhood. "I actually play my mother," she said. "That's why I took this movie role. Because it was so similar to my youth experience, only I play my mother and Winona [Ryder] plays me, and that's kind of the reason I took it, because my mother was really nuts and Mrs Flax is really nuts, and I had a little sister."

Eventually, Cher would even use old photos of her mother as the basis for Mrs Flax's costumes. "Mrs Flax *is* my mother," she continued. "They are one and the same person. The dresses were taken from old Polaroids my mother had from the sixties. The dresses work. Mrs Flax doesn't have to open her mouth too much—look at her and you get a quick sense of who she is."

Cher also liked the script because in some ways its gentle feel reminded her of her most recent movie success. "It's very reminiscent of *Moonstruck*," she explained. "It's a sweet look at people who are totally out of their minds and doing the best job that they can, but they're just cracked. The story's not even mostly about me. It's about Charlotte, and I play her mother."

Mrs Flax's two young daughters, fifteen-year-old Charlotte and nine-year-old Kate, were initially to be played by British actress Emily Lloyd and Christina Ricci. British character actor Bob Hoskins was cast as Lou Landsky, the shoe-store owner. The director was the Swedish filmmaker Lasse Hallström, best known for *My Life As A Dog*.

Filming began in October 1989, but almost immediately Cher began to complain that she felt audiences would have trouble believing that the fair-haired and fair-complexioned Lloyd could be her daughter. Cher believed that another young actress—Winona Ryder, who had darker coloring more like her own—would be much more suitable.

Ryder was at this point no more widely known than Lloyd, having appeared only in the cult film *Heathers*, but she and Cher immediately bonded and Cher finally insisted that Ryder replace Lloyd. But it was not just Lloyd with whom Cher had difficulties. She had also been having problems with Hallström. The director was reportedly keen to amend the script, changing it so that Kate, Mrs Flax's younger daughter, dies toward the end of the film. Hallström felt that this would be more memorable and dramatic. Cher did not think audiences would want that kind of serious drama. She wanted the emphasis to be much more on the comedic aspects of the script, and to keep things lighthearted overall. Hallström was duly fired, and another month passed while the studio looked for a replacement director.

The studio's next suggestion was Frank Oz, who had recently directed *Little Shop Of Horrors* but was far better known for his work with The Muppets. Cher was unconvinced from the start, sarcastically asking how Oz's credentials were relevant, since there were no marionettes in *her* film. She agreed to meet him and, at the studio's insistence, try working with him. But the trial did not work out; Cher felt that, like Hallström before him, Oz was focusing too heavily on the serious, dramatic aspects of the plot rather than making a 'feel-good' movie. She was also concerned—as was the studio—that Oz worked too slowly. The picture was now quite significantly behind schedule.

Finally, at Cher's suggestion, a new director was brought in. Richard Benjamin had made his name as an actor in films like *Goodbye Columbus*, *Westworld*, and *Catch 22*, but had more recently turned his hand to directing films such as *My Favorite Year* with Peter O'Toole, *City Heat* with Clint Eastwood, and *The Money Pit* with Tom Hanks. Cher had in fact wanted to work with Benjamin before, when he had been planning a film called *Going To The Chapel* just after she had finished *Mask*, but the project had fallen through.

Cher was convinced Benjamin understood her vision for the movie and would direct it well, and so, finally, Benjamin was appointed. It had not been an easy situation for anybody on the film. "Winona and I cried every night and every day," Cher told *Premiere* magazine. "It was just the worst experience of my life."

However, with Benjamin on board, Cher felt that the movie could really now begin to take shape. "Once the director got fired, it was much better," she remembered. "The new director, Richard Benjamin, was really fabulous, but we were behind schedule by that time so we were always playing catch-up."

Cher may have gotten her own way as far as the director was concerned, but she had also developed a reputation for being demanding and difficult. "Look, I'm only difficult if you're an idiot," she retorted. "If you don't know more than I know, then I'll be really difficult. I know you're not supposed to say it, but nobody ever says anything if an actor gets fired. If a director gets fired, everybody has a heart attack."

Cher may have had issues with the movie's first couple of directors, but in the meantime she and Winona Ryder had become very close, with Cher developing a maternal and sisterly bond toward the eighteen-year-old actress. Cher even arranged for Ryder to stay in the same Boston apartment building that she herself was living in during filming, instead of the hotel where most of the crew was staying. Perhaps inspired by the improvisational rehearsals Norman Jewison had arranged for her with her onscreen family in *Moonstruck*, she also invited both Ryder and Christina Ricci for dinner and a sleepover before filming began so that the three of them could spend some informal time together.

As far as the film's plot is concerned, the central focus really is on Charlotte rather than Mrs Flax, but Cher still made a lasting impression on the movie by bringing out the sassy comedy of the script. Unlike some of her past roles, she also seemed to bring to the part an outlandish glamour that was very much her own, although to some critics this made her character less believable.

Hal Hinson of the *Washington Post* nevertheless felt the casting worked well. "All of the women characters here are seen as exotics," he wrote. "For some this notion might be hard to swallow. But Cher, who's the most otherworldly of modern actresses, makes the suggestion seem altogether reasonable. Her Mrs Flax is deliciously trashy—kitsch in high heels." The acting establishment also agreed, and Cher was nominated for a Golden Globe Award as Best Supporting Actress. Cher had had to wait a while before finding the right role but in the end, her choice had turned out to be a good one.

This was not to be Cher's only area of success with the movie. The soundtrack featured a selection of early-sixties hits from the pre-Beatles era by artists such as Franki Valli, Eydie Gormé, and the now mostly forgotten Shelly Fabares. John Kalodner once again supervised the score and Cher recorded versions of the 1964 Betty Everett hit 'The Shoop Shoop Song (It's In His Kiss)' and Barbara Lewis's 'Baby I'm Yours.' Both songs were produced by Peter Asher.

'The Shoop Shoop Song' was added to the movie's soundtrack and ran over the closing credits. It was released as a single, with 'Baby I'm Yours' on the B-side, to coincide with the movie's release in November 1990. The single failed to make the US top twenty, so 'Baby I'm Yours' was released as a single in the UK. This similarly failed to graze even the British top fifty, so 'The Shoop Shoop Song' was finally issued instead. This time it was a different story. The single went to number one on May 4 1991 and remained at the top of the British charts for five weeks. It also hit the top spot in Austria, Norway, Spain, New Zealand, and Ireland, and made the top ten in France, Germany, Belgium, the Netherlands, Sweden, Switzerland, and Australia.

It was her first solo number one since 'I Got You Babe.' "You could have just knocked me over with a feather," she said, "because in America the song wasn't a big hit at all. It was just an OK song, you know, but I was shocked it was number one."

It was the kind of surprise that Cher could more than cope with. On the back of the song's phenomenal success, she made a promotional video which shows her in a studio in front of large video screens, as per the 'Heart Of Stone' clip. This time she was dressed as Mrs Flax, complete with hair in the black-fringed flip wig and polka-dotted wiggle dress from the movie. Winona Ryder and Christina Ricci appear as back-up singers, dressed in identical dresses and wigs.

C

Shortly after finishing filming *Mermaids*, Cher was delighted to be contacted by the director who had given her her first serious acting role, Robert Altman. This time Altman was offering her another film role—albeit a cameo as herself.

Altman was making a satire on the Hollywood film industry, lightly disguised as a gentle murder mystery. Titled *The Player*, the film was notable as much as anything for its star-studded cast, with what amounted to a who's who of Hollywood A-listers appearing in walk-ons, bit parts, or simply as themselves. Cher's role fell into the latter category alongside the likes of Angelica Huston, Burt Reynolds, Rod Steiger, Harry Belafonte, Bruce Willis, Julia Roberts, Jack Lemmon, and Susan Sarandon.

The film's main plot line follows a studio producer, played by Tim Robbins, who becomes involved in a murder and also begins a relationship with the victim's girlfriend, played by Greta Scacchi. Roughly midway through the film, Robbins invites Scacchi on a date and takes her to a glamorous Hollywood gala evening.

The event is filled with the crème de la crème of Hollywood—both fictional and real-life. Among the guests is Cher, who causes an immediate sensation by arriving in what an onscreen commentator describes as a "fire-engine red" beaded gown with a plunging neckline. However, the dress code for the event is black and white; Cher is the only one wearing any color. Her dress, just like the outfit she had worn in the 'If I Could Turn Back Time' video, shows off the extensive tattoo on her left upper arm—an undulating line in the form of a necklace with a heart-shaped pendant.

Accompanied by Peter Gallagher, her date for the evening, Cher has only one audible line in the film: "Are we having fun yet?" Later on, we see her seated at a table chatting to Academy Award nominated actress Sally Kirkland. We can't hear what they're saying, but Kirkland later recalled that she and Cher were both very interested in "holistic or spiritual things" and had been comparing experiences with these matters.

The film was well received and continues to enjoy a cult following. From Cher's point of view it had been a brief and enjoyable experience but it also suited her as it took very little of her time. Since finishing the Heart Of Stone tour, she had concentrated on her acting, and she was glad now to return to music once more to record her third album for the Geffen label: *Love Hurts*.

The relative peace and tranquility of the recording studio came as a welcome change after the physical demands, tight schedules, and overall pressures of acting or performing live. "When I came off the road after eight months," she later explained in the album's press release, "I was really whipped. I had never done a tour like that by myself, and it was a blast, but it kicked my butt. Recording has always been so terrifying and so hard but going into the studio this time was a nice break for me—no audience, no camera, no makeup. This time I felt like I was doing an album for myself."

It was also the first time in some years that Cher had been able to allocate specific time for recording, rather than squeezing in sessions between film work. She was delighted to be able to concentrate on one thing. "I do my best singing when I'm not doing other things," she said. "When there's a movie, too, it infringes on my focus."

When it came to choosing a songwriting and production team for the album, both Cher and Kalodner took the 'if it ain't broke, why fix it?' approach. As with the album's two most recent predecessors, they decided to use the same combination of multiple producers and different songwriters. Consequently, the overall sound has the same soft-rock feel, which had by this time become Cher's musical stock-in-trade.

It was a style to which Cher felt genuinely connected. "Part of the reason this was an easy album to make is that the music is closest to what I like—

guitars, rock'n'roll, but not too heavy," she explained. "But every track is different, too. What bothers me about radio is you get only one kind of music from each station. On this album, the producers left their marks on their songs, making every track unlike the one before."

As with *Cher* and *Heart Of Stone*, Diane Warren once again proved a rich source of material, providing three songs: opening track 'Save Up All Your Tears,' 'Love And Understanding,' and 'When Lovers Become Strangers.' Just as before, many of the songs' lyrics deal with disappointment in love and the pain of separation, but rather than making them sound maudlin or self-pitying, Cher's hard-hitting delivery and the take-no-prisoners hard-rock production make her sound as though she is every inch in control.

These were all songs to which Cher had felt a personal connection, and to which she felt she could bring something of herself. "I don't write the songs I sing," she explained, "but when I hear a piece of material and it … connects, I do it. It's like, I don't write the movies either but I can act out my character. When you feel a certain way, you feel it. It's something you can't explain. It just is."

One track she clearly connected with was 'Save Up All Your Tears,' a hard-nosed power ballad with a catchy, sing-along chorus in the trademark Warren style. Co-written by Desmond Child, it had originally been recorded by Welsh rocker Bonnie Tyler. Cher gives it what had by now already become her own standard treatment, belting it out alongside some similarly predictable rock guitar. 'When Lovers Became Strangers' is more of the same, while 'Love And Understanding' is a more up-tempo rocker, complete with full string orchestration.

Continuing with the heartbreak theme, Cher also decided to explore the work of other songwriters. Aside from the Warren and Child compositions there are various other cover versions. One is Kiss's 'A World Without Heroes,' written by Cher's ex-beau Gene Simmons and Paul Stanley with Lou Reed/Alice Cooper producer Bob Ezrin. Lamenting the fact that "a world without heroes is like a bird without wings," Cher gives an impassioned homage to the world's heroes alongside some searing rock guitar by Toto's Steve Lukather.

In a similar vein is 'I'll Never Stop Loving You,' co-written by seventies heartthrob David Cassidy and previously recorded by stadium-rockers Heart, which in Cher's hands becomes yet another bombastic, arena-filling anthem. However, the album is not entirely uniform in mood. The catchy, poppy 'Could've Been You' would prove to be a big favorite with Cher's fans. Written and originally recorded by Bob Haligan Jr, who also wrote songs for British rock band Judas Priest, it is a paean to an ex-lover focusing on the things they've missed out on. The way Cher sings it, you have no doubt that she means every word.

The title track is the song Cher felt closest to. It had originally been a hit for The Everly Brothers way back in 1960; Cher herself had recorded it in 1975 for her *Stars* album and was always keen to sing it in her live shows. Now, still feeling the hurt of her split from Rob Camilletti, it was a song she related to in every way. "I'm a better performer than I am a singer," she explained in the press release for *Love Hurts*, "but I can sing honestly— there's no bullshit. When I sing a song, it's always about me. That's not narcissistic. It has to be personal. I have to hear how it relates to me. Love hurts—that's the truth. I know it from experience," she continued, laughing. "Put it this way, I can do a convincing job of singing that song."

Cher's 1991 version of the song takes the gentle pace of the original and slows it down still further, eking out every inch of drama and pathos from the lyric and giving it the full eighties power-rock treatment.

Love Hurts—Cher's 26th solo album—was released in June 1991. She dedicated the album to the current man in her life, Richie Sambora—and, in acknowledgement of the theme of heartbreak running through the album, to "every man that ever made me shed a tear." The front cover artwork has her looking like some kind of Gothic Greek Goddess, her dark hair curled above her head in a diamond tiara against a background of Medieval-looking leaves and wings.

The Gothic theme continued with a special 'collector's edition' of the CD. Inside a hinged wooden box, fans were treated not only to the album but also to thirteen specially designed Gothic Tarot cards bound together in a rice paper ring. Each card featured an image of Cher alongside the words "I hate and I love. Why I do so, perhaps you ask. I know not, but I feel it and I am in torment." The lines were taken from the work of Catullus, one of ancient Rome's most famous poets and philosophers. This may have been a slightly unusual approach for a showbusiness star but by referencing such an early source, Cher was merely following in the well-worn heavy metal tradition of looking to ancient texts for inspiration.

Four singles were released from the album—'Love And Understanding,' 'Save Up All Your Tears,' 'Love Hurts,' and 'Could've Been You'—and when it came to making videos, Cher's points of reference were clearly considerably more contemporary. Although his romance with Cher was by now over, Rob Camilletti appears once again in the video for 'Love Hurts.' The video for 'Save Up All Your Tears' on the other hand was almost as risqué as the one for 'If I Could Turn Back Time.' This time there were no sailors and no cannons to upset anyone. It was just Cher's outfits that caused the controversy—or at least one in particular. First up is a skimpy, pale pink negligée, followed by a similar black number. The third outfit looks like something Bob Mackie might have dreamed up if Queen Cleopatra had worked in a bondage parlor.

After that, Cher appears in a revealing black bustier supported by gold chains on either side and flowing batwing sleeves made of what looks like chainmail black leather, above a severely high-cut black leather thong and fishnet stockings. This is all rounded off with a long, Cleopatra-style fringed straight black wig. At various points during the song, as Cher tosses her hair back and dances to the music, the camera scans to the rear, where the audience is treated to several glimpses of her famous tattoo.

In case any fans had missed the video, Cher had Herb Ritts photograph her in the same outfit. The resulting derriere-revealing images were later used to promote her subsequent Love Hurts tour of Europe. "Cher's Back!" the posters saucily proclaimed.

Tongue-in-cheek controversy and Cher had long been regular playmates, and the liaison had certainly never harmed her career. 'Save Up All Your Tears' was a top forty hit in both the USA and UK, where it reached number thirty-seven in the charts, while 'Love And Understanding' was the album's biggest hit, reaching number seventeen in the USA and number ten in the UK. 'Love Hurts' and 'Could've Been You' were both also European hits.

As a whole, the album was generally well received by the critics. "With a few exceptions," *Billboard* concluded, "the overall musical direction is more straightforward rock'n'roll this time, which is the perfect environment for her unique vocal style." *Entertainment Weekly*'s review was similarly complimentary. "For all the fakery that surrounds her, Cher remains weirdly genuine; an earnest sellout who—bless her soul—knows no other way."

Cher herself was confident that the public would enjoy the album. "People who like my singing are going to love this album," she predicted. "People who don't like my singing? They might still like this one." She was not entirely wrong. *Love Hurts* reached only number forty-eight on the *Billboard* charts in June 1991 but eventually sold enough copies to be certified Platinum in the USA.

However, in the UK, it was a different story: the album went straight to number one and stayed there for five weeks. The UK version of the album also includes her recent chart-topper from *Mermaids*, 'The Shoop Shoop Song,' while later European pressings of the album had different artwork, with a simple cover portrait of Cher reclining against a white background wearing a red wig.

Cher promoted the album further in Europe during April and May the following year, playing sold-out shows in twelve countries on her eight-week Love Hurts tour. The album itself eventually sold some fourteen million copies worldwide, making it the second best-selling album of Cher's career.

"If I had not come back to a music career, I would have missed doing this album," she said. "That would have been a real disappointment in my life. But you can either swim or die at points in your career. I swam. I'm a gutsy kind of gal."

C

With *Love Hurts* and 'The Shoop Shoop Song,' Cher had re-established herself as a major chart-topping star in Europe and to capitalize on this newly regained status, Geffen decided to release a European-only hits album.

Entitled simply *Greatest Hits: 1965–1992*, the album is a somewhat oddly compiled collection of sixteen of Cher's singles, nominally spanning her entire career. It contains only one track from the sixties—the inevitable

'I Got You Babe'—and only two from her MCA days in the seventies: 'Dark Lady' and 'Gypsys Tramps & Thieves.' The rest of the album is drawn largely from her Geffen years, with no less than eight songs from this period, including 'If I Could Turn Back Time,' 'We All Sleep Alone,' and 'Heart Of Stone,' as well as one of her early entrées into the faux-rocking arena, 'Dead Ringer For Love,' her collaboration with Meat Loaf.

The album also features three previously unreleased new songs, recorded under John Kalodner's stewardship during the recent album sessions. Opening the album is the first of these, 'Oh No, Not My Baby,' originally a hit for pop-soul singer Maxine Brown in 1964. It was one of a host of hits written by Carole King in her early days in New York with her husband of the time, Gerry Goffin, and very much follows on from the style of 'The Shoop Shoop Song,' conjuring up the same early sixties romantic innocence.

Also harking back to an earlier era, this time to the seventies, was a cover of reggae star Jimmy Cliff's 'Many Rivers To Cross,' which had been recorded live at The Mirage in Las Vegas during the filming of Cher's recent televisual *Extravaganza*.

The third new number—'Whenever You're Near,' a love song in the gutsy power-ballad vein specially written for Cher by Jack Blades and Tommy Shaw—brings things back up to date. All three new songs went on to become top forty hits in the UK, while the album itself debuted at number one. *Greatest Hits: 1965–1992* subsequently became the biggest-selling European album of Cher's career, and for many years was a sought-after import in the USA.

When Geffen Records A&R man John Kalodner had first persuaded Cher to return to the recording studio in 1987, she had had no idea how successful their partnership would be. Under Kalodner's direction she had now made three albums and scored some of the biggest hits of her solo career. However, the *Greatest Hits* albums would prove to be her last release for the Geffen label, and her next musical outing would see her pursuing a new direction altogether.

CHAPTER 15
Walking In Memphis

For most American stars, breaking into the UK market is just an added bonus. But for Cher, Britain had played a key role in her career from the very start. By the nineties, she had become a regular fixture at the top of the European charts, so when it came to recording her next album, it was perhaps little surprise that she should look to the UK for inspiration.

While the success of *Greatest Hits 1965–1992* had further confirmed Cher's status as a major star in Europe, her recent releases had generally been much less successful in America. She had had a surprise one-off US hit in January 1994, when she duetted with alternative MTV cartoon heroes Beavis & Butt-Head on a comedy version of 'I Got You Babe,' which made the top forty, but other than that she hadn't had a major solo chart hit since 'If I Could Turn Back Time.' Consequently, when it came to planning her next studio album, it seemed natural to focus on the British and European markets.

Having recorded three albums with Geffen, she also felt it was time for a change. With Geffen, Cher had reinvented herself in the public imagination as a stadium rock diva par excellence, but despite the success of the soft rock formula, she knew it was time to move on. "There was a lot of upheaval [at Geffen]," she later recalled, "and I wasn't at all happy. David [Geffen] was gracious enough to let me go, and when we looked around for a new company a lot of people on the West Coast recommended Warners UK."

Not only did the British arm of Warner Bros come strongly recommended, but the company's chairman—legendary industry mogul Rob Dickens—was also a longstanding fan of Cher. She consequently signed the deal and began plans for a new album.

From the beginning, Cher worked closely with Dickens, much as she had with John Kalodner on her Geffen albums. "I've always liked her voice,"

Dickens said at the time, "and she made it plain from the start that this would not be a superstar vehicle, but a fully realized music project. We worked together on the songs and although we sometimes disagreed on details, we were both committed to producing an adult piece of work."

Cher and Dickens also discussed the idea of moving away from the power ballads that she had become so closely identified with on her Geffen albums. Although those songs had been hits in the UK and Europe, by this point in the mid nineties their sound and style had become rather dated. The charts were now full of the pop R&B sound of hit acts like Boyz II Men, and even Madonna had recently made an album, *Bedtime Stories*, in the same vein. It therefore made sense to consider material by different writers in a fresher, smoother style.

"It was me experimenting with me," Cher later explained. "I didn't want to sound like I've always sounded on records, because I'm kind of bored with it. Some songs like 'If I Could Turn Back Time' I like, but on a lot of albums, I think I'm kind of pukey! The problem with having a really distinctive voice is that if you like it, great, but if not, people can't stand [your album] and you're blown out of the water by the first three songs."

As with her previous albums, Cher would use a combination of different producers rather than having one person oversee the entire album. "I don't like working with one producer," she continued, "I like the idea of producers picking up songs they like, because that way they do their best job in the songs they pick, whereas if they do the whole album, it seems that they only love their songs and the rest they just do."

Rob Dickens agreed and felt that using different producers would also help give Cher the opportunity to extend her voice and emphasize its range and possibilities. "That's why we used four different producers," he said. "Each could bring something new and choose the particular songs they wanted to work on."

When it came to deciding on who to work with, Dickens enlisted four of the top names in the British music industry. Chris Neil had worked with Celine Dion and Mike & The Mechanics; Greg Penny had previously worked with Elton John and kd lang; and Steve Lipsom was best known for his work with Annie Lennox. The fourth producer, Trevor Horn, had been responsible for some of the biggest hits of the past two decades, including Frankie Goes To Hollywood's 'Two Tribes' and 'The Power Of Love,' Seal's 'Kiss From A Rose,' and the ABC album *The Lexicon Of Love*. He had also worked with Paul McCartney, Grace Jones, and Tina Turner.

The plan was to record the album in London—a city that Cher knew well. "I've been coming to London since I was 18 years old," she told Patrick Humphries of the *Times* in 2001, "and I always feel homey here. I always feel like I'm not a foreigner." It therefore made sense for her to stay in the English capital for a while. "I was gonna work over there and I just decided I like it [there] and it would be really cool to go over and live there for a year," she later told David Letterman. "Elijah came. I was working there and just hanging out."

However, when it came to choosing a London neighborhood, Cher's choice was perhaps more than a little unconventional. Usually a visiting star of Cher's stature would stay in one of the more exclusive, upscale enclaves of the city such as Mayfair or Knightsbridge. Cher took the surprising decision to rent an apartment in Wapping, in the Docklands area of East London. The area had historically been an extremely poor, run-down part of town, but during the eighties it had been radically redeveloped, with new sky-rise office blocks and yuppie riverside apartments filling the old storeroom warehouses. It was more likely to be home to stock market traders than showbiz superstars, but Cher seemed to like it. "London's great," she told *Music Week*. "I love my building and my neighbors and, because I'm from California, I don't even mind the cold weather."

When it came to driving on the other side of the road, Cher was slightly less at ease. After an English journalist asked if there was anything about living in London which left her reeling with culture shock, she replied: "Yes—how unbelievably weird you guys drive, and how old ladies with bicycles can be on the same lane as traffic. Going round the roundabouts is insanity—it's a cluster-fuck. I'm almost always killing couriers and old people ... partly because I'm dyslexic and I'm never really sure which side of the street to look at. Every time I get home I think: thank God I made it. You English seem so respectable, but when you get behind the wheel of a car, you're all Jeffrey Dahmer."

While Cher was getting to grips with the day-to-day aspects of British culture and road safety, she was also tackling several songs that were very much about America. A case in point was one of the album's standout tracks, 'Walking In Memphis,' which would provide her with another huge UK hit.

The gospel-tinged pop ballad had originally been an American top twenty hit for singer-songwriter Marc Cohn in 1991, and is Cohn's unofficial homage to Memphis, Elvis Presley, and Carl Perkins, whose *Blue Suede Shoes* Elvis covered. It was a subject close to Cher's own heart. She had discovered rock'n'roll herself as a teenager when her mother took her to an Elvis concert and immediately related to Presley's unorthodox, irreverent stance. "For me, Elvis was a singing James Dean, and I was really rebellious," she recalled. "When I was growing up in Southern California, the role models were Sandra Dee and Doris Day, and everyone but me was cute and perky and blond. I was dark and moody and strange looking."

It had in fact been Dickens's idea for Cher to record the song but she was initially unconvinced. "Rob Dickens persuaded me to do this," she explained. "I've always liked it but didn't think that it seemed right for me, but he said that we should at least try it out, and I'm really pleased with the result." By the time producer Chris Neil had finished the song, there was little doubt that it was indeed right for Cher, who very much makes it her own in a rousing rendition complete with gospel-style back-up singers.

'Walking In Memphis' is one of several covers on the album that not only has its roots in the American Deep South or country rock/blues but also was originally written from a man's point of view. Another is Eagles main-man Don Henley's 1985 hit 'Not Enough Love In The World.' Cher had been keen to record the song for some years and now adapted it to be sung from a woman's point of view before producer Steve Lipsom gave it a bright, poppy feel.

Lipsom also produced another of the album's covers—'I'm Blowing Away,' originally recorded by Bonnie Raitt and Linda Ronstadt—and was partly responsible, along with Rob Dickens, for persuading Cher to cover the James Brown classic 'It's A Man's World,' which was to provide the album's title.

As with 'Walking In Memphis,' Cher had once again been unsure whether to tackle the song. "I didn't want to go that far," she said, "but it was Rob's idea and Lipsom forced me." The result was very much a new departure for Cher. In sharp contrast to the hard-rocking bravura of her previous albums, her version of the song takes a languorously slow, gentle pace, complete with angular but lush string arrangements. The only nod to her earlier rocking stance is the guitar solo toward the end.

Continuing with this newly smooth approach is Cher's cover of another American soul classic, 'I Wouldn't Treat A Dog,' originally recorded by one of her favorite vocalists, rhythm & blues supremo Bobby Bland. Producer Greg Penny suggested the song to her, and once again the overall feel is very much in keeping with the prevailing up-tempo R&B sound of the time, with Cher eking every inch of heartfelt lament out of the lyrics.

Other cover versions include Tina Turner's 'Paradise Is Here' and 'The Sun Ain't Gonna Shine Anymore,' originally recorded by Franki Valli but better known as one of The Walker Brothers' biggest hits. The Walkers' version had featured an epic, overblown orchestral production very much in the Phil Spector style and as Cher had appeared with The Walker Brothers on TV several times in her Sonny & Cher days, she remembered the song well.

This time, rather than trying anything too new, her version very much follows the format of the Walker Brothers version. Her new vocal follows Scott Walker's interpretation, while the production similarly echoes the full, chiming sound of the original.

Despite using a range of different production styles, when it came to choosing material, Cher was still keen to record new songs as well as well-known classics. "I wanted to make as varied an album as possible," she explained, "taking on different styles and recording news songs as well as old favorites."

"I worked really hard to have more control and not use my vibrato and other things," she added. "I didn't like my voice. It's still me—you know it's me, and there's no getting around it. But on some songs, like 'One By One' and 'The Gunman,' you don't know it's me right away."

When it came to choosing new songs, Cher wasn't afraid to take some risks. 'The Gunman,' written by Paddy McAloon of British indie band Prefab Sprout—one of producer Trevor Horn's favorite songwriters—was a radical departure. The slow, moody ballad has no obvious sing-along hooks or choruses, and although the track features a smooth, glossy, string-filled production, it takes a significantly different approach from virtually anything Cher had recorded before. It even has a spoken intro, in which Cher speaks of eyes meeting on "some narrow street" and love leaving her "at his feet."

Once again, Cher had in the first instance been hesitant about recording the song, but this time it was Horn who persuaded her. "I didn't think this was for me," she later admitted, "because I don't usually sing in this style, but Trevor Horn told me not to be nervous and I relaxed into it."

Horn's slick touch is very much in evidence on 'The Gunman,' as it is on the album's penultimate track, 'Shape Of Things To Come.' Horn co-wrote the latter song specifically for Cher with former 10cc member Lol Crème, and for many it is one of the album's forgotten classics. Cher gives one of her best vocal performances, while the production offers an intriguing mix of Madonna's pop-R&B and gothic moodiness all set to a pounding beat. Although it was a style far removed from her earlier material, she sounds relaxed and natural on the track—possibly thanks to the fact that she seemed to work very well with Horn, while he in turn clearly had considerable respect for her as an artist. "Cher's an intelligent and articulate singer," he told *Music Week*. "A lot of people who work in films do not easily switch across to music, but we had a great time working together. It was actually very informal and there was a strong element of fun about the whole proceedings."

In fact, once Cher got into the swing of working with new material, new musical styles, and new producers, she was delighted with the results. She even persuaded Warner Bros to extend the album's length. "Originally we were heading for ten or eleven tracks," she said, "but when I found out we could go for fourteen songs, I really persisted. There is a lot of variety there." It was, she felt, her "best album ever."

It's A Man's World was initially released for Christmas 1995 in the UK and Europe only. Cher was hopeful that her adventurous new approach would be a hit not only with her existing fans but also some new ones. "This is the last chance to sway a few more people," she told Q magazine. "I'd like them to say: I didn't know she could actually sing—I thought she was just loud! Before, my songs have been larger than life … these are *like* life, and in some cases, smaller than life. I mean, when I hear it, it sounds effortless in some strange way."

It did indeed sound effortless, and although *It's A Man's World* was certainly a departure for Cher in terms of musical genres, when it came to lyrical content there was still a familiar unifying poignancy to nearly all the tracks. "It's kind of a sad record," she told *Billboard*. "I have two speeds— really sad and kick ass—but this is a bittersweet kind of album."

The British public seemed to find it more sweet than bitter, and Cher's gamble paid off. The album went to number ten in the UK album charts and yielded Cher no fewer than four top-forty hit singles: 'Walking In Memphis,' which reached number eleven; 'One By One,' a super-slick, smooth R&B ballad, which reached number seven; 'Not Enough Love In The World,' which went to number thirty-one; and 'The Sun Ain't Gonna Shine Anymore,' which hit number twenty-six.

The video for 'Walking In Memphis' is still considered by many to be one of Cher's finest. Shot entirely in filmic black-and-white, the promo is set in the fifties and shows Cher dressed in a relatively sedate full skirt and fishnets—not dissimilar to Marilyn Monroe's look in *Bus Stop*—boarding a Greyhound-style bus to Memphis. There we see her dressed as a young (male) Elvis fan, guitar in hand, checking into a motel, where she immediately puts up her Elvis poster.

The US version of the album was issued some months later, in June 1996, although this time there were several significant differences in the releases. Firstly, the songs run in an almost entirely different sequence, while three tracks were radically re-cut and remixed for the US market, including 'One By One,' the disco remix of which did at least provide Cher with a top ten Dance hit on *Billboard*.

The artwork was the same for both versions of the album: a portrait of Cher by top British photographer David Scheinman, with Cher as Eve, holding a scarlet apple in her hand with a snake draped across her chest. The first US pressings also included an engraved 'limited edition' hologram of the cover image, but seemingly none of this was enough to convince the American public. Well over a decade later, the album has still sold fewer than a quarter of a million copies since its release. In hindsight, it seems that remixing the album was a mistake. Many of Cher's American fans considered the original UK release to be far superior to the US edition and sought out the original British album on import.

The US version did nevertheless win the favor of the critics, with Stephen Holden of the *New York Times* particularly impressed. "From an artistic standpoint, this soulful collection of grown-up pop songs … is the high point of her recording career," he wrote. "Capped by an iconoclastic rendition of 'It's A Man's, Man's, Man's World,' James Brown's ode to male supremacy, the album evokes the hard emotional lessons learned by a woman who has loved too well, but not wisely … the album suggests that Cher, who has been saddled with the tabloid image of a boy-crazy perpetual adolescent, has achieved a kind of emotional maturity."

Many, like Holden, still consider the album to be one of Cher's best works, but the singles were to prove the record's most successful legacy. Both 'Walking In Memphis' and 'The Sun Ain't Gonna Shine Anymore' were used subsequently in an episode of the cult sci-fi series *The X-Files*, with the former still standing as one of Cher's most enduring hits.

C

Cher used the relatively quiet time between the UK and US release of *It's A Man's World* to return to the film world for a new movie, *Faithful*. Although six years had passed since her last major role, there had nonetheless been other small non-musical projects. She had recorded various infomercials in America, as well as *Cherfitness—A New Attitude*. She had also made a brief appearance in *Prêt À Porter (Ready To Wear)*, Robert Altman's 1992 follow-up to *The Player*.

Once again, Cher appears in a cameo role as herself, and once again the plot features a murder, this time with several other concurrent sub-plots that take on the world of *haute couture* fashion. Set in Paris during the annual week of fashion shows by leading international designers, the film likewise features an A-Z of stars both from Hollywood and the fashion world, including Sophia Loren, Marcello Mastroianni, Lauren Bacall, Forest Whitaker, Rupert Everett, and Julia Roberts, as well as Jean Paul Gaultier, Naomi Campbell, and Jerry Hall.

Cher is first glimpsed on a television screen, arriving at fashion house Bulgari's runway show wearing tight black leather pants. We then see her being interviewed by a reporter, played by Kim Basinger, who questions her about her philosophy on fashion. "I'm as much of a fashion follower as I am a perpetrator," Cher explains, before elaborating: "I'm a victim as well as a perpetrator of all of this. And I think it's not about what you put on your body, I think it's more about what you are on the inside."

It was the ultimate post-modern movie scenario: a twentieth century celebrity, famous for her wardrobe and glamour, appearing as herself in a movie by an auteur director, playing a scene in which she's interviewed on a television show. It was also a brilliant send-up of the fashion élite, and Cher seemed to enjoy every minute of it.

Larger movie roles had nevertheless proved harder to come by. Although she had received several provisional scripts, none of them had felt quite right. Among the roles Cher turned down was the part eventually played by Susan Sarandon in *Thelma & Louise*. "I didn't like the ending very much ... the killing and the suicide," she explained. "I didn't believe, so it was difficult for me. I'm sure I would have done a good job of it, but it wasn't ... you know, things are meant to come to you."

She did, however, receive a script she liked based on a play by actor and writer Chazz Palminteri, best known for his roles in films such as Woody Allen's *Bullets Over Broadway* and *The Usual Suspects*. *Faithful* told the story of a depressed housewife whose husband is having an affair. The wife begins to contemplate suicide but changes her mind when she is faced with a hired killer sent by her husband to murder her. The plot then centers on the relationship between the wife and the hired killer as she attempts to seduce him into letting her free. The tension builds, leading the audience to question who has really hired whom.

Cher took the central role of the housewife, with her onscreen husband played by seventies heartthrob Ryan O'Neal, and the killer by Palminteri himself. The film was directed by actor, screenwriter, and director Paul Mazursky and co-produced by Robert De Niro and Peter Gatien, the owner at the time of one of the New York A-listers' favorite haunts, the Limelight club. As with many films originally written for the stage, *Faithful* carries the feel of the fourhanded theater work on which it was based, and feels slightly constrained by association. The plot is based on an engaging premise, but when the film opened in New York City on April 3 1996, the critics were almost unanimously unimpressed. Nearly all found the movie heavy-handed but their main preoccupation seemed to be with what had happened to Cher's face in the years since *Mermaids*.

Cher had very clearly had several plastic surgery procedures in the intervening years, including collagen implants in her lips, rhinoplasty (aka a nose job), and tooth capping, as well as what appeared to be eye-lifting. The results had in fact already been visible in some of Cher's recent promo videos, such as 'Walking In Memphis,' and the process had begun with her teeth, which Cher had been unhappy with for some time. "When I saw my face in *Mask* especially," she explained, "I thought I just want to get my teeth fixed, and my nose is huge. I don't want to see that close-up on that nose and those teeth anymore, so I went and had it done."

Cher may have been pleased with her new look, but most critics found that her various 'improvements' had radically lessened her facial mobility, meaning her expressions were now limited. Not perhaps ideal for an actress. The public seemed to agree with the critics, and the movie died at the box office, closing a mere fortnight after it opened.

Cher was stoical. "It was no loss," she told the *New York Times*. "At least the reviews said it was nice to see me acting again." Later on, she nevertheless confessed that she had never been entirely sure about the script, and that she considered the film to have been "a mistake." But the experience had not put her off making movies. On the contrary, she had begun to start thinking about directing herself, and even Chazz Palminteri was now convinced that Cher could be a success behind the camera as well as in front of it.

"When you become a star," he said, "and you're not hungry anymore, one of the things that keeps you a star is your work ethic. Cher's very regimented. She gets up at a certain time, works out, has a chef that cooks certain things for her to stay in great shape, has a voice teacher come every few days for a singing lesson and a chiropractor who gives her adjustments. She's also one of the smartest people I've ever met ... Mark my words, she will become an A-list director one day, guaranteed."

Palminteri was right—at least in part. Cher's next screen move would mark her first foray into the director's chair. Although it may not have instantly catapulted her into the A-list of directors, it was a phenomenally successful first effort, and one that saw her working with a glittering cast.

If These Walls Could Talk was a three-part mini-series made by Demi Moore's production company for the HBO network. Each episode was set in the same house during a different decade and focused on three different women going through abortions, albeit under circumstances which of course differed considerably due to the social mores of the time. The idea was that each of the three vignettes—set in 1952, 1974, and 1996—would illustrate the prevailing social attitudes.

Cher had originally been offered a part in the third half-hour episode, set in 1996, but as soon as she saw the script she knew she wanted to have a deeper involvement beyond just acting in the film. One of the reasons, she later said, that the subject struck a chord with her was that in the seventies, after she had had Chastity but before she had become pregnant with Elijah, she herself had had an abortion. Having considered the role, she then told the producers that she would only appear in it if she could direct it. They agreed.

Although she had made numerous films, directing her first feature was still an unsettling and nerve-wracking experience. "The first day I walked on the set, I was pretty terrified," she later remembered, "but I thought, well, I'm here, I might as well just do it. And soon I was thinking this is so much fun! It was definitely a lot of work, and it really tested my stamina. But I loved it from the beginning."

Once she settled into the flow of the movie, she began to use specific techniques she had learned from directors she had worked with herself, such as Robert Altman, Mike Nichols, and Norman Jewison. In particular she was keen to give the actors the freedom of their own interpretations and offer positive feedback after individual scenes.

The first two episodes starred Demi Moore and Sissy Spacek, while Cher's 1996 segment tells the story of a college student played by Anne Heche, who gets pregnant by a married professor. When he breaks up with her, she decides on an abortion, but just as she is undergoing the operation, a violent anti-abortion protest starts up.

Cher plays the abortion doctor; among the crowd during the protest scenes, playing a photographer, is none other than her ex-amour Rob Camilletti. Continuing the personal touch, Cher also used 'One By One,' from her recent album *It's A Man's World*, over the closing credits. Nobody seemed to mind. On the contrary, it was a surprise success, becoming HBO's highest-rated movie ever. It even spawned a sequel in 2000, starring Sharon Stone and Ellen DeGeneres.

The critics were similarly impressed and the series garnered nominations for no fewer than three Emmys, including Outstanding Made For Television Movie, and three Golden Globes, including Best Mini-Series Or Motion Picture Made For TV. Cher couldn't have been happier. "It was so exciting for me," she recalled. "There was an unbelievable amount of satisfaction. Whenever you try something new, there's always the chance that you're going to be embarrassing. But I was better than I thought I'd be. Not as good as I'd like to be, but I'm on my way."

The success of *If These Walls Could Talk* was a surprise even for Cher, and life was to throw up further surprises still for her before long. Some better than others.

CHAPTER 16
If You Believe

S hortly after New Year's Day 1998, Cher flew to London, where she
was due to make a personal appearance at Harrods, the world-famous
luxury department store. Early in the morning of January 6, she was
woken by a phone-call from daughter Chastity. The operator apologized for
putting a call through so early but explained that it was an emergency.

"Mom," said Chastity, "Dad's dead."

Since Cher's appearance on *Late Night With David Letterman* in 1988,
Cher had maintained a more or less cordial relationship with Sonny Bono,
despite her frequent public jibes at his expense. She had made it clear that
she didn't agree with his politics—particularly since he had been elected to
Congress in 1994 and become (Republican) mayor of Palm Springs—but
that she bore him no real ill will. Whatever differences they may have had
in the past, he had nevertheless played a hugely significant role in her life
and the news left her devastated.

Bono had been at the Heavenly Ski Resort in Lake Tahoe with his wife
Mary and their two small children on a post-Christmas skiing holiday. He
had been a regular visitor to the area for some twenty years and was a highly
experienced skier, but on January 5 he unexpectedly hit a tree and died
almost immediately from his injuries.

As soon as Cher heard the news, she cancelled her engagement at
Harrods and arranged to return to Los Angeles on the first available flight.
When she arrived, a limousine was waiting to take her straight to the Bono
family home in Palm Springs.

Cher spent the next few days with Chastity, Bono's wife Mary and their
children, and other close family members. As the days passed, Mary began
to make arrangements for the funeral—and, to Cher's surprise, asked her if
she would make the eulogy.

Cher was initially reluctant, worried that she would be overcome by her own grief or in some way fall short of what she felt she owed Bono. "I didn't want to blow it," she later explained. "I felt I had to repair all the damage and misconceptions about Sonny."

When the day of the funeral arrived, it emerged that Cher would not only be addressing their friends and family. The ceremony was also going to be broadcast live on CNN. She found the prospect more nerve-wracking than virtually anything she had ever done. She admitted to being terrified, but remembered an old tip she had heard Judy Garland mention about locking her knees to hide the trembling. "I had no control," she said. "My face was making all kinds of movements, I had to lock my legs and grit my teeth."

Although Cher had managed to control the trembling, when it came to her emotions, she found herself unable to suppress her tears. "He was the greatest friend," she told the congregation. "When I was young, there was a section in *Reader's Digest* called 'Most Unforgettable Character I Ever Met.' For me, that person is Sonny Bono, no matter how long I live or who I meet. That person will always be Sonny for me."

Cher's emotional delivery at the funeral surprised some observers. After years of her critiques and put-downs of Bono, some found it hard to believe that her grief had been genuine. Cher was deeply upset by the suggestion. "I think it hit home for me the most when people thought I was acting at Sonny's funeral," she later recalled. "That's the definitive experience of people getting it so wrong that you just don't know where anybody's coming from. I was so blindsided by that. And that day, I actually did give a thought to packing it in and saying: you know what? Fuck all you guys, you don't get it anyway. I'm out of here."

The funeral concluded with the congregation singing one of Bono's compositions, Sonny & Cher's 1967 hit 'The Beat Goes On.' The song's title was also used as the epitaph on his headstone when he was buried at the Desert Memorial Park in nearby Cathedral City, California. Some months later, Cher appeared with Mary Bono in Los Angeles to receive a Sonny & Cher star on the Hollywood Walk Of Fame For Television.

Cher also paid further tribute to Bono in the CBS TV special *Sonny & Me: Cher Remembers*, calling her grief "something I never plan to get over." Later that year, she published her book, *The First Time*, in which she wrote:

"After Son and I split up, I would always say that leaving him was the toughest thing I would ever have to face. But that turned out to be not exactly true. The toughest thing was him leaving me."

C

Having dealt with the shock of Sonny's unexpectedly sudden death, Cher once again needed to think about recording another album. She had worked very successfully with new label Warner Records UK and Rob Dickens on *It's A Man's World*, but now Dickens had a new suggestion for her altogether.

"Do you want to make a dance album?" he asked.

"No, I don't," she replied, without hesitation.

"I didn't want to do the album," she later told Patrick Humphries of the *Times*. "I thought: what are people going to think? All of a sudden, Cher goes dance! Where has she been, and why is she doing this now? I just thought people were going to hate me, and I think I was totally full of shit. Rob said: if it's a good album, they won't think that. I thought, well, maybe, but I wasn't sure."

Cher was also uncertain whether a dance record was the most appropriate project for a woman who was now over fifty, but Dickens had his own reasons. "Every gay guy I know is a huge Cher fan," he recalled. "They just love her as an icon. She has this huge gay following and they love Hi-NRG dance records. So the idea was to repay their faith and loyalty to her over the years, to make a record for them."

Eventually, Dickens suggested a compromise: he would send Cher two songs in a dance style, and if she liked them, she would record them and they would go from there. 'Dov'è L'Amore' and 'Strong Enough' were duly dispatched to Cher; thankfully for Dickens, she was immediately impressed. "There was something about those two that I got kind of hooked into," she said.

The tracks had been written by the up-and-coming team of Mark Taylor and Paul Barry, who worked for the British production house Metro. They had previously worked for Dickens on releases by pop singers Gina G and Dannii Minogue before Dickens approached them to see if they could come up with something equally successful for Cher. His plan was for the two songs to then be produced by hip New York dance producer Junior Vasquez, but when Vasquez sent back his provisional rough mix, Dickens rejected it. Instead, he decided to ask Taylor and fellow Metro producer Brian Rawlings to work with Cher and produce their own songs.

As Cher had successfully recorded her previous album in London, it was decided that she would return to the capital to work with Metro on the two new tracks during the spring of 1998. However, this time, she would not be working in any of London's state of the art, internationally renowned recording studios, but at Dreamhouse, the small, three-studio complex Metro ran amid the suburban hills of Kingston, Surrey, on the outskirts of London.

It was not a space normally frequented by superstars, and was radically smaller and considerably less plush than most of the studios Cher was used to, but she was not bothered by the lack of glamour. "We worked in a small space that really wasn't that nice," she explained. "I'm sure if they're gonna get other major artists, they're gonna have to spruce up the old studio little a bit! But I couldn't care less. Honest to God, I have *so* two distinct parts of my personality. I have me at the BRIT Awards, which is all smoke and mirrors, and then I have me which is just funky down-to-earth and not very interested in glamour."

Cher felt the benefits of the relaxed, un-starry atmosphere. "Mark and I worked in the teeniest space," she continued. "We just sat around by ourselves and it was really very unpretentious. It was fun but it was not very superstar like, and I think there's a vibe that goes along with that." Despite the lack of superstar trappings, Cher, Taylor, and Barry quickly developed a strong working rapport. "They were very smart," she recalled. "They tricked me into it, because I'm kind of stubborn. So we started recording and I really liked those guys … and all of a sudden, it was a dance album!"

The song that had originally converted Cher to the project, 'Dov'é L'Amore,' was to become one of the album's strongest tracks, and a future single. But despite having an Italian title and lyrics, the song's sound is very much Spanish; almost like an updated version of Madonna's eighties hit 'La Isla Bonita,' complete with hand-clapping and flamenco guitar courtesy of The Gypsy Kings, one of Cher's favorite groups.

In fact, the Metro team would have given the song Spanish lyrics, given the chance, but had to make do with what they could get. In search of words that were at the very least non-English, they had asked staff at an Italian restaurant across the road from their studio. "They needed lyrics right away," Cher explained, "so they went across the street and said: tell me how to say this—so that's how basically you get a Spanish-sounding song with Italian lyrics."

The other song that Metro and Rob Dickens had initially sent Cher, 'Strong Enough,' would likewise become another of the album's most popular tracks. Rather than going for the pop/dance hybrid of 'Dov'è L'Amore,' 'Strong Enough' is an out-and-out homage to the Hi-NRG seventies disco of Donna Summer and Gloria Gaynor, with 'I Will Survive'-style strings and a pounding beat.

Lyrically, the song—written by Mark Taylor and Paul Barry to a brief from Dickens—is very much a tale of survival over heartbreak and betrayal, sung from the point of view of a woman who has found out that her lover has been unfaithful and is determined to end the relationship regardless of how painful it may be for her. It seemed that Metro shared Dickens's vision of Cher as a gay icon, and the song's theme of triumph over adversity very much fits into the 'gay disco' canon. "Come hell or waters high, you'll never see me cry," she sings. "I'm strong enough to live without you."

Cher was surprised that this was the kind of song she had inspired. "The weird thing for me was Rob told the boys to 'go write a Cher song'—and that's what they came up with," she said. "But I just thought, boy, if you tell someone go write a Cher song and they come back with that, what does that mean? I guess people just think I'm like this kick-ass woman with Nazi boots jumping around, but it seems like a strange song for someone to just distil down to me. I am able to handle anything that comes my way but I'm not able to handle it quite as easily as anyone thinks. I am tough because I've been in this business so long and it's definitely not for sissies so I guess I am strong, but I'm not hard."

She did nevertheless admire the song's basic sentiment of survival. "I didn't really think of it so much as a female song—it wasn't like 'I am Woman' by Helen Reddy. I just thought of it as people being strong enough to survive having their hearts broken. It's a little song that reminds you [not to] fold your tent up and go away."

When it came to deciding on how the song should ultimately sound, the seventies-style disco production was, in fact, Cher's own idea. "If I'm going to go dancing," she explained, "I wanna go on a night when they're playing seventies hits, because that's my favorite music to dance to." She also knew instinctively that this particular sound would work best for the song. "That was the only way to get into that song," she said. "The boys tried a whole bunch of different ways to do it [but] I told them it wasn't gonna work."

Eventually the Metro team conceded that Cher was right and the disco style was agreed. Meanwhile, Cher was now fully persuaded that Dickens's idea for a dance album might work after all, and as the first two tracks seemed to have gone so well, she agreed to continue working with Metro both on further compositions of their own as well as tracks from other writers.

Although Rob Dickens had originally only planned for Metro to write one or two songs, once they started working with Cher, everyone was so pleased with the results that Taylor and Rawling ended up producing a total of six songs on the album, including two further Hi-NRG numbers, 'All Or Nothing,' 'Runaway,' and what would become the album's title track, 'Believe.'

"We just went song by song," Cher remembered, "and then the boys from Metro started writing and that was great too because I got to influence it. It was a real kind of backroom experience ... no one came to see what we were doing, but it ended up being brilliant."

Rob Dickens's original choice of producer, Junior Vasquez, finally got involved on the gospel tinged dance ballad 'The Power,' while top US producer Todd Terry oversaw three tracks: the self-penned Chicago-house track 'Taxi Taxi,' 'Love Is The Groove,' and, at his own suggestion, a dance reworking of Cher's 1989 Warren & Child hit 'We All Sleep Alone.'

The standout is of course the title track, co-written by Metro's Paul Barry and what Cher would later describe as "a cast of thousands." Produced by Mark Taylor and Brian Rawling, the song would turn out to be not only one of the landmark recordings of the decade in terms of its subsequent influence, but also of Cher's entire career.

Brian Higgins, a British songwriter and producer responsible for numerous hits by Girls Aloud, Pet Shop Boys, and Sugababes, had written 'Believe' with fellow songwriters Matt Gray, Stuart McLennen, and Tim Powell. A demo for the song had been sitting around the Warner Bros offices in London for several months as an option for different artists, but although the record company liked the chorus, nobody was entirely sure about the rest of the song. Some months later, when it came to finding material for Cher, Dickens remembered it. Knowing that Cher had liked Metro's other songs, he approached them to rework the song.

When Paul Barry and another Metro writer Steven Torch were sent a demo version of the song, however, neither was particularly impressed. They set to work rewriting the song on their guitars, and by the time they had finished, all that remained of the original was the chorus—which, apart from a few minor chord changes, they left more or less intact. The rest of the song sounded completely different.

"The lyrics for the chorus were already there," Mark Taylor recalled, "but our guys added the lyrics, melody, and chords for the verses and middle-eight, then put the whole thing back together again." They then sent the song back to Dickens, who suggested a few small changes, before it went on to Cher.

Cher liked it immediately, but after rehearsing the song in the studio she began to be less sure about the lyrics to one of the verses and decided to remedy it herself. "I was singing in the bathtub," she recalled, "and it seemed to me the second verse was too whiny. It kind of pissed me off, so I changed it. I toughened it up a bit."

In the end, it was the song's production that would really cement its place in musical history, but finding the right sound was not an easy process. In fact, it was quite the opposite.

"We knew the rough direction to take," explained Mark Taylor, "because Rob [Dickens] had said he wanted to make a Cher dance record. The hard part was trying to make one that wouldn't alienate Cher's existing fans. We couldn't afford to have anyone say: I hate this because it's dance— then we would have turned off loads of people who are used to hearing Cher do rock ballads and MOR songs. ... The only way you can achieve sales of

1.5 million is to appeal to both camps. Getting that right was the most difficult part—and was the reason why I ended up doing the track twice!"

Taylor was halfway toward completing a first version when he decided to reject it outright. He didn't even want anyone else hear it. "It was just too hardcore dance—it wasn't happening," he continued. "I scrapped it and started again, because I realized it needed a sound that was unusual, but not in a typical dance record sort of way. This was tricky, because dance music is very specific. To get what I was after I had to think about each sound very carefully, so that the sound itself was dance-based but not obviously so."

Taylor stayed up all night in the studio alone, feverishly trying to find a sound that would work for Cher. When the sun finally came up the next day, he had found what seemed to be a solution, even though it sounded unlike anything Cher had done before.

The effects he had put on the track also meant that parts of the vocal didn't even sound recognizably like Cher. He was pleased with the results, but was much less sure what Cher's reaction would be. Indeed, he was hesitant as to whether he should even let her hear it. "It was a bit radical," he later said. "Basically, it was the destruction of her voice, so I was really nervous about playing it to her. In the end, I just thought it sounded so good, I had to at least let her hear it—so I hit 'play.'"

Taylor needn't have worried. "She was fantastic," he remembered, "She just said it sounded *great*, so the effect stayed. I was amazed by her reaction, and so excited, because I knew it was good."

In the decade since 'Believe' was recorded, the effect Taylor used has of course been used on countless hits, and is now commonplace. But when the record was initially released, the sound was radically new and caused such a sensation that Taylor was inundated with journalists asking how he had done it. Keen to keep his technique a secret, Taylor initially claimed that he had used a vocoder on the track. It was only several years later that he finally admitted that the effect had in fact been created by using the now well-known Autotune pitch-correction software. Instead of using the program as it is intended, Taylor set it at a rate too fast for the audio it was processing, thereby creating the highly distinctive vocal 'hiccup' effect. The sound subsequently became known as 'the Cher effect.'

The other main vocal effect on the track came from a suggestion by Cher herself. She had heard a song by British soul singer Roachford, which had what Taylor later described as a kind of "telephoney" quality. "I'd bought this Roachford CD and said: can you do this?" Cher recalled. "And [Taylor] said no, so I was playing around with the pitch machine, and if you do it really fast, it does a strange thing. I said: can we do *that*? He said: well, let me work on it—it'll take a while to work out how to do it on the song. The next day he'd done it, so we put it on everything!"

Recording 'Believe' took ten days, but once it was completed Cher was convinced they were onto something. "I had to go home to Los Angeles," she recalled, "and I said: if you let anyone change this, I'm gonna rip your fucking throat out!"

However, when Rob Dickens first heard the track he was less than convinced, worrying that the unusual effects on Cher's voice were a step too far. "Of course they wanted to change it," Cher recalled. "I said over my dead body; they said it won't be a hit this way; I said I don't really care … the truth was, I wasn't sure if it was going to be a hit or not. I just loved it so much that I just wanted it to be that way."

In the end, Cher got her own way, and the pitch-altering effects did indeed stay on several other tracks. The *Believe* album took six weeks to record, but although Cher was uncertain how it would fare, she was glad to have done something new.

"We took the songs further," she said. "We were braver—or desperate, I'm not sure which it was. It's a fine line: sometimes it starts out as one, then when it's a success, you can say: oh, this is bravery!"

Taking risks in the studio was nothing new for Cher. Her first ever experiences of a recording studio had been with Phil Spector and Sonny, neither of whom were strangers to the idea of experimentation. With this perhaps in mind, she dedicated the album to her late ex-husband, with a simple note in the CD booklet: "In memory of Son."

Believe was released in the fall of 1998, but as with *It's A Man's World*, Warner Bros decided to issue the album in Europe and other international territories first, with the USA to follow. The strategy paid off: by the time the album came out in the USA in November, it was already a global hit.

Believe went straight to number one in the UK, and when it was eventually released in the USA, it reached number four, remaining at the top of the charts for a year and half, eventually selling over four million copies. It was certified gold or platinum in thirty-nine different countries. In 1999, the album also received two Grammy Awards nominations, for Record Of The Year and Best Pop Album, and won the Award for Best Dance Recording.

The 'Believe' single, meanwhile, was even more successful, topping the charts in twenty-three countries, including the UK, where it spent seven weeks at number one. In 2011, it was still the UK's all-time best-selling single by a female artist. In the USA, the song debuted at number ninety-nine on the *Billboard* Hot 100 Chart in December 1998 and finally peaked at number one the following March. It also reached number one on the US Hot Dance Music/Maxi Single chart, remaining in the top ten for a whole year. Who could have guessed that a dance tune with a strange sound effect would prove the biggest global hits of the decade?

'Strong Enough,' 'All Or Nothing,' and 'Dov'è L'Amore' were subsequently released as follow-up singles, and all were hits. 'Strong Enough' made the top twenty in most countries apart from the USA, where it did at least become a hit on the *Billboard* dance charts. 'All Or Nothing' reached the US top forty, while 'Dov'è L'Amore' made it to number one on the Hot Dance Singles Sales and Hot Dance Club Play listings.

C

While Cher had been in London recording the *Believe* album, she had been thinking about her movie career. Apart from *Faithful*, which had not made much of an impact at the box office, her last major role was in *Mermaids* some eight years earlier. Since then, her only other parts had been cameos in *The Player* and *Pret À Porter*, but she had recently been sent a new script that she liked very much.

Written by Franco Zeffirelli, best known for his 1968 movie of Shakespeare's *Romeo And Juliet* and his 1977 TV mini-series *Jesus Of Nazareth*, *Tea With Mussolini* was based on the Italian director's own childhood experiences before and during the Second World War. The plot is centered on Luka, the illegitimate young son of a married local businessman who is taken under the wing of a clique of eccentric English ladies and unofficially adopted by them. At the edges of the women's social circle is Elsa, a wealthy, glamorous American socialite and art collector. It was this part that was being offered to Cher.

In the script the generous and *bonne vivante* Elsa, who is also Jewish, begins an affair with an Italian playboy who, unknown to her, proceeds to swindle her into signing over her money and property to him while he betrays her to the Nazis. It is therefore only a matter of time before she will be deported, and the movie's denouement focuses on the English ladies' attempts to arrange her escape.

Cher liked the script and the idea of working with Zeffirelli, but what appealed to her even more was the prospect of working with the British actresses due to star alongside her in the movie. All were Oscar-winners or Oscar-nominees, and were among the leading names in British theater: Dame Joan Plowright, Dame Judi Dench, and Dame Maggie Smith.

There was no question that she would take the part. "Who could give up the chance of working with those women?" she later asked. "I would have paid *them*. And I liked the script and the story."

Even so, Zeffirelli was thrilled that Cher had agreed to the role. "She was heaven-sent," he said. "We had already cast the three English ladies but we were still fighting to find the right American lady. There was the usual list: Glenn Close, Diane Keaton, Susan Sarandon. But then I wondered: what happened to Cher? You know, her career goes up and down like the waves of the ocean."

Cher was initially slightly intimidated by the prospect of working alongside three such illustrious doyennes of the British stage, but the experience turned out to be a particularly enjoyable one. "[I was] scared to death," she recalled, "but then when I got a chance to actually hang around with them they were great. Judi is very shy; Joan was the most ... forthcoming. And, of course, I'm such a huge Maggie Smith fan that I really couldn't talk very much around her! It took me such a long time to actually speak to her without being nervous. But I loved to sit around and listen to the three of them talk. They have stories and they are *so* funny in that really English way. I wish I could have taped it—they were brilliant!"

In the movie we see Cher make several grand entrances in fabulously glamorous thirties hats, skirt suits, and evening gowns. She even gets to sing the thirties standard 'Smoke Gets In Your Eyes' in one scene, but although her character at first appears to be a superficial socialite, as the movie progresses we see that she is in fact generous and altruistic and has more depth than is at first apparent.

Cher particularly liked that aspect of her part, as well as the costumes and the atmosphere on set, but when she saw the final cut she was disappointed, feeling that her best scenes had ended up on the cutting room floor. "My scenes were cut to ribbons," she said. "They were much longer when we filmed them. They made more sense. Now they seem disjointed. But maybe I'm looking at my performance and judging the film by it. I don't know. I shouldn't knock it. A lot of people really like the movie."

Indeed, *Tea With Mussolini* is a beautifully filmed, atmospheric period piece with an exceptional cast, and when it opened in 1999 it was clear that many people really admired it. Roger Ebert of the *Chicago Sun Times* noted that "people keep forgetting what a good actress [Cher] can be," while Mick La Salle of the *San Francisco Chronicle* was especially effusive: describing Cher's performance as "warm, spontaneous, and heartfelt," he went on to say that she is "wonderful in the film. Cher hasn't had an important role in years, but *Tea With Mussolini* should turn things around for her. I've never been a fan but with this movie, I finally 'got' Cher. It's a role that allows her to be seen, that lets her create a vivid character while showing off what is best about her as a screen personality. ... Plowright is lovely, but somehow it's Cher who lingers in the mind when the film is over."

Cher had yet again proved that she could rise to a challenge. The small, intimate, ensemble cast, meanwhile, would prove a sharp contrast to her next project.

C

The runaway success of *Believe* had taken almost everyone by surprise, not least Cher. But while some artists might have taken time out to bask in the glory, particularly having now also completed filming on *Tea With Mussolini*, Cher decided to go out on tour.

She had not been out on the road since 1992, but her recent success had made her a regular fixture on some of the highest-profile events in the American calendar. In January 1999, she sang 'Believe' at the American Music Awards telecast, and later the same month appeared at the Super Bowl XXXIII—America's top rated TV event of the year—to sing the National Anthem.

However, the Do You Believe Tour was to be on a scale unlike anything Cher had ever done before. Running from June through September, the tour would take in more than twenty-five North American cities and some fifty-four shows. The dates were sold out in every city, so perhaps it was unsurprising that she was a little anxious about what lay ahead of her.

"I'm looking forward to touring," she told the BBC. "I'm a little bit scared but I think being onstage is the thing I do best. I just haven't done it in a million years and you always feel like 'oh my god' but you have to be frightened a little bit to do a good job. You have to remember that that's what it is. It's not really nerves—it's excitement. Because you have to go out there and you have to be big enough for 20,000 people to see you and feel you and so you have to *be* bigger than you are and you have to pump yourself up to be tall.

"But I am always frightened. I always think: what am *I* gonna do out here? How am I going to pull this off? But then you start to do it and the starting to do it is the thing that's the magic part. The moment that you open your mouth or step out onstage and you no longer exist. That's when something else takes over and starts to do your job."

Cher may have been nervous, but when the tour opened at the America West Arena in Phoenix, Arizona, on June 16 1999, nobody would have known. As the thousands-strong crowd awaited her arrival, vast video screens flashed images of Cher from the sixties onward. The stage, meanwhile, featured a backdrop painted with a *trompe l'oeil* effect to look like stone in front of which stood a pair of twenty-foot asymmetrical staircases linked by a high balcony. Then the houselights dimmed and Cher rose up from the balcony, dressed in a typically fantastical and bizarre Bob Mackie combo, singing not one of her own hits but U2's 'I Still Haven't Found What I'm Looking For.'

If some fans were slightly disappointed by her choice of opening number, when it came to costumes, nobody could have complained. Some had thought the Heart Of Stone tour had been elaborate, but this show was going to be even more so. With some tickets costing $60–75 and others being sold by scalpers for up to $600, Cher was keen to make sure her fans felt they were getting their money's worth.

The show featured nine costume changes in total, and Cher's opening outfit was certainly memorable. Comprising a bronze-and-copper meshed bodice with a black, Crusaders-style crucifix and a seemingly African-influenced fringed skirt, this was rounded off with Egyptian-style slave bangles and a curly, waist-length red wig. Cher herself would later jokingly describe it as her 'Bozo The Clown meets *Braveheart*' look.

The U2 opening number led into Cher's recent hit single 'All Or Nothing,' followed by 'The Power' from *Believe*. After that it was time to revisit some of her hits of yesteryear. Unlike her previous tour when she had focused solely on her current material, this time Cher intended to give her fans what they wanted and sing songs from almost every decade of her career. "We've got a lot of territory to cover," she told the audience in Phoenix, Arizona. "I'm gonna do songs I haven't done since the seventies."

After changing into an eighteenth-century pirate outfit—complete with three-cornered black hat and silver frock coat—Cher treated the audience to 'We All Sleep Alone' and 'I Found Someone' before wowing the crowds with a series of further show-stopping costumes, hats, and wigs ranging from elegant, beaded evening gowns to a highly revealing 'If I Could Turn Back Time'-style bodysuit.

Other hits included earlier triumphs like 'Gypsys Tramps & Thieves,' 'Half-Breed,' and 'Take Me Home.' Cher also had a new song which was to become a particular live favorite—for her fans and indeed for Cher herself. In the past, she had found herself getting fed up with certain songs, particularly on tour. 'Believe' was not one of them.

"As a singer who doesn't necessarily love going around singing her own songs," she explained, "there are certain songs you don't get fed up with. Like on the road, when you've sung a song a *million* times, I never get fed up with 'The Shoop Shoop Song,' just cos it's so fun. I never get fed up with

'Turn Back Time,' but 'do you believe in life after love': I think is the coolest thing I've ever heard and there's no time when I go to sing that song that I don't get caught up in it. You know what's great about having a hit song that's this great? You just always get to sing it. It's always yours and it's always cool."

Cher's fans certainly thought it was cool, as did the critics. The *Washington Post* called the show a "dynamic, over-the-top extravaganza," while the *New York Times* said Cher had "a quintessential rock voice ... spectacularly styled with a rough and tumble vaudevillian edge."

The opening dates of the tour were sold out in every city, but they also, unsurprisingly perhaps, proved to be extremely tiring.

A tour on this scale would have been hard on any artist, but Cher was by now fifty-three years old, and although she had no shortage of energy the physical strain was beginning to take its toll. By the end of July, after a month and a half of performances, Cher was so exhausted that she had to postpone her shows in Detroit, Cincinnati, and Indianapolis. By early August, after a recuperating break, she was well enough again to resume the tour and reschedule the canceled dates.

Not only did she then complete the North American leg of the tour, she also continued on to a European leg, taking in thirty-five shows in thirteen countries. If that wasn't enough, she then concluded the tour by playing an extensive final series of dates around the USA, taking in Las Vegas, Los Angeles, Chicago, Toronto, Miami, Washington DC, Boston, and Philadelphia. Although she had by this time been across America three times on the tour, there seemed to be a kind of cyclical logic for Cher to be ending on home turf. "After traveling all over the world," she explained, "I really wanted to end my tour at home."

With such a comprehensive tour schedule, it seemed unlikely that any Cher fans wouldn't have been able to catch her show at least once. But those who couldn't still had the possibility of seeing one of the shows on TV. One of the earlier dates at the MGM Grand in Las Vegas was shown on the HBO TV channel on August 22 1999, although this particular broadcast ended up being a cause for yet more controversy when critics discovered that the supposedly 'live' broadcast had in fact been taped the night before. The show was nevertheless eventually released as a video and DVD complete with 3D cover art.

The critics' complaints did little to dent Cher's delight at the tour's overall success. Besides, as she explained to one magazine, when it came to reviews, the only people whose opinions she really cared about, other than her fans, were her own children. So she was especially pleased when her son Elijah told her he had enjoyed her show. "Everything I do embarrasses Elijah," she said. "But you know what he said about the concert? 'My friends and I actually thought your show was good, Mom. It was good.' That was better than a rave review in the *New York Times*, because he never has anything good to say."

The Do You Believe Tour was also Cher's highest-grossing tour to date, bringing in some $160 million. She had now played standing-room-only shows to nearly a million fans and she couldn't have been happier.

Not only had the tour been a phenomenal success but 'Believe' itself had broken records on several fronts, with Cher becoming the oldest female artist ever to have a number one hit. She had also set another record as a solo artist for having the longest gap between chart-toppers, her last US number one having been 'Dark Lady' back in 1974. If that was not enough, 'Believe' became one of the best-selling singles of all time, and is still one of fewer than thirty singles to have sold more than ten million copies worldwide.

Cher had once again surprised both her critics and her public, but if her choices had seemed unpredictable in the past, they were to seem even more so in the future.

CHAPTER 17
Living Proof

As the new millennium began, Cher was at an all-time high. She had just had her biggest ever hit with 'Believe,' and had also just completed a phenomenally successful international tour. She was therefore in the fortunate position of having a number of options. She could take some time off, although that would be uncharacteristic; she could look at possible movie options; or, alternatively, she could think about recording a new album.

Never one for choosing the obvious route, Cher decided to take the road least expected. Instead of capitalizing on the success of *Believe* and following in its dance-oriented footsteps, her next album would be a different kind of record altogether.

Firstly, it wasn't really a new album. Back in the spring of 1994, Cher had been invited to a writers' retreat organized by Sting's manager, Miles Copeland. Held biannually in a fairy-tale castle just outside Bordeaux in rural France, the retreat offered a place for singers and songwriters to meet and collaborate. Other musicians attending in 1994 included Pat MacDonald (the singer, guitarist, and main songwriter with American post-punk outfit Timbuk 3), Patty Smyth (the lead singer in Scandal, not to be confused with her better-known namesake, Patti Smith), country star Ty Herndon, and Brenda Russell.

Although she is rarely thought of as a songwriter, Cher had in fact written songs before. She had penned 'My Song (Too Far Gone)' for her 1979 album *Take Me Home* and had also written poetry since she was a young girl. In terms of songwriting, she had most recently also amended the lyrics to 'Believe,' so although the idea of her writing her own material came as a surprise to others, it did not to Cher.

"I wrote the second verse to 'Believe,'" she later noted, "so it's not like I don't do it, it's just not the main focus of my life. I rewrite all the movies I'm in—there are moments in every movie that I've had to change or readdress because I have kind of a strange speaking pattern. By luck or whatever, people always allow me to make changes."

Consequently, although Cher still didn't think of herself as a fully-fledged writer as such, she was nevertheless pleased to accept the invitation. "I didn't really choose it," she explained. "I just thought it would be fun to go to this writers' thing. I've always written poetry and it never occurred to me really that I would put the poetry to music. I just thought: you know what? They invited me; they asked me to come as a writer. Well, this is unique, this is strange—I'm not really a writer but what the hell, I might as well try."

In preparation for the trip, Cher found herself going through a sudden and intensive period of writing. "Even before I left [for France]," she remembered, "there was magic. The week before, I would wake up in the middle of the night and write, and write, and write." She then flew to Paris, rented a car, and drove a couple hours across the French countryside to the wine-growing region of Bordeaux.

During her time at the castle, Cher began to work with Pat MacDonald on setting her lyrics and poems to music. By the time she got home to America she had almost an album's worth of songs, which she decided to record with the help of musicians from the band on David Letterman's *Late Show*, led by Paul Shaffer and producer Bruce Roberts.

Of the ten tracks they completed, eight were written by Cher, and the feel of the songs is markedly different from any of her previous work. Unlike either her earlier soft-rock power ballads or her subsequent up-tempo dance material, these were singer-songwriter ballads, with Cher's voice set to low-key accompaniments, often featuring acoustic guitar or country-style steel guitar. The stark lyrics dealt with subjects ranging from the fate of neglected World War II veterans to Kurt Cobain's suicide and Cher's own painful childhood experiences. She would later describe the overall sound as resolutely 'dark.'

In the poignant 'Our Lady Of San Francisco,' Cher sings about a homeless woman she had once met; another track, 'Disaster Cake,' relates to her daughter Chastity, who had come out as gay some years earlier to much media attention. After admitting to being shocked initially, Cher had since reconciled herself with her daughter's sexuality—so much so that 'Disaster Cake' was written about an ex-girlfriend of Chastity's whom Cher had taken in after they split up. "I wrote the song about Chastity's ex-girlfriend, Heidi," Cher explained in the liner notes. "She was staying at my home trying to get her life together. I tried to talk to her, but people have always got to learn for themselves! Around my house we call it 'learning the hard way.'"

Perhaps the darkest song on the album is 'Sisters Of Mercy,' in which Cher draws on her own early childhood and lambasts the Catholic nuns at the orphanage where she was temporarily sent as a baby. "Your faith is not faithful," she sings, "Your face has no grace." She then goes on to describe the nuns as "sisters of suffering" and "daughters of hell."

The song would later cause considerable controversy, not least among the nuns, but Cher was more than willing to explain the harrowing episode that had inspired it. Shortly after Cher was born, her mother, Jackie, had found herself pregnant again. Unable to care for Cher, Jackie took her to an orphanage as a temporary measure. Cher's father then walked out on Jackie for the second time, so she decided to have an abortion. She then went to retrieve Cher, only for the nuns to refuse to return the child to her, telling her she was an unfit mother and insisting that she had to put Cher up for adoption. "My mother said the [nuns] were so cruel to her," Cher recalled. "She was so without any resources and she felt the weight of this huge establishment against her. That's why I wrote the song."

The songs were all deeply personal. Cher's favorite track of them was 'The Fall (Kurt's Blues),' a gentle country-rock number featuring steel guitar and a slightly more driving rhythm than the rest of the album. It was inspired by the death of Nirvana's Kurt Cobain. "One morning I woke up and heard Courtney Love reading his [suicide] letter on the radio," Cher recalled. "And so the next morning, at 5am, I just wrote this song all in one sitting. Then I put it to music."

As well as the Cher originals, the album also includes a newly remixed version of an old Sonny Bono number from 1970, 'Classified 1A,' which

Cher had initially released as a single just prior to 'Gypsys Tramps & Thieves,' and another track, 'Born With A Hunger,' by Canadian singer-songwriter Shirley Eikhard, who had written Bonnie Raitt's nineties hit 'Something To Talk About.' Two other songs earmarked for the album didn't make the final cut. "There was one, a really great one ... called 'Obviously Caucasian,' which I wrote about my son," she recalled. "Because he's running around like some guy from East LA, and yet he's this blond-haired, green-eyed, palest person you ever saw, so I just wrote this song about him with this really cool guy named Bink, who was at the castle, but we never really got it together. There's another song I wrote about myself called 'Phoenix' ... I got the words, but could never quite pay enough attention to get it into real song form."

Unlike most of her previous studio albums, *not.com.mercial* took just two days to record. Cher approached the sessions in a very laid-back, unpretentious manner. "We were just making demos," she said, "and it was kind of like a garage thing, you know what I mean? It was a studio but it was a very do-it-yourself kind of deal."

Once she had completed the album, the question was: should she release it? At this point, in early 1995, she had just signed a new record deal with Warners UK, and the label's chairman, Rob Dickens, was unconvinced as to whether Cher's new material was suitable for commercial release. It was "really nice stuff," he explained, but it was also out of sync with current musical trends, and therefore "not commercial." Consequently, he refused to put it out.

Over the next few years the album remained unreleased but not entirely forgotten—at least not by Cher, who thought of it as her most personal project and gave individual prototype copies of the album to friends and family members for Christmas. "I just thought of it as this thing that made me happy," she explained, "but that no one would be able to share but my immediate friends and my family, 'cause it's really personal."

Then, some five years later, a friend suggested the possibility of Cher releasing the album via her website, cher.com. The internet was clearly the perfect outlet for a project such as this, which didn't necessarily fit in with her usual remit, despite the fact that, by her own admission, Cher was "beyond computer illiterate." "I'm not very web-savvy," she explained, "because I'm dyslexic, so I can't make heads or tails of it. I can't type. I have a hard time seeing letters. If they make the software where you can talk into it, I would love that."

Not.com.mercial was eventually released on November 8 2000. In a typically tongue-in-cheek move, the inspiration for the album's title came from Rob Dickens's earlier remark about the record. No singles were ever drawn from the album, but 'Born With The Hunger' was later included on the international version of *The Very Best Of Cher*.

Because of the nature of its internet-only release, sales figures have never been available for the album, but Cher was just happy to have it released. "I don't have any expectations," she told the *Los Angeles Times*. "It's so personal. I'm just sharing it with other people who might be interested." More than a decade later, the album remains popular with Cher's fans and is testimony to her little-known ability as a songwriter.

C

Despite having taken the unusual step of self-releasing *not.com.mercial* immediately after *Believe*, when it came to recording her next new studio album, Cher was still happy to be guided by—or at least advised by—Rob Dickens at Warners UK in terms of what form her next album should take. It had after all been his idea for her to record a dance album, and given the success of *Believe* it made sense to continue in the same vein.

Many artists would have been daunted by the prospect of a follow up but Cher seemed remarkably relaxed. When British music writer Patrick Humphries asked her if, in the light of *Believe*'s extraordinary success she'd found making her next record harder, she replied: "I don't think I thought about it. I know that seems hard to believe, but it's absolutely true. I just thought the way I made the *Believe* album: you just go in, you pick the songs you like, and you do your best, and people are either going to like it or not."

As with the previous album, the plan was for Cher to record in London again, with the Metro team once more at the helm. Also as before, the process began with Cher choosing songs from an initial selection commissioned by Dickens. "I was in Rob's office," she recalled, "and he played me a whole bunch of songs. Some popped out, some didn't."

Among the tracks to pop out was 'The Music's No Good Without You,' written by Metro's Mark Taylor, Paul Barry, and James Thomas. Cher was struck by the chorus and also liked the song's originality and poignancy. "It doesn't sound like something you've heard a lot," she explained. "It kind of sounds like me but not like me. It just has a very haunting feel about it."

It would eventually become the first single released from the album in Europe and Australia, and the finished version, to which Cher also contributed, certainly does have a slightly haunting, ethereal quality—mainly thanks to the Metro team's use once again of various electronic effects on Cher's voice. The sound is not dissimilar to 'Believe,' but although there is certainly a similarity in feel Cher was adamant that the two tracks had very little in common.

"It doesn't remind me at all of 'Believe!'" she insisted. "It does have some effects but I don't think the effects sound anything like 'Believe.' I don't think that's what you go away with. There's only one place where my voice is just my voice, and that's the bridge and it's only a couple of lines, but it's got a vibe to it. I would say this is a record that's more about the vibe and less about what's being said."

Although she felt that "what was being said" was not so important, the lyrics and subject matter are classic Cher: a woman in the aftermath of a breakup who finds that, now the relationship is over, the "music's no good" without her ex-lover, but is nevertheless determined to survive her sorrow. "It's no good me dwelling on the past," she sings. "I have to live each day like it was my last."

Several other songs on the album continue the 'torch song' theme, including 'Love Is A Lonely Place Without You'—an impassioned electro-house ballad written by Taylor and Barry with Metro writer Steve Torch, which again talks about the aftermath of a failed relationship—and 'When The Money's Gone,' which poses the question: "Will you love me, baby / When the money's gone?" It's a sentiment to which Cher—a highly successful, wealthy woman who had had several relationships with less successful men—must surely have related. Written by singer-songwriter Bruce Roberts and Donna Weiss, it had originally been recorded by Roberts himself on his 1995 album *Intimacy*, with backing vocals by Elton John. Cher's version meanwhile has a decidedly up-tempo, Hi-NRG disco feel.

While Cher and the album's Metro producers may not have been consciously trying to recreate the sound of *Believe*, much of the album nevertheless uses electronic effects. 'A Different Kind Of Love Song' was written by the Norwegian songwriter and producer Sigurd 'Ziggy' Rösnes in conjunction with Swedish songwriter Johan Aberg and American songwriter Michelle Lewis. At one point, even Cher thought the song had been "vocoder'd to death," but she felt that it was "such a great song, and that's the way the demo was, [so] I didn't want to shy away from it."

She must nevertheless have been pleased that one track, 'Rain Rain,' featured her voice in a completely unadorned, un-meddled-with form. Written by Shelly Peiken and Guy Roche, the team best known for having written and produced Christina Aguilera's 1999 number one hit 'What A Girl Wants,' it is one of several more straightforward love songs on the album. A slow, R&B-tinged ballad, it struck a chord with Cher, who felt she had "never done a song like this before" and "really loved it."

Featuring Cher's voice in the raw, as it were, gave her the chance to show off the work she had been doing to improve her vocal technique. Despite having made numerous hit records since the sixties, she had never formally learned how to sing, and had recently decided to rectify this.

"I sang my whole life without any singing lessons whatsoever," she told Australia's *TMF Extra* in 2001. "There was an eight-year period where I was concentrating on my acting, and then I went and made a record and I had no chops whatsoever, so I started taking lessons from a teacher. She didn't really try to change my style—she just helped me get my voice in shape and added notes at the top. It's like going to a gym and having an instructor, because your voice is a muscle and it needs to be strong. The stronger it is, the better you sing. I actually think I sing better on this album than I ever have in my life."

Something else that helped Cher with her vocals was Taylor's suggestion that, rather than spending day after day cooped up in Metro's not-so-spacious studios, it might be more comfortable for her to record in her temporary English home. Although Cher had spent more than three decades in recording studios, she still felt that this was not the best place for her voice.

"When I go into the studio I'm so nervous," she explained, "I feel like the best place that I sing is onstage in front of people. So to go into the studio is scary for me. I have to work really hard to not be self-conscious."

The change of location proved an immediate success. "I'd just fall out of bed," she recalled, "and come down and sing, and it was really fun and easy going." In fact, once the album was finished, Cher was pleased with every aspect of it. "I'm really proud of this record," she said. "I was really proud of *Believe* and I can't say that about most of the records in my life. I think that a lot of my recording life I wasn't happy with more than one or two songs on an album, but these last two albums I've made—*Believe* and *Living Proof*—are the best two I've ever made."

One of Cher's favorite tracks on the album was 'Song For The Lonely,' another Taylor–Barry–Torch composition, which despite its title is anything but downbeat. The song's driving dance beats belie the heartfelt lyrics, in which Cher asks: "When your dreams won't come true / Can you hear this prayer?"

'Song For The Lonely' was recorded during the summer of 2001, but after the tragic events of September 11 that year, Cher decided to dedicate the track to "the courageous people of New York, especially the firefighters, police, Mayor Giuliani, Governor Pataki." She later explained that the song "has so much meaning for me, because even though we recorded it before the World Trade Center bombings, for me it's so much about the spirit that I saw after those bombings that I just relate that song to it. It's all about spirit, it talks about heroes and about people being there for each other even when they're lonely and they have a tragedy, so somehow that song just really speaks to me."

The song was later released as the first US single from the album, accompanied by a video in which we see Cher singing the song as she walks the streets of New York. Although she is dressed in an ordinary, contemporary outfit of jeans, Puffa jacket, and woolly hat, the other people in the background are clearly from the nineteenth century. The city is shown in the sepia, brown-tinged hue of old photographs.

As iconic New York City buildings suddenly sprout up, the picture turns to black-and-white and then to color, moving through various eras to the present day. Intercut with the city scenes we see Cher singing the song dressed in a glamorous, off-the-shoulder white evening gown, topped off with a blond, fringed wig. The idea is seemingly that she represents redemption in the form of an angel of hope.

Once *Living Proof* was released, Cher still needed to convince the press that she was not intentionally following the *Believe* format. "I didn't make any attempt to do any *kind* of record," she told *TMF Extra*. "I was just trying to make a really good record with really good songs and have it sound really cool."

Ironically, for all Cher's insistence that the new record had not been made with *Believe* in mind, the working title she and the Metro team had jokingly given it was 'SOB' or 'Son Of *Believe*.' This was obviously not going to stick, however, and eventually Cher was inspired by a line in 'A Different Kind Of Love Song,' in which she sings: "We have living proof / There is some kind of light that flows through everything."

C

As with *Believe* and *It's A Man's World*, Warner Bros decided to stagger the album's release by issuing a European edition first and then following it a few months later with a US version. *Living Proof* was consequently released in Europe in November 2001, with the American release following in February 2002.

The first single in America was 'Song For The Lonely,' which made it to the top forty on many US airplay charts despite only peaking at number eighty-five on the *Billboard* Hot 100. It was followed by 'The Music's No Good Without You'—which had been the album's lead single in the UK—and 'A Different Kind Of Love Song.'

In the USA, 'The Music's No Good Without You' was released only as a club single, rather than as a regular single, and made it to number nineteen on the *Billboard* Hot Dance Club Play chart. In Europe, meanwhile, it reached number eight in the UK and was likewise a hit in Canada, Italy, Romania, Taiwan, and beyond.

With the single's success in Britain, Cher became the only female recording artist to have had top ten hits in every decade from the sixties onward. 'The Music's No Good Without You' was also the first single by an American act to reach number one in Russia, and similarly went to number one in Poland.

Living Proof debuted at number nine on *Billboard* with sales of 114,000 copies in its first week. Warners later re-released the album in the USA with shortened 'radio edit' versions of 'Song For The Lonely' and 'A Different Kind Of Love Song,' but there was no additional promotion. This edition of the album was subsequently nicknamed the 'WalMart version,' since the chain store was the only outlet known to sell it.

Although *Living Proof* was unable to repeat the extraordinary success of its predecessor, it sold more than respectably and yielded its fare share of hits. In addition, in 2002, one of the album's lesser-known tracks, 'Alive Again,' was used by German TV network ARD as the official song for the German Olympic team at the Salt Lake City Winter Olympics.

C

With the album released, the next step for Cher was to take to the road. But if her Believe tour had been lavish, Cher's follow-up—timed to coincide with the US release of the *Living Proof* album in 2002—was even more spectacular. There was the usual array of dazzling, revealing Bob Mackie costumes but also even more extravagant sets, flashily edited videos on giant screens, and show-stopping dance routines.

"It's like going to a circus with music," Cher explained. "That's the best thing about it. You could be any age and still have a good time. Unless you hate me—in which case don't come! Go do something else."

Cher also announced that the tour was to be her last. Although she enjoyed the shows themselves, the traveling involved was tiring, and she was also wary of disappointing her fans as she got older. "It's just got to be [the last tour]," she told Australia's Fox TV channel. "I've been doing this now for forty years. I won't get better. It'll be the law of diminishing returns.

That's why it has to be over. Not because I want to give it up, just because it's the time."

Later on, when journalists were skeptical as to whether this really would indeed be her last tour, she quipped: "I'm approaching eighty, and if I did that thing everyone does, come back in five years, I'd be driving around in one of those carts you know, the ones with the joysticks you see in Costco. There are two reasons people come back: because, like the Stones, they're broke. Again. Or they're old divas who can't wait to be out among their adoring fans. But this, this truly is it."

By way of a warm-up, Cher appeared as one of five co-headliners at the fifth annual *VH1 Divas* event, recorded at the MGM Grand Las Vegas on May 23. After Celine Dion and Anastacia opened the show with a rendition of AC/DC's 'You Shook Me All Night Long,' Cher took to the stage to sing 'Believe' and her new hit 'Song For The Lonely.' She closed her short set with 'If I Could Turn Back Time,' sung as a duet with Cyndi Lauper, who had appeared as a support act on the Believe tour and would do so again during some of the Living Proof shows. Cher later returned for an all-star tribute to Elvis Presley, for which she sang 'Heartbreak Hotel' dressed as The King, complete with leather jacket and slicked-back hair.

The initial plan for the Living Proof tour was for it to comprise three months' worth of dates across North America, taking in more than fifty cities from New York, Pittsburgh, and Milwaukee to Chicago, Portland, Denver, and Oklahoma.

As fans eagerly awaited Cher's arrival onstage, the show began with a short movie on the giant screens showing Cher as a young girl leaving her home. The clip then gradually moved through different stages of her life: from a selection of her music videos and live shows to excerpts from *The Sonny & Cher Comedy Hour* and *The Cher Show*. The final section then showed a series of still images of Cher from the seventies and eighties before concluding with a montage of her single and album covers.

While the crowd watched the screens, Cher went though her last-minute preparation ritual for the show with her dancers backstage. "I arrive late always because if I have too much time it makes me nervous," she told the UK's Heart FM radio station. "I do my vocalizing, and then I go out and all the kids are around and we just do this group-football kind of prayer and it's kind of like a team of us and we have to be kind of pumped up and feel good and get energy from somewhere so we hold hands and I lead us. Sometimes it's really hysterical and sometimes it's dull but then sometimes it's good and then we all scream 'Amen' and I go into my offstage quick-change room and get ready."

As the final introductory images flashed on the giant screens, Cher descended onto the stage like some kind of magical snow queen on high, resplendent in a white fur-lined, sequined cloak, standing on what looked like the roof of a cylindrical brass chandelier, singing an up-tempo dance mix of U2's 'I Still Haven't Found What I'm Looking For.'

Dancers swathed in black and seemingly dressed as Greek Orthodox nuns then helped remove the cloak and matching headdress to reveal another outfit that was this time more like Cleopatra reinvented as a cabaret dancer. A riot of sequins and tassels, the combo comprised a brief black bolero over a skimpy body-stocking covered only by gold sequined tassels suspended from a thong-style belt around Cher's waist, like the flimsiest grass skirt, and topped off with a matching gold skullcap. "Ladies and gentlemen, and flamboyant gentlemen," she announced to the thousands-strong crowd. "Boys and girls and children of all ages. Welcome to the Cher-est show on earth."

Although she opened once again with the U2 song, as she had done on the Believe tour, for the rest of the show Cher gave her fans what they wanted, mixing current hits with selections from her back catalog. The set continued with 'Song For The Lonely' and 'We All Sleep Alone.' By now more dancers had appeared and the circus style show began in earnest as acrobats swathed in yards of silk began to leap from the rafters.

After leaving the stage briefly, Cher reappeared for one of the most flamboyant parts of the show. Dressed in what looked like a Vegas-style Indian sari in pinks, purples, and turquoise, she appeared astride a seven-foot high, brightly colored *papier-mâché* elephant to perform 'All Or Nothing.' With Cher surrounded by dancers in similarly Indian-style dress, the overall effect was like something out of *Aladdin*.

Adding to the overall drama were the sets and lighting, which featured various exotic touches such as oriental style hanging lanterns, vast panels of twinkling lights, and grandiose staircases. These were the creation of set designer Jeremy Railton and lighting designer Abigail Rosen Holmes, who had previously worked with Janet Jackson and the Barnum & Bailey Circus Company.

For the Living Proof tour, the pair worked closely with director and choreographer Doriana Sanchez to create something eye-catching, memorable, and different from the usual rock paraphernalia. "It's probably the most theatrical music tour that any of us have done," Railton said. "Abigail had a theater approach to the show rather than just a concert lighting job. We had a lot of fun."

Cher had also had her say and was delighted with the results. "Dory, the director, and I worked on the set," she explained. "We had seen it in a Gaudí book, and we worked on it with Jeremy, and I remember coming in to the theater in Toronto where we were rehearsing and seeing it for the first time. That was pretty spectacular for me. When you're up there, you just can't imagine what it looks like. You can't get the feeling."

Many aspects of the lighting and set had in fact been inspired not just by Cher but also by her home. "Cher is all girly and glittery and sparkly," Holmes explained, "so there's shiny glitter everywhere you look on this tour. Her house inspired parts of the design. She has beautiful Mediterranean, medieval, Moorish, and Indian art influences in it, and they carry into the design. I used some Arab and Moorish art images and then modified them. Also, the lanterns were inspired by some lanterns that hang in one of the Gaudí cathedrals in Spain. So all of that region's art and architecture is reflected in the set."

Alongside the exotic sets, there were also further costume and wig changes, ranging from a sequined 'circus ringleader' outfit—complete with silver sequined top hat—to floor-skimming evening gowns. For a new rendition of 'Bang Bang (My Baby Shot Me Down),' Cher appeared in an outfit that could best be described as Hollywood Cavegirl—or, as the *New York Daily News* put it: "like Conan The Barbarian's favorite concubine."

During the course of the show, while Cher left the stage to change costumes, there were further video clips, including a selection of Sonny &

Cher performing some of their most popular numbers, before Cher re-appeared to sing 'All I Really Want To Do,' her first solo hit. Another break featured clips from her films, including *Silkwood*, *Moonstruck*, and *Mermaids*, before Cher reappeared to sing 'Just Like Jesse James,' 'Heart Of Stone,' and 'The Shoop Shoop Song (It's In His Kiss).'

The grand finale was a rendition of 'If I Could Turn Back Time' in which Cher appeared in a getup not dissimilar to the notorious thong-and-body-stocking look she had worn in the video years earlier. The crowd clearly loved every minute of it. And they were not to be disappointed by the encore. After a few minutes of the audience stomping and clapping, Cher re-emerged for the last time, once again descending on the golden chandelier, this time in front of a shimmering disc. Dressed in an Abba-style silver jumpsuit fringed with lace and diamante at the arms and legs, topped off with the red fringed wig from earlier on, she sang the song that would remain her ultimate crowd-pleaser—'Believe'—as dancers somersaulted through the air around her.

Cher had said she wanted to make the show as memorable as possible, and she told the crowd at one show why. "I wanted to make a spectacular, spectacular show because I'm never doing this again," she explained. "Give me a frickin' break ... I have been a frickin' diva for forty frickin' years and it's not easy!"

It may not have been easy, but that did not mean Cher was at all keen for the tour to end. On the contrary: after she had played the initial run of US dates, the tour was extended, and extended, and extended again. It would eventually continue for a record-breaking 350 shows on three continents. The first leg of the tour continued from Toronto across North America from June 2002 to January 2004. From May through July 2004 she then toured Europe, taking in no fewer than fifteen countries, before returning to the USA and Mexico. During late February and March of 2005 she extended the tour again to Australia and New Zealand before finally returning to North America for one last stint, closing at the Hollywood Bowl on April 30. It was perhaps fitting that the tour's final date should be held at this historic LA venue—it was where she had made her debut US appearance with Sonny Bono so many years earlier.

Inevitably, many observers wondered why the tour had been extended so many times. The answer seemed to lie somewhere between the tour's phenomenal success—selling out stadia and arenas in virtually every city it went—and Cher's reluctance to bring it to an end.

"I really don't want to stop," she told the *Toledo Blade*. "They're making me stop! I told the tour managers I haven't done Vermont or Delaware, and they said: there are no venues big enough, dear. And then I said go out and build some! After that, physical restraint was mentioned. But seriously, I figured if I didn't stop, I was going to go into permanent Marlene Dietrich mode—'And these are the songs I sang for audiences in Alaska, Ohio, Connecticut'—and then I'd keep falling off my elephant and eventually become a recluse."

There seemed little danger of either thing happening. "Every place we could possibly put this show, we've played it," Clear Channel Entertainment's Brad Wavra, the tour's producer, revealed. "We did two shows in Council Bluffs, Iowa. We played Billings, Montana, twice in three months. This is the biggest tour in history by a female artist. She crushed any other female artist."

Cher would eventually perform to nearly three-and-a-half million fans enthusiastic around the world, but the tour was also a success with the critics. *Newsweek* magazine called it "flawless," while the *Boston Globe* described it as "everything a Cher fan could want." As if to complete the critical acclaim, the tour also won an Emmy award.

Nevertheless, during such a long-running tour, there were, perhaps inevitably, some moments of controversy—some of them by design, others beyond her control. During the final leg of the tour, she caused a mini media furor by mentioning some of the new, younger female artists who had recently come to fame in what several of the artists considered a less than favorable light.

Cher herself felt it was all much ado about nothing. "All right! Jessica Simpson, Britney Spears, Jennifer Lopez!" she began from the stage on her final night at the Hollywood Bowl. "I'll tell you something that happened and this is the truth. One night I got so excited by you guys. And then I said: oh, they're a bunch of little hos, aren't they? Yes! But don't you know, two of them were really angry and didn't think it was a joke. No, no, I'm not gonna mention any names, but … well, all right—but—that's a … big butt! Yes. She was a little pissed off, you know. But I don't blame her. It's just my sense of humor, you know … I call myself a stupid bitch; they're little hos … so, whatever! I have to proceed with the show and those girls are coming, so we have to prepare ourselves."

Another controversial incident dealt not with the show itself but Cher's offstage activities. In October 2003, whilst playing dates in Washington DC, Cher found time to spend a few hours at the Walter Reed Medical Center, the US Army's flagship medical facility. There she met various young soldiers, recently returned from the Iraq war, nearly all of whom had been severely injured or maimed.

The soldiers made such an impression on Cher that a couple of weeks later she felt compelled to speak out about what she had seen. She had always been a big fan of the C-SPAN (Cable Satellite Public Affairs Network) channel, which specializes in rolling coverage of government proceedings and public affairs, and in particular the *Washington Journal*, a daily morning show in which politicians, government officials, and journalists answer questions from the hosts as well as calls and emails from the public.

On Sunday October 26, shortly after 7am, Cher phoned in to the show. After waiting on hold for five minutes she was put through to the host Peter Slen, to whom she introduced herself simply as a "caller from Miami."

"Thank you for C-SPAN," she said, before explaining what she wanted to talk about. "I would like to say I had the occasion the other day to spend the entire day with troops that had come back from Iraq and had been wounded," she began. She then went on to detail the soldiers' circumstances, including mention of "a boy about nineteen or twenty who had lost both his arms."

Wary of bogus callers, Slen was keen to verify the caller's credentials. He asked her where exactly she had met the soldier, to which Cher explained that it had been at Walter Reed. Was she a volunteer, Slen wondered?

"No," Cher replied. She had just been working in DC that day.

"What kind of work do you do?" Slen asked.

"I'm an entertainer," Cher replied.

The game of twenty questions continued for a while longer as Slen then asked Cher if she worked for USO (United Service Organizations Inc), the non-profit organization that provides entertainment and morale-boosting services to the US military overseas.

"No," explained Cher. "I actually was called by the USO. But I'm just an entertainer. I really don't want to go much beyond that."

By now, Slen had worked out who his caller was, recognizing her distinctive speaking voice while also being aware that she had spent the day with troops at Walter Reed on October 10.

"Is that Cher?" he asked.

Cher finally admitted that it was, before returning to the topic at hand. "These boys had the most unbelievable courage. They felt it was their duty. And it took everything I have as a person to not break down … I just think that if there was no reason for this war, this was the most heinous thing I'd ever seen … And also I wonder, why are Cheney, Wolfowitz, Bremer, the President—why aren't they taking pictures with these guys? I don't understand why these guys are so hidden, why there are no pictures of them."

She then also chided the news media for not including the "devastatedly wounded" in their coverage. "Don't hide them," she said. "Let's have some news coverage where people are sitting and talking to these guys and seeing their spirit." She went on to explain that she watched *Washington Journal* every day and "really appreciated" it, saying that she felt that C-SPAN, along with the BBC news service outside the USA, were the most reliable sources of independent, unbiased news coverage, and as such were her "favorite sources." With that, the call ended and the show returned to its normal, more prosaic agenda.

The next day the press was full of the story. "Celebrities voice their political opinions in many ways," the *Washington Times* noted. "They sign petitions, make donations, appear at rallies, and sound off on late-night talk shows. And sometimes they just stay on hold. That is what Cher did yesterday."

The fact that a celebrity of Cher's stature had been happy to phone in to the program and remain on hold for several minutes seemed to some to be the most newsworthy aspect of the story. "A celebrity on hold at 7:16am is not typical," a C-SPAN spokesperson told the *Washington Times*. "But it's business as usual. Cher came in like just another regular caller with something on her mind."

Cher had always had strong views on politics, and despite having once acknowledged that she's "not supposed to have any opinions about politics, because I'm famous," she had never been shy of making them publicly known. While Sonny Bono was alive, she had made clear her shock at his becoming a Republican politician, and publicly stated that she did not agree with his politics.

Meanwhile, her 'Heart Of Stone' video had presented clips of the Vietnam War in a way that made her own sentiments on the subject very clear, and she had recently appeared on numerous European TV chat shows wearing a pendant with the insignia of the Campaign For Nuclear Disarmament (CND).

Her concern for the veterans of both Iraq and Afghanistan has also continued over the years, and a large proportion of her charitable work is still devoted to them. Recently, she has stated that she plans to join President Obama's Veterans Task Force. "I was buying helmet inserts for guys who were in Iraq," she told *Vanity Fair*. "Football players have more protection on their heads than the guys over there do."

More generally, she has also often expressed concern about the ineffectiveness of her fellow human beings as a whole and governments in particular. "I have a lot of ambitions about making the condition of our lives better," she told one interviewer, "but I don't think that government is really the place to do it because I think they're all really ... can I say 'full of shit' on English television?"

But despite her avowed lack of faith in the traditional bodies of power, she has always made clear her own commitment to creating a more socially and economically equal society. "I would be willing to pay a lot more taxes," she explained, "because I make a lot more money, but I don't want to give [the government] more to just fuck things up more. It really should fall on people like me to get together and do things to help the people in this country. If you're not worrying about how to put food on your table, you [should be] worrying about why other people don't *have* food on *their* table."

The days of Cher herself having to worry about putting food on the table were certainly long past. By the time she played the final night of her Living Proof tour in Los Angeles in April 2005, the shows had grossed nearly $250 million. It was in fact the most successful tour Cher had ever staged. In 2003, she was listed among the highest-earning touring acts of the year— second only to Sir Paul McCartney. After this kind of success, nobody would have been in the least surprised if Cher had decided to retreat from the public eye for a little while, but as ever she had other ideas.

CHAPTER 18
You Haven't Seen The Last Of Me

If Cher's fans had been concerned that Living Proof: The Farewell Tour would be their final opportunity to see her live, they need not have worried. It may well have been the last time she would go on the road, but this did not mean that she was never going to perform again.

On the contrary, in February 2008 Cher announced that, as of May, she would be playing a series of 200 shows at the Colosseum Theater at Caesars Palace, Las Vegas. The shows would run for three years, with Cher alternating some seasons between Elton John and Bette Midler.

In earlier years, Cher had complained about the repetitive nature of playing Vegas, but there were benefits to be had—both financially and logistically, because, with a long run, she could play live without the wearying travel involved in a tour. She also found a pleasing symmetry in playing the venue where she had started out with Sonny so many years earlier. "I've come full circle," she said. "I'm back and I plan to give my fans the best experience yet. I think everybody knows I only do things in a big way."

The plan was for a ninety-minute spectacular designed specifically with the 4,300-seater Colosseum in mind. This time the idea was for the new show to be still more impressive than the last. As with the Living Proof and Believe tours, the show was once again to be staged and choreographed by Cher's long-standing friend Doriana Sanchez, whom she had first met some twenty-one years earlier. Cher had spotted Sanchez when she appeared as a star dancer in the hit 1987 film *Dirty Dancing* and invited her to her home to see if she would give her dance lessons. The pair immediately became friends as well as collaborators and Sanchez subsequently choreographed many of Cher's videos and live shows.

"What we were trying to do this time was make it bigger and better than our last tour which was very successful," Sanchez said at the time. "We wanted this to be *as* spectacular but even more, and we could do more because we were in a sit-down situation."

The spectacular featured fourteen dancers and four 'aerialists' (aka trapeze artists), each of whom had been handpicked by Sanchez and Cher. There were state-of-the-art videos, special effects, and dazzling sets, not to mention a gondola and a golden chariot. There would also be, as one might have expected, a series of some twenty-five show-stopping Bob Mackie outfits.

Cher had come to Mackie with several suggestions, and the designer had only four weeks to turn those ideas into reality. "It was like building a battleship, with all the pieces and layers," he said. "It was full, long days and lots of nervousness." The costumes were indeed completed nevertheless and the show opened on May 6 2008.

After a fast-edited introductory video sequence, Cher appeared onstage, making exactly the kind of grand entrance her fans had come to expect. Determined to top the opening segment of the Farewell Tour, this time Cher descended from the rafters in a golden chariot, resplendent in a glittering floor-length cape with what looked like gilded feathers stretching upward and outward in every direction. The outfit was topped off by an elaborate Egyptian-style gold headdress, an asp, and yet more grandiose feathers. It was one of Cher's favorites. "When she put that gold cape on in the fitting," Bob Mackie recalled, "she just smiled, like: look what I got! She couldn't help herself. She was like a little girl."

Musically, meanwhile, the show was to be a kind of 'greatest hits' of Cher's career, in the same way as the Farewell Tour had been, taking in her biggest successes from every decade. The choreography followed suit, as Sanchez explained: "Her music has spanned four decades, so there's everything in it: there's contemporary, there's ballet, there's hip-hop, there's gypsy dancing ..."

Just as the music and choreography spanned different styles, Cher's costumes similarly ran the gamut from ostrich-feathered, diamante-festooned, Ziegfeld-style showgirl to gypsy princess. As Booth Moore of the *Los Angeles Times* wrote: "[Cher's] new show is an eyeful of deliciously glittery costumes that hark back to the wonderfully tacky, pre-

Celine Vegas of Liberace and feather-flocked revues. She plays the gypsy in a jingling skirt, the sultan in genie pants that are little more than ropes of gold and crystal embroidery draped across her thighs, the Indian chief in a feathered headdress and sixties-era Cher in a Mod red mini-dress. Through seventeen costume changes, she shares and bares—bellybutton, hips, and butt cheeks."

Other outfits included a black sixties-style mini-dress with fluted sleeves worn with pink heels and a curly fuchsia pink wig for 'The Shoop Shoop Song,' a peasant girl blouse and jeans for 'Walking In Memphis,' and a geometrically patterned teal feathered hat and coat, adorned with flashing lights, for her rendition of the disco classic 'Don't Leave Me This Way' (first made famous by Thelma Houston and later by The Communards).

The lights had been one of Cher's own ideas, and she had gone to Mackie to see if it were possible. "It was easy," Mackie remembered. "First, we made a pattern, and I marked where the lights would go, then we had it beaded, and they pulled the beads out where the lights were going to be. Then we sent it out, and it was done."

Cher saved one of her most eye-catching numbers for the encore of 'Believe'—a flesh-colored body-stocking dripping with diamante, jewels, and sequins combined with another feathered headdress—this time in silver—over a wig made of silver dreadlock-style chains. As Mackie later explained, Cher had firm ideas about the kind of effect she wanted. "Cher told me that she wanted to be more naked," he told the *Los Angeles Times*. "It's not vulgar, but it's quite shocking. It's like we dipped her in glue and rolled her in diamonds. Not enough of them to cover up the girl."

Cher has always been the first to admit her penchant for revealing outfits. "My mom told me that I used to run around when I was three years old naked singing," she told a British radio interviewer a few years earlier. "So I said: well, mom, nothing's changed."

Some of the outfits may indeed have been miniscule but they were still dazzling as ever, and as an added bonus there was a further display of Cher's outfits from yesteryear outside the theater for fans to admire before or after the shows. Glamorous costumes such as the red Pocahontas-style outfit from the mid seventies and the corset-dress from the Believe tour were housed in glass cases like the museum pieces they had by now become.

Audiences were clearly delighted with the shows, and such was the overwhelming demand for tickets that within three months of the dates being announced, an additional eighteen performances were added. During the course of the show's three-year run, Cher played to thousands of fans including many of her fellow celebrities, among them Liza Minnelli, Marie Osmond, Bette Midler, Barry Manilow, Joan and Jackie Collins, Carrie Underwood, Pink, and Larry King.

On the final night she thanked her musicians, singers, dancers, crew, "teamsters," and managers. Later, on her official website, she offered an additional thank you to her fans. "Cher would like to thank all of the fans who came to Las Vegas to see nearly 200 shows, who survived the flying cart, and to all of the fans who, for one reason or another, couldn't make it," the message read. "2011 was the last show of three years of Las Vegas. What's next? Only Cher knows."

C

While Cher had been busy focusing on her music with both The Farewell Tour and the Colosseum shows, she had not entirely neglected her acting career. She had accepted two small roles, both of which involved playing herself, and both of which were in comedies.

Although she had previously been known for straight acting roles, comedy had always been a key part of her stage persona, right back to the days of deadpanning wisecracks at Sonny's expense onstage and on their television show. Indeed, when Francis Ford Coppola first commented that she should try acting back in the seventies, it was because he had been impressed by her comic timing during her Vegas stage shows.

Perhaps it was not so surprising therefore that some three decades later she made a cameo appearance on one of America's biggest TV sitcoms, the NBC series *Will & Grace*. Although her scene in the episode entitled 'Gypsies Tramps & Weed' lasted only a couple of minutes, it subsequently became one of the most talked about moments in the series' history. One of the main characters in the show, Jack, is obsessed with Cher, and when his idol appears in person before him, he is so surprised to meet her that he cannot believe she is really who she says she is, accusing her of being a female impersonator doing an impression of herself. The ensuing repartee between them played up to Cher's own naturally sassy, deadpan delivery and when 'Gypsies Tramps & Weed' aired on November 16 2000, it was watched by some twenty-two million viewers. It received the second highest rating of the show's eight-year run.

Cher's other comedic outing came in 2003 when she appeared in a feature film entitled *Stuck On You*, written and directed by Bobby and Peter Farrelly, whose earlier comedies *Dumb & Dumber* and *There's Something About Mary* had gained a cult following. The plot centers on a pair of conjoined twins, played by Matt Damon and Greg Kinnear, who move to Hollywood so that one of them, Walt (Kinnear), can try his luck at becoming an actor.

The part offered to Cher was that of a diva-like movie queen who, according to the script, is a prima donna with a monstrous ego and a tendency to throw tantrums at the merest provocation. Keen to extricate herself from a TV movie she feels is too much of a comedown from her past work, she insists on hiring Walt—and, by extension, his brother in the hope that this will be disastrous enough to fold the entire project.

It was an odd part for Cher to play inasmuch as her character was nominally based on herself but with a different personality. Consequently, despite agreeing to take the role, Cher soon had misgivings. "I was petrified," she said. "As an acting role it was *very* difficult. How do you that without looking stupid?" She was also concerned that people might think the character was based on her real-life persona. "You'd have to do something *so* bad to get me to scream," she continued. "The truth is if I get really angry I go the other way. I just go completely inside, walk away, and if it's real bad I'll probably never speak to you again."

Eventually, Cher grew more comfortable with the role and enjoyed the whole experience. "One of the big things they did for me was that they let me rewrite some of the things because I have such a special way of speaking," she explained. "You can't just tie me down to the script because some of the words are not words that I would use, you know? They were great about that."

There was a good feeling on set, and Cher got on well with the directors and her co-stars, Kinnear and Damon. "It's like being with the Marx Brothers, all those guys," she recalled. "They were hysterical." Her co-stars likewise enjoyed working with her. "She was very cool and very game for everything we did," said Kinnear, while Damon noted that she was "nothing like this woman that she's playing."

In between tour dates and filming, Cher even managed to find time to record a song for the movie: 'Human,' a smoochy electronica-rock track produced by David Foster that harked back to her epic power ballads of the eighties and nineties. However, although the song was eventually used over the movie's closing titles, it was never released as a single.

Released in December 2003, *Stuck On You* received generally strong reviews, as did Cher's performance in it. Roger Ebert of the *Chicago Sun Times* called the film "funny, but also kind-hearted," while *USA Today* noted that it "may be just the light and humorous break we need from all the serious epic films of the holiday season."

Despite having played herself in various guises in recent times, however, Cher had not had a significant acting role since *Tea With Mussolini* in 1999. This was not due to any lack of interest or commitment on Cher's part, but more to do with a lack of suitable offers and the intensive demands of her touring and recording schedules.

"You get lots of scripts but you don't get things you want to do," she explained. "If there had been great movies, I would have done those, but the only thing that I've missed that I wanted to do was *Mamma Mia*. I wanted to have the chance to work with Meryl [Streep] again, but I was on the road, so I couldn't do it."

Eventually, Cher received a new script that she liked almost immediately. The plot told the story of a small-town girl, Ali, who heads to Los Angeles with dreams of making it as a singer. Once there, she finds a job as a cocktail waitress at the Burlesque Lounge, a cabaret revue run by a former dancer, Tess. This was the part intended for Cher, and although Ali is the main focus of the movie, Tess acts as a mentor to her and encourages her to pursue her dream of becoming a performer.

As had been the case in the past with some of her most successful movies,

Cher felt a personal connection to the part of Tess, particularly in the way the character's relationship with Ali echoed Cher's relationship with her own mother. "My mom and her friends were all successful women," she said. "Not money-wise, but they were role models. Her friends were painters, singers, actors, and songwriters—women who'd been married and divorced and brought up their children and hung out together and worked. They were the most gorgeous women I've ever seen in my whole life."

Cher also conceded that although she herself was still fortunate enough to have a flourishing career of her own, there were nevertheless similarities. "Tess, my character, is very close to me," she admitted. "She's not as old as I am, but she is an artist; she's strong. She's having a hard time, and she is moving over so someone else can take over. In real life I don't think I'd love doing that."

The other main factor that appealed to her about *Burlesque* was the fact that it was a musical. Although Cher belongs to that small elite of singers who have successfully managed to sing and act, she had strangely never really combined the two. She was delighted to have the chance. "I really wanted to sing in a movie," she said, "and I thought: I'm never going to get this opportunity again."

Cher was also well aware that, having turned sixty in 2006, the likelihood of her being offered many more singing and dancing parts in the future was perhaps slim. But although she was delighted to be playing the role, she was also nervous after such a long gap since her last major part. "I was terrified," she said. "That's the way I roll. You go scene by scene, but I knew everything worked with Stanley [Tucci, who plays the nightclub manager] and with Peter [Gallagher, who plays Tess's ex-husband, the club's owner]."

As with her live shows, the nerves vanished once filming started. Cher's relaxed friendship with Gallagher in particular ended up having an impact on the script. She had become used to amending and adapting her scripts as she wished, and with *Burlesque* she did so once again. "Peter and I had a great relationship, which wasn't there on paper," she explained. "He and I changed that relationship completely. We were very adversarial on the page, but then we started to work and it didn't come out that way. We didn't even try, and nobody said anything. We had this relationship that just started being funny at one point, and that's what we decided to go with."

Cher also added a scene with Ali, played by Christina Aguilera, inspired by her own experiences with her mother: a poignant moment in which the older, more experienced Tess shows Ali how to make herself up in her dressing room. But while some aspects of the onscreen relationship between the two women reminded Cher of her own mother, she also found herself offering the kind of sisterly support, encouragement, and guidance to Aguilera that Meryl Streep had shown Cher at the beginning of her own acting career.

"I kind of did for Christina what Meryl Streep did for me in *Silkwood*," she explained to the UK's *Mail On Sunday* newspaper. "I just said to her: I have your back, I'm here to support you; don't worry, I will help you in every way I can, I will never make you look stupid or do anything to hurt you. So we became friends."

When they first started work on the movie, Cher hadn't known very much about Aguilera, but as they got to know each other she liked what she discovered. "Christina is wonderful," she continued. "I knew she had a big voice and was a really good singer and wore too much makeup, and that's pretty much all I knew about her. When I met her on this movie we talked a lot about life and work and acting. It was interesting to watch a girl who's had courage and was going to try something she didn't really know how to do [acting] but just does it anyway. I like to see that in a woman."

Aguilera, meanwhile, was thrilled at the friendship and support she received from Cher. "Cher's been incredible," she explained. "She has just since day one embraced me with open arms. It's meant the world to me. Her emails of encouragement and support are like unwrapping little pieces of candy and getting the best sensation from it. ... For some reason I feel like we're old girlfriends, we'll talk and talk ... I just find her the most fascinating person I've ever met."

Cher had developed close friendships with several of her co-stars in the past, but whereas in the past she and her fellow actors had often found themselves battling against dictatorial directors, the atmosphere on the set of *Burlesque* was rarely anything other than harmonious. Indeed, writer and director Steve Antin was also grateful, like Aguilera, for Cher's support and easy-going approach.

"Cher is really down-to-earth, very nurturing, incredibly funny and fun, a great storyteller, and creates a great environment on the set," he said. "She was really supportive of me as a director and a filmmaker. Whatever I wanted or needed, she was really willing to go there, so that I was happy. She often [asked] me: did you get what you want? And I'd say yes, do you feel good with what you did? If you didn't, let's do it one more time. She would say no, I feel good, and we would move on. We really had that quite a bit."

In contrast to her earlier movie experiences, Cher was now the veteran working with the younger director. She may not have made a musical before, but when it came to filming her musical numbers she was very much on home ground. She sings two key songs in the movie, the first of which is 'Welcome To Burlesque,' a sultry, cabaret-style tango, complete with syncopated rhythms and gypsy violin … and more than a nod to Joel Grey's 'Wilkommen' from *Cabaret*. In fact, much of *Burlesque*—particularly in terms of choreography—can be seen almost as an homage to Bob Fosse's dance routines in the 1972 movie.

Cher's main number comes later on in the film, when she sings 'You Haven't Seen The Last Of Me.' The song had been written specially for her by her old friend and hit-writer Diane Warren, and as with so many of the songs she had sung in the past, the lyrics once again tell of a woman who has overcome hardship and adversity but survived to tell the tale. "I've been brought down to my knees," she sings in the chorus, "And I've been pushed way past the point of breaking / But I can take it / I'll be back." The song also makes it clear that she is determined not to be cast aside in favor of the younger talent emerging around her. "I'm gonna stand my ground," she sings. "You're not gonna stop me … don't count me out so fast."

For Cher, the lyrics very much encapsulated her feelings about her own place in music at the time. "That song had a lot of meaning for me," she said. "When I started this character, I thought: this is hard, to play supporting [role] to this girl and know that this is what's potentially happening in my life. I have to move over. Not that I'm doing it gracefully.

You'd have to pull me over … I'm old and there was too much truth in this film for me a couple of times, so that song was really meaningful. It was not exactly my life, but it was my life in that movie."

In January 2011, 'You Haven't Seen The Last Of Me' climbed to number one on *Billboard*'s Dance/Club Play chart, enabling Cher to retain her record as the only performer to have reached the top of at least one *Billboard* chart in every decade since the sixties. Later the same month, it was named Best Original Song at the Golden Globes. When songwriter Diane Warren received the award from Jennifer Lopez and Alec Baldwin, she thanked Cher for being an "eternal bad-ass" and making sure the song was in the movie. "We've never seen the last of Cher," Warren said, "and thank God we never will."

Following the song's success at the Golden Globes, Cher was hopeful that it might be equally successful when it came to the Academy Awards, but in the end it was not nominated. She was clearly disappointed, and in a somewhat uncharacteristic display of pique decided to air her frustration publicly.

However, rather than broadcasting her feelings in print or on television, she opted to use the new social media technology of the day instead. Ever in tune with the zeitgeist, she decided to 'tweet' her feelings. "OK this is me being a baby!" she wrote. "My heart is broken! I was upset after winning the Golden Globe … not to be nominated by the academy, but the Music Voting process is different than the acting, directing, etc etc."

Cher had also heard a rumor that Academy Awards co-host James Franco had been planning to dress up in a *Burlesque* style outfit to sing 'You Haven't Seen The Last Of Me,' but that the idea had been dropped. How cool would it have been, she asked, "to have YOUR SONG sung by James Fkn Franco in Your Outfit! … Oh well I'm all sour grapes!"

Cher ended her Twitter outburst with a note of defiance: "I'll keep this song alive." But the disappointment soon passed, and while Cher may not have won the Academy Award, the movie was clearly a hit with the public. Released on November 24 2010, it became the third highest-grossing film on its first day, and by the end of the weekend had brought in $17.3 million at the box office. By the end of February 2011, that figure had risen to $89.4 million worldwide. It was a success by anyone's standards.

C

As much as she is known as a singer, an actress, and an entertainer, to many of her fans Cher is, more than anything, the ultimate survivor. There are even jokes on the internet about how, in the event of a nuclear catastrophe, all that will be left will be "cockroaches and Cher."

Increasingly, she has come to symbolize a resilience and invincibility—both professionally and personally—that is central to her appeal. She may have achieved the extraordinary feat of scoring hits in every decade since the sixties, but her career has nonetheless not been without its lows. She is also a woman who can be seen to have had her fair share of life experience, from a difficult childhood through two divorces and numerous relationships.

In fact, many of her hits since the eighties deal with surviving heartache and coming out the other side, stronger and wiser. As she sings in 'Believe': "I know that I'll get through this / Cos I know that I am strong."

Cher is the first to admit that she has amazing staying power. Back in 1990, when ABC News' Diane Sawyer asked her which of her lyrics she liked to sing most, she immediately thought of Jimmy Cliff's 'Too Many Rivers To Cross.' "I've been licked, washed up for years, and I merely survived because of my pride," she said, quoting back the lyrics. "It's me! It says everything about me in those two lines. I've been on my way out for twenty-five years. At this rate I'll be 100 before I'm gone!"

To many, Cher also epitomizes the idea of the outsider who has overcome hardship and adversity to reach the upper echelons of fame and wealth. Like a modern-day Cinderella, she is the poor girl from the valleys of California who looked radically different to the cookie-cutter blond, blue-eyed ideal that was so prevalent when she was growing up in the fifties and yet still managed to become a star—mostly through her own determination and hard work.

"I invented someone who was funny and interesting: not the most beautiful person on the block, and yet still could convey that kind of feeling across," she told Barbara Walters in 1985. "I think that you can invent your life as you go along. You're born with a huge piece of paper or a canvas and you can put anything on it you want to."

Cher clearly did invent her stage persona, but over the years she has also become known as a mistress of reinvention. With her changing image and regular forays into different musical genres, she perfected the art of chameleon-like change long before younger acts like Madonna or Lady Gaga. It's no real surprise that her fans—and in particular her gay fans— love her for it. She is the ex-outsider made good in a panoply of flamboyant costumes; the ultimate gay icon.

"Gay men never leave you," she told *Attitude* magazine in 2011. "When my career was in the toilet, as it was many times over the years, they were just there. I think they understand that I know what it's like to be an outsider. So I get them. We get each other."

For all her fatalist, outsider allure, Cher has always taken a more than practical approach to her physical survival and is rigorously disciplined. "I don't drink, I don't smoke, I don't do drugs," she explains. "I live like a nun when I'm performing. I get up at ten o'clock and work out for an hour and a half. At night I like to watch Turner Classic Movies, then I fall asleep at two o'clock. I go dancing and swimming and surfing. I do everything except Pilates, which is really boring. I've worked out my whole life, even when I was young. My sister always read books and I was always racing the kids down the street and climbing the highest trees."

Working out and keeping fit is obviously no bad thing at any age, but at sixty-five and with an estimated $600 million in the bank, Cher could easily retreat to an island in the sun to reflect on past glories. But then she wouldn't be Cher. "I could retire now," she said recently, "and think to myself: I've done more work than five people, and be happy with it, but I am not ready to do that. I like working."

In fact, far from taking it easy, Cher has no shortage of new projects on the horizon. There is talk of her playing a Mother Superior in a Farrelly Brothers remake of the comedy classic *The Three Stooges*, while the summer of 2011 saw the release of *The Zookeeper,* an animated family movie in which Cher voices the part of a lioness whose lion husband is played by Sylvester Stallone.

She also has a new album in the pipeline, for which she has once again been exploring new musical territory, this time in America's Country music capital of Nashville. Her new album is said to be "country flavored" and rumor has it that she has once again collaborated with her old friend and hit songwriter Diane Warren. Cher herself has also said that Pink has written two songs for the project, as well as hinting that there could be another duet between her and Christina Aguilera.

Furthermore, she has also made various mentions of her desire to direct movies. "As artists we're always striving to keep doing something," she said recently. "If you're an artist, you want to create. When people say you have achieved everything, why do you keep working, my reply is: did someone [tell] Picasso: You've done enough paintings, you painted every day, how long are you going to keep doing it?"

In true survivor style, Cher is determined to prove her reputation for indestructibility, and for the time being at least she has no intention of shrinking from the limelight. "I just like what I do," she says, "and I wouldn't do it if I didn't. I don't think I'm going any place yet. They're going to have to carry me out feet first."

Selected Discography

SONNY & CHER ALBUMS

Baby Don't Go—Sonny & Cher & Friends (Reprise, 1965, US #69)

Look At Us (Atco, 1965, US #2, UK #7)

The Wondrous World Of Sonny & Cher (Atlantic/Atco, 1966, US #34, UK #15)

In Case You're In Love (Atlantic/Atco, 1967, US #45)

Good Times (Original Film Soundtrack) (Atlantic/Atco, 1967, US #73)

Sonny & Cher Live (Kapp/MCA, 1971, US #35)

All I Ever Need Is You (Kapp/MCA, 1971, US #14, UK #7)

Mama Was A Rock And Roll Singer, Daddy Used To Write All Her Songs (Kapp/MCA, 1973, US #132)

Live In Las Vegas Vol. 2 (Kapp/MCA, 1974, US #175)

SONNY & CHER SINGLES

'The Letter' (as Caesar & Cleo) (Vault, 1964)

'Love Is Strange' (as Caesar & Cleo) (Reprise, 1964)

'Let The Good Times Roll' (as Caesar & Cleo) (Reprise, 1964)

'Do You Wanna Dance' (as Caesar & Cleo) (Reprise, 1964)

'Baby Don't Go' (Reprise, 1964, US #8, UK 11)

'I Got You Babe' (Atco, 1965, US #1, UK #1)

'Why Don't They Let Us Fall In Love' (Atco, 1965)

'Just You' (Atco, 1965, US #20)

'Sing C'est La Vie' (Atco, 1965)

'The Letter' (Atco, 1965, US #75)

'But You're Mine' (Atco, 1965, US #15, UK #17)

'What Now My Love' (Atco, 1966, US #14, UK #13)

'Have I Stayed Too Long' (Atco, 1966, US #49, UK #42)

'Little Man' (Atco, 1966, US #21, UK #4)

'Living For You' (Atco, 1966, US #87, UK #44)

'The Beat Goes On' (Atco, 1967, US #6, UK #29)

'Good Combination' (Atco, 1967, US #56)

'A Beautiful Story' (Atco, 1967, US #53)

'Plastic Man' (Atco, 1967, US #74)

'It's The Little Things' (Atco, 1967, US #50)

'All I Ever Need Is You' (Kapp, 1971, US #7, UK #8)

'A Cowboy's Work Is Never Done' (Kapp, 1971, US #8)

'When You Say Love' (MCA, 1972, US #32)

'Real People' (MCA, 1972)

'Mama Was A Rock And Roll Singer, Papa Used To Write All Her Songs' (MCA, 1973, US #77)

'The Greatest Show On Earth' (MCA, 1974)

SOLO ALBUMS

All I Really Want To Do
(Imperial/Liberty, 1965, US #16, UK #7)
The Sonny Side Of Chér
(Imperial/Liberty, 1966, US #26, UK
#11)
Chér (Imperial/Liberty, 1966, US #59)
With Love, Chér (Imperial/Liberty, 1967,
US #47)
Backstage (Imperial/Liberty, 1968)
3614 Jackson Highway (Atco, 1969, US
#160)
Gypsys, Tramps & Thieves (aka Cher)
(Kapp/MCA, 1971, US #16)
Foxy Lady (Kapp/MCA, 1972, US #43)
Bittersweet White Light (MCA, 1973, US
#140)
Half-Breed (MCA, 1973, US #28)
Dark Lady (MCA, 1974, US #69)
Stars (Warner Bros, 1975, US #153)

I'd Rather Believe In You (Warner Bros,
1976)
Cherished (Warner Bros, 1977)
Two The Hard Way (as Allman &
Woman) (Warner Bros, 1977)
Take Me Home (Casablanca, 1979, US
#25)
Prisoner (Casablanca, 1979)
Black Rose (Casablanca, 1980)
I Paralyze (Columbia, 1982)
Cher (Geffen, 1987, US #32, UK #26)
Heart Of Stone (Geffen, 1989, US #10,
UK #7)
Love Hurts (Geffen, 1991, US #48, UK #1)
It's A Man's World (WEA, 1995, US #64,
UK #10)
Believe (WEA, 1998, US #4, UK #7)
not.com.mercial (Artistdirect, 2000)
Living Proof (WEA, 2001, US #9, UK #46)

SOLO SINGLES

'Ringo, I Love You' (as Bonnie Jo
Mason) (Sceptor, 1964)
'All I Really Want To Do'
(Imperial/Liberty, 1965, US #15, UK #9)
'Where Do You Go' (Imperial/Liberty,
1965, UK #25)
'Bang Bang (My Baby Shot Me Down)'
(Imperial/Liberty, 1966, US #2, UK #3)
'Alfie' (Imperial/Liberty, 1966, US #32)
'I Feel Something In The Air'
(Imperial/Liberty, 1966, UK #43)
'Sunny' (Imperial/Liberty, 1966, UK #32)
'Behind The Door' (Imperial/Liberty,
1966, US #97)
'Mama (When My Dollies Have Babies)'
(Imperial/Liberty, 1966, US #124)
'Hey Joe' (Imperial/Liberty, 1967, US #94)
'You Better Sit Down Kids'
(Imperial/Liberty, 1967, US #9)
'The Click Song' (Imperial/Liberty, 1968)
'Take Me For A Little While'
(Imperial/Liberty, 1968)

'Yours Until Tomorrow'
(Imperial/Liberty, 1968)
'For What It's Worth' (Atco, 1969, US
#125)
'The First Time' (Atco, 1969)
'Chastity's Song (Band Of Thieves) (Atco,
1969)
'Gypsys, Tramps & Thieves'
(Kapp/MCA, 1971, US #1, UK #4)
'The Way Of Love' (Kapp/MCA, 1972,
US #7)
'Will You Love Me Tomorrow' (MCA,
1972)
'Living In A House Divided' (MCA,
1972, US #22)
'Don't Hide Your Love' (MCA, 1972, US
#46)
'Am I Blue?' (MCA, 1973, US #111)
'Half-Breed' (MCA, 1973, US #1)
'Carousel Man' (MCA, 1973)
'Dark Lady' (MCA, 1974, US #1, UK
#36)

'Train Of Thought' (MCA, 1974, US #27)
'I Saw A Man And He Danced With His Wife' (MCA, 1974, US #42)
'Rescue Me' (MCA, 1974)
'A Woman's Story' (MCA, 1974)
'Baby, I Love You' (MCA, 1974)
'Just Enough To (Keep Me Hangin' On) (Warner Bros, 1975)
'These Days' (Warner Bros, 1975)
'Geronimo's Cadillac' (Warner Bros, 1975)
'Long Distance Love Affair' (Warner Bros, 1976)
'Pirate' (Warner Bros, 1977, US #93)
'War Paint And Soft Feathers' (Warner Bros, 1977)
'Take Me Home' (Casablanca, 1979, US #8)
'Wasn't It Good' (Casablanca, 1979, US #49)
'It's Too Late (To Love Me Now)' (Casablanca, 1979, UK #87)
'Hell On Wheels' (Casablanca, 1979, US #59)
'Dead Ringer For Love' (Meat Loaf Featuring Cher) (Epic, 1981, UK #5)
'Rudy' (Columbia, 1982)
'I Paralyze' (Columbia, 1982)
'I Found Someone' (Geffen, 1987, US #10, UK #5)
'We All Sleep Alone' (Geffen, 1987, US #14, UK #47)
'Skin Deep' (Geffen, 1988, US #79)
'Bang-Bang' (Geffen, 1988)
'After All' (Cher & Peter Cetera) (Geffen, 1989, US #6, UK #84)
'If I Could Turn Back Time' (Geffen, 1989, US #3, UK #6)
'Just Like Jesse James' (Geffen, 1990, US #8, UK #11)
'Heart Of Stone (Geffen, 1990, US #20, UK #43)
'You Wouldn't Know Love' (Geffen, 1990, UK #55)
'Baby I'm Yours' (Geffen, 1990, UK #89)
'The Shoop Shoop Song (It's In His Kiss)' (Geffen, 1990, US #33, UK #1)
'Love And Understanding' (Geffen, 1991, US #17, UK #10)
'Save Up All Your Tears' (Geffen, 1991, US #37, UK #37)
'Love Hurts' (Geffen, 1991, UK #43)
'Could've Been You' (Geffen, 1992, UK #31)
'When Lovers Become Strangers' (Geffen, 1992)
'Oh No Not My Baby' (Geffen, 1992, UK #33)
'Whenever You're Near' (Geffen, 1992, UK #72)
'Many Rivers To Cross (Live From The Mirage)' (Geffen, 1993, UK #37)
'I Got You Babe' (Cher With Beavis & Butt-head) (Geffen, 1993, US #108, UK #35)
'It Ain't Necessarily So' (Cher & Larry Adler) (Mercury, 1994)
'Love Can Build A Bridge (Cher, Chrissie Hynde & Neneh Cherry With Eric Clapton) (RCA/Curb, 1995, UK #1)
'Walking In Memphis' (WEA, 1995, UK #11)
'One By One' (WEA, 1996, US #52, UK #7)
'Not Enough Love In The World' (WEA, 1996, UK #31)
'The Sun Ain't Gonna Shine Anymore' (WEA, 1996, UK #26)
'Paradise Is Here' (WEA, 1996)
'Believe' (WEA, 1998, US #1, UK #1)
'Strong Enough (WEA, 1999, US #57, UK #5)
'All Or Nothing' (WEA, 1999, UK #12)
'Dov'è L'amore' (WEA, 1999, US #104, UK #21)
'Più Che Puoi' (Eros Ramazzotti With Cher) (BMG International, 2001)
'The Music's No Good Without You' (WEA, 2001, UK #8)
'Song For The Lonely' (WEA, 2002, US #85)
'A Different Kind Of Love Song' (WEA, 2002, US #105)

'When The Money's Gone' (WEA, 2003, US #114)
'Love One Another' (WEA, 2003)
'Bewitched, Bothered And Bewildered'
(Rod Stewart & Cher) (J Records, 2003)
'You Haven't Seen The Last Of Me' (RCA, 2010)

FILMS

Wild On The Beach (20th Century Fox, 1965)
Good Times (Columbia Pictures, 1967)
Chastity (American International Pictures, 1969)
Come Back To The Five & Dime, Jimmy Dean, Jimmy Dean (Viacom, 1982)
Silkwood (20th Century Fox, 1983)
Mask (Universal Pictures, 1985)
Suspect (Tri-Star Pictures, 1987)
The Witches Of Eastwick (Warner Bros Pictures, 1987)

Moonstruck (MGM, 1987)
Mermaids (MGM, 1990)
The Player (Fine Line Features, 1992)
Prêt-à-Porter (Miramax, 1994)
Faithful (Miramax, 1996)
If These Walls Could Talk (HBO, 1996)
Tea With Mussolini (Universal Pictures, 1999)
Stuck On You (20th Century Fox, 2003)
Burlesque (Screen Gems, 2010)
Zookeeper (MGM, 2011)

Bibliography & Sources

Bego, Mark *Cher—If You Believe* (Taylor 2004)

Biskind, Peter *Easy Riders, Raging Bulls: How The Sex'n'Drugs'n'Rock'n'Roll Generation Saved Hollywood* (Bloomsbury 1998)

Biskind, Peter *Star: The Life & Wild Times Of Warren Beatty* (Simon & Schuster 2010)

Bono, Sonny *And The Beat Goes On* (Pocket Books 1991)

Bronson, Fred *The Billboard Book Of Number 1 Hits, Updated And Expanded 5th Edition* (Billboard 2003)

Brown, Mick *Tearing Down The Wall Of Sound, The Rise And Fall Of Phil Spector* (Bloomsbury 2007)

Boyer, Paul S., Clifford E. Clark Jr., Joseph F.Kett, Neal Salisbury, Harvard Sitkoff and Nancy Woloch (eds) *The Enduring Vision: A History Of The American People* (DC Heath 1996)

Cher and Jeff Coplon *The First Time By Cher* (Warner Books 1999)

Dellar, Fred *The NME Guide To Rock Cinema* (Hamlyn 1981)

Dickson, Paul *From Elvis To E-Mail: Trends Events And Trivia From The Postwar Era To The End Of The Century* (Federal Street 1999)

Ertegun, Ahmet *What'd I Say: The Atlantic Story 50 Years Of Music* (Orion 2001)

Goodall, Nigel *Cher. In Her Own Words* (Omnibus 1992)

Jones, Alan and Jussi Kantonen *Saturday Night Forever—The Story Of Disco* (Mainstream Publishing 1999)

Larkin, Colin *The Virgin Encyclopedia Of Popular Music, Concise Fourth Edition* (Virgin 2002)

Knobler, Peter and Greg Mitchell (eds) *Very Seventies: A Cultural History Of The 1970s, From The Pages Of Crawdaddy* (Simon & Schuster 1995)

Kutner, Jon and Spencer Leigh *The 1000 UK Number One Hits* (Omnibus 2005)

Marsh, Dave *The Heart Of Rock And Soul: The 1001 Greatest Singles Ever Made* (Penguin 1989)

Murrells, Joseph *The Book Of Golden Discs: The Records That Sold A Million* (Barrie & Jenkins 1978)

Oldham, Andrew Loog *2Stoned* (Vantage 2003)

Quirk, Lawrence J. *Totally Uninhibited—The Life And Wild Times Of Cher* (William Morrow 1991)

Pegg, Nicholas *The Complete David Bowie* (Reynolds & Hearn 2004)

Sounes, Howard *Seventies: The Sights, Sounds And Ideas Of A Brilliant Decade* (Simon & Schuster 2006)

Southall, Brian *The A-Z Of Record Labels. Second Edition* (Sanctuary 2003)

Taraborelli, J. Randy *Cher—The Unauthorised Biography!* (Pan 1989)

Wexler, Jerry and David Ritz *Rhythm And Blues: A Life In American Music* (Knopf 1993)

Williams, Richard *Out Of His Head: The Sound Of Phil Spector* (Abacus 1974)

CHAPTER 1 "Johnny was very charming" Suzy Kalter, *People*, July 8 1978; "I felt like an outsider" Dotson Rader, *Parade*, 21 November 2010; "I was away from home" / "My mother once" Bego; "I actually raised my sister" / "When I was little" / "Sonny's lifestyle was" / "I need someone to cook" / "I was pretty naïve" Goodall; "He was very showy" / "I sounded too much" Taraborrelli; "They were young" / "Mortified would have been" / "I hadn't seen" / "Something is different" Cher and Coplon; "When I was just" Biskind, *Star*; "Cher had a honking voice" Brown.

CHAPTER 2 "Sonny Bono greeted us" Oldham; "We had these managers" / "When we got to England" / "I don't have any regrets" / "We call it folk'n'roll" Goodall; "I said really" Ertegun; "We stretched the capacity" / "A great little circus act" / "Cher's tonal quality" Taraborrelli; "We didn't have much" *Sonny & Cher Live In Las Vegas Vol II*

liner notes; "At the time Dylan" Ken Sharp, *Look At Us* liner notes; "A majestic example" Larkin; "Love redeems everything" Marsh; "The people in England" / "My dear, you're lovely" Cher and Coplon; "Real space cadets" *Playboy*, 1975; "I've always dressed like this" / "We were really honored" / "About a hundred policemen" Keith Altham, *NME*, October 22 1965; "A bad case of Doris Day" *After Dark*, February 1979; "When he finally proposed" / "While we've got" Mike Grant, *Rave*, October 1965; "We have a big advantage" Penny Valentine, *Disc Weekly*, September 4 1965.

CHAPTER 3 "Not releasing our version" / "The freight elevator" / "I had received many letters" / "The concert went without" Cher and Coplon; "We loved the Cher version" / "We don't know where" Derek Taylor, *KRLA Beat*, July 7 1965; "I was terrified of the crowd" Goodall; "Cher isn't the most subtle singer" Tim Sendra, allmusic.com.

CHAPTER 4 "People ask why" Goodall; "Even by third-season standards" manfromucle.org; "The parties made good" Quirk; "That was our death sentence" / "It was Billy's first feature" / "He must have needed" Cher and Coplon; "He had seen a couple" Taraborrelli.

CHAPTER 5 "Son's straight-ahead" Cher and Coplon; "In case of a tie" Wexler; "Not only did I lose" / "I was bored with music" / "A philosophic, loving interpretation" / "We were going to be" Bono; "Every cent he could" Taraborrelli; "I remember going" Goodall.

CHAPTER 6 "Cher and I hesitated" / "Silverman sent us" / "He wanted to use Snuffy" Bono; "We'd go on stage through the casino" / "We began joking around" / "We were pretty ragged" / "We were like" / "Whole families watched" / "It was the first time" Cher and Coplon; "Comically cartoonish versions" / "Sonny was now singing" Bego; "I played Sonny the song" / "They were going to sign" / "Nobody would ever play it" / "He was looking for something" / "It wasn't well recorded" *All I Ever Need* liner notes; "I knew exactly" Bronson; "Snuffy was so funny" Melody Nelson, rocksbackpages.com; "I knew that was" / "When we had the track done" / "I've been involved" Taraborrelli; "Sonny & Cher may" John Mendelsohn, *Rolling Stone*, February 3 1972; "The genius of Snuff Garrett" cherscholar.com; "Her voice on the record" Quirk; "Cher didn't even realize" justplaincher.net.

CHAPTER 7 "I really worked" / "I said, yeah" Taraborrelli; "Setting preteen fashions" Gene Sculatti, *Creem*, November 1972 "Cher is no Streisand" Jaan Uhelszki, *Creem*, January 1974.

CHAPTER 8 "Both fiercely competitive"

/ "Cher wasn't into this" Taraborrelli; "She's recording an album" / "I wanted to be mad" / "It was the strangest thing" / "Anybody with two eyes" / "Gregg makes a great villain" / "I would never have" / "I realized it was" Cher and Coplon; "Unknown to me" / "One of my great misjudgments" / "We were playing the largest" / "From what I heard" / "He had to compete" Bono; "Stardom made Sonny" Dotson Rader, *Parade*, November 21 2010; "A dark lamentation" Brown; "*Stars* is certain" John Mendelsohn, *Phonograph Record*, May 1975; "A bull in the bedroom" / "I think I married Gregory" Quirk; "Drugs and alcohol" Michael Gross, *Swank*, 1977; "Their performance on stage" Ruth Gruber, *United Press International*, November 16 1977; "I wouldn't have gone" Lois Armstrong, *People*, April 10 1978; "Elijah's never been close" Goodall.

CHAPTER 9 "I was a working single mother" / "Nothing else compared" / "People weren't used to" Cher and Coplon; "Neil wanted Cher to fit" / "The best thing about her" Bego; "I thought she would" / "She was ahead" Taraborrelli; "Very few other records" Jones and Kantonen; "It was nice except" Mike Weatherford, *Las Vegas Review Journal*, May 6 2008.

CHAPTER 10 "Les is the person" Michael Musto, *US*, November 11 1980; "That's what makes it" / "Black Rose isn't *my* band" / "I'm very pleased" Andy Secher, *New York Daily News*, October 7 1980; "That's what art is" / "I did it" Taraborrelli.

CHAPTER 11 "As far back as" Patrick Humphries, *Times*, 2001; "Las Vegas is my gig" / "It's like a play" Jim Farber, *Rolling Stone*, October 16 1980; "I couldn't get arrested" / "Too old, too tall" / "You're so good" / "You know what?" / "I thought he was" Cher and Coplon; "I never had any qualms" / "What Cher has" / "In the interrogation Scene" / "She has a wonderful" Jan Hoffman, *Premiere*, February 1988; "I believe I have found" Darcy Diamond, *Los Angeles Herald Examiner*, June 5 1981; "That was a good one" / "John Kalodner was" / "I was at some" / "It was my favorite" Dean Ferguson and Johnny Danza, dancemusic.about.com; "How do I know" / "The first time I" *Los Angeles Herald Examiner*, January 11 1983; "I don't really know" Frank Rich, *New York Times*, February 19 1982; "I was the curiosity factor" / "Let's not make a statement" / "I panicked" / "Before shooting" *Cosmopolitan*, January 1984; "I cried a lot" Roderick Mann, *Los Angeles Times*, December 5 1982; "I ran into the bathroom" / "She is tough" Jim Jerome, *People*, 1985; "I felt Cher's persona" Nina Leeds, *US*, April 8 1985; "Cher has an element of danger" *USA Today*, March 14 1985; "He wasn't very nice" / "I'm going to take that" Jancee Dunn, *Rolling Stone*, September 19 1986; "I don't really like" / "Peter tells you exactly" *Movie Magazine*, Spring 1983; "When I finally saw" / "The director didn't want me" Jim Watters, *New Woman*, February 1988; "Once we started" / "It really wasn't my idea" / "Once I actually got" Jacob Dahlin, *Jacobs Stege* (Swedish TV); "Filming a movie" / "It was disappointing"/ "I was devastated" Jay Gissen, *Cable Guide*, March 1989; "It makes it more" *Q*, May 1992.

CHAPTER 12 "As much as I" / "I don't know where" / "It kind of reminded" / "I much prefer playing" Donald Chase, *Los Angeles Times*, March 1 1987; "The reason I was" / "We sit down" *Moonstruck* DVD commentary; "Too

much fun" Jay Gissen, *Cable Guide*, March 1989; "Her comic timing is" Jan Hoffman, *Premiere*, February 1988; "It's hard for me" Cher and Coplon.

CHAPTER 13 "I was constantly sick" *People*, May 28 1998; "I think the album" / "Someone once asked" Kenny Kerner, *Music Connection*, October 1 1989; "I wanted to look" / "I seize moments" / "Every night I'm standing" *Primetime Live*, ABC-TV 1990; "When they pulled" / "I'm getting too old" / "I decided not to" *Vanity Fair*, November 1990; "Kenny, let's get pops" Stuart D. Bykofsky, *USA Today*, August 18 1989; "At my house" *Entertainment Tonight*, CBS-TV, April 3 1990; "A kind of Las Vegas" Jon Pareles, *New York Times*, May 12 1990.

CHAPTER 14 "I couldn't find anything" / "It's very reminiscent" Jay Gissen, *Cable Guide*, March 1989; "I actually play my mother" / "Once the director got fired" Goodall; "Much of the material" John O'Connor, *New York Times*, February 4 1991; "Holistic or spiritual things" Bego; "I'm only difficult if" *Vanity Fair*, November 1990.

CHAPTER 15 "There was a lot" / "I've always liked" / "That's why we used" / "How unbelievably weird" / "Rob Dickens persuaded" / "I wanted to make" / "I didn't think it was" / "Originally we were" *Music Week*, November 28 1995; "It was me experimenting" / "I don't like working" / "I didn't want to" / "I worked really hard" Jim Bessman, *Billboard*, May 18 1996; "I didn't like the ending" / "When I saw my teeth" Goodall; "For me, Elvis was" / "It was no loss" / "When you become" / "From an artistic" Stephen Holden, *New York Times*, June 30 1996; "The first day I walked" / "It was so exciting" Cher and Coplon; "This is the last chance" *Q*, February 1996.

CHAPTER 16 "I didn't want to blow it" / "I had no control" *People*, May 29 1998; "I think it hit home" Mim Udovitch, *Rolling Stone*, April 15 1999; "We just went" / "There was something" / "We worked in" / "They needed lyrics" / "The weird thing" / "That was the only way" / "Of course they wanted" / "I'm looking forward" / "As a singer who" *Do You Believe In Cher?* BBC Radio 2, March 1999; "A cast of thousands" / "They were very smart" / "I'd bought this Roachford CD" / "We took the songs" / "Who could give up" Patrick Humphries, *Times* (UK), 2001; "Every gay guy I know" / "I was singing in" / "She was heaven-sent" / "My scenes were cut" Benjamin Svetkey, *Entertainment Weekly*, April 23 1999; "If I'm going to go" Dean Ferguson and Johnny Danza, dancemusic.about.com; "The lyrics for the chorus" / "We knew the rough direction" / "It was a bit radical" *Sound On Sound*, February 1999; "Everything I do" Michael Logan, *TV Guide*, August 21–27 1999.

CHAPTER 17 "I wrote the second" / "There was one" / "We were making demos" Lawrence Ferber, ewelthrope.blogspot.com; "I didn't really choose" / "I just thought of" artistdirect.com, 2000; "Even before I left" *not.commercial* liner notes; "My mother said" Ting Yu, *People*, November 27 2000; "One morning I" Benjamin Svetkey, *Entertainment Weekly*, April 23 1999; "I'm not very web-savvy" James Oliver Cury, *Entertainment Weekly*, February 19 1999; "I don't think I thought" Patrick Humphries, *Times* (UK), 2001; "It doesn't sound like" / "It has so much meaning" / "Such a great song" /

. "When I go into" / "I'm really proud" *TMF Extra* (Australian TV, 2001); "It's like going to" Darren Kelly May, Heart FM (UK radio 2004); "I'm approaching 80" *USA Today*, May 2 2005; "It's probably the most" / "Cher is all girly" Catherine McHugh, *Live Design*, October 2002; "I really don't want" Liz Smith, *Toledo Blade*, February 4 2005; "Every place we could" Ray Waddell, *Boston Globe*, October 31 2003; "I was buying helmet inserts" / "I would be willing" Krista Smith, *Vanity Fair*, December 2010; "I have a lot of ambitions" Goodall; "I didn't think" / "One of the big" Thomas Chau, *Cinema Confidential*, December 9 2003; "You'd have to do" *The Early Show*, CBS-TV, December 2003; "It's like being" Prairie Miller, *NY Rock*, December 2003; "She was very cool" eonline.com, December 2003.

CHAPTER 18 "I've come full circle" cher.aeglive.com, February 2008 / "What we were trying" / "Her music has spanned" better.tv, March 2008; "When she put that" / "It was easy" / "Like building a" Booth Moore, *Los Angeles Times*, May 18 2008; "You get lots of scripts" / "I was terrified" / "Peter and I" / "Cher is really" / "The song had a lot" Christina Radish, *Collider*, November 16 2010; "My mom and her friends" / "Tess, my character" / "I really wanted to sing" / "I kind of did" / "Christina is wonderful" / "Gay men never leave you" / "I don't drink" / "I could retire" Elaine Lipworth, *Mail On Sunday*, November 27 2010; "Cher's been incredible" Sal Morgan, novafm.com.au, November 2010; "I've been licked" *Primetime Live*, ABC-TV, 1990; "As artists we're always" / "I just like what I do" theage.com.au, January 4 2011.

INDEX

Words in *italics* indicate album titles unless otherwise stated. Words in 'quotes' indicate song titles. Numerals in **bold** refer to illustrations.

'A Cowboy's Work Is Never Done,' 76, 93
Academy Awards, 40, 48, 66, 86, 91, 159, 164, 169, 170, 185, 189, 195, 257
'After All,' 179, 191
Aguilera, Christina, **128**, 148, 235, 255–6, 260
'Alive Again,' 238
All I Ever Need Is You, 75–6, 81
'All I Ever Need Is You,' 75, 76, 79
All I Really Want To Do, 27, 29–30, 31
'All I Really Want To Do,' 28, 95, 185, 242
'All Or Nothing,' 218, 222, 226, 240
Allman And Woman, 108–9
Allman Brothers Band, The, 101, 110
Allman, Duane, 101
Allman, Gregg, 100–4, 107–12, **118**
Allman, Elijah Blue, 107, 112, **123**, 175, 176, 181, 183, 185, 203, 211, 228
Altman, Robert, 152–3, 154–5, 159, 189, 194, 208, 211
American Music Awards, 225
And The Beat Goes On (book), 65, 74, 95
Atco/Atlantic, 48, 51, 56, 67, 68, 81, 84
Average White Band, 102

'Baby Don't Go,' 13, 21, 48, 69
'Baby, I Love You,' 99
Backstage, 51–2
Baldwin, Alec, 257
Baldwin, Red, 11
'Bang Bang (My Baby Shot Me Down),' 31, 84, 173, 241

Barry, Paul, 215, 217, 218–19, 234
Battiste, Harold, 10, 16, 22, 27, 30, 36, 37–8, 50, 51, 54, 63, 83
'Beat Goes On, The,' 37, 38, 40, 48, 77, 84, 214
Beatles, The, 12–13, 18–19, 22, 23, 24, 41, 42, 47–8, 49, 50, 54, 77, 83, 193
Beatty, Warren, 8–9, 151, 155
Beavis & Butt-Head, 201
'Behind The Door,' 50
Believe, 215–22, 224, 226, 229, 233, 235, 236, 237
'Believe,' 218–21, 222, 225, 228, 229, 234, 238, 239, 242, 250, 258
Benjamin, Richard, 192
Best Of Sonny & Cher, The, 48, 49
Bishop, Joey, 66
Bittersweet White Light, 82, 85, 86, 90, 91, 131
Black Rose, 129, 139, 144–7, 150, 183
Black Rose, 145–6
Bogart, Neil, 129–31, 134, 137, 146
Bogdanovich, Peter, 42, 159–60, 161–2
Bolton, Michael, 172, 173, 178, 180
Bon Jovi, Jon, 172–3, 174, 178, 180
Bono, Mary, 177, 213, 214
Bono, Sonny, 8, 9–14, 15–21, 25, 26, 27, 28–30, 32, 33, 34–5, 36, 37, 38, 39–40, 42–7, 49, 50, 51, 53, 54, 55, 56–7, 61–9, 72, 75, 76, 78, 79, 80, 82, 83, 85–8, 90, 91, 93, 94, 95–6, 98, 100, 103, 104, 106–8, 111, **114**, **115**, **117**, **120**, 132, 141, 150, 168, 173, 174, 175, 176–7, 182, 213–15, 221, 231, 242, 246, 248, 251
'Born With The Hunger,' 232, 233
Bowie, David, 104–5
Braille Institute Of America, 32

Buddah Records (label), 129
Burlesque (movie), 254–7
'But You're Mine,' 34
Byrds, The, 27–8

Caesar & Cleo, 13–14, 21, 22, 27
Cage, Nicolas, **123**, 167, 170
Camilletti, Rob, 168, 174–5, 180, 185, 197, 198, 212
Cammareri, Ronny, 167
Cannes Film Festival, 162
Capps, Al, 71, 79, 90, 96, 97, 108
'Carousel Man,' 92, 96
Casablanca Records (label), 129–30, 131, 133, 135, 137, 138, 146, 148
Celebration At Caesars Palace, A, 138–40
Charles, Ray, 8, 53, 75, 104
Chastity, see Sun, Chastity
Chastity (movie/soundtrack), 56–63, 64, 141
'Chastity's Sun,' 92, 134
Cher, 172–5, 178, 180, 185, 196
Chér, 35–6
Cher … And Other Fantasies (TV special), 135
Cher At The Colosseum, 248–51
Cher Enterprises, 98
Cher Show, The (TV show), 100, 104–5
Cher … Special (TV special), 130–1
cher.com, 232
Cherished, 108
Cher's Golden Greats, 83
Child, Desmond, 149, 172, 173, 174, 179, 196
'Classified 1A,' 69, 75, 99, 231
Cliff, Jimmy, 200, 258
Cobain, Kurt, 230, 231
Columbia Records (label), 148
Come Back To The Five & Dime, Jimmy Dean, Jimmy Dean (play/movie), 152–5, 165, 170, 189
Cooke, Sam, 10, 33

Coppola, Francis Ford, 57, 151, 251

'Could've Been You,' 197–8

Crouch, Jackie (aka Georgia Holt, Cher's mother), 5–9, 11, 152, 170, 204, 231, 254, 255

Damon, Matt, 252

'Danny Boy,' 78

Dark Lady, 96–7

'Dark Lady,' 96–7, 132, 134, 200, 228

Davies, Ray, 29

'Dead Ringer For Love,' 130, 147–8, 200

DeCarlo, Joe, 35, 48, 57, 64, 69, 103

Decca Records (label), 68

de Paola, Alessio, 57, 62

DeShannon, Jackie, 10, 29

Dickens, Rob, 201–2, 204, 215–16, 217, 218–19, 221, 232, 233, 234

'Dream Baby,' 27, 28

Do You Believe Tour, 225–8, 238, 239, 250

Dr John, 36, 51, 55

'Don't Hide Your Love,' 81

'Don't Talk To Strangers, Baby,' 45, 47

'Dov'è L'Amore,' 215, 216, 217, 222

Dreamhouse Studios, 216

Dudek, Les, 143–6

Dusty In Memphis, 54

Dylan, Bob, 16, 17, 27–8, 29, 36, 37, 38, 52, 55, 83, 84, 95

Eagles, 94, 140, 186, 204

Emmy Awards, 212, 243

Ephron, Nora, 159

Ertegun, Ahmet, 14, 15–16, 17, 48, 53, 75, 77, 94

Esty, Bob, 131–2, 133–4, 135, 136, 137, 146

Everett, Betty, 193

Everett, Rupert, 209

Faithful (movie), 208–10, 222

Farrar, John, 148–9

Farrelly, Bobby and Peter, 252, 259

First Time, The (book), 7, 9, 11, 28, 47

'First Time, The,' 80, 81

Foxy Lady, 79–82, 86–7, 91

Friedkin, William, 40–2, 43, 44, 48, 56–7

Gaga, Lady, 259

Garrett, Snuff, 69–73, 75–6, 79, 80, 81–2, 86, 89–90, 91–2, 96, 97, 108–9, 132, 135

Gaynor, J.C., 137, 139

Geffen, David, 94–5, 97, 99, 101, 103, 104, 105, 171, 172

Geffen Records (label), 171–2, 174, 178, 180, 195, 199, 200, 201–2

Gold Star Studios, 11, 16, 27, 30, 35, 54, 68, 78, 94, 98

Golden Globe Awards, 155, 159, 193, 212, 257

Good Times (movie/soundtrack), 35, 39–49, 62, 76

Gorrie, Alan, 102

Gouldman, Graham, 50

Grammy Awards, 222

Greatest Hits: 1965–1992, 199–200, 201

Greene, Charlie, 13, 14, 15, 18, 19, 20, 22, 23, 29, 32, 35, 40

Griffin, Merv, 66, 145

Gypsys Tramps & Thieves, 72–4, 79, 91, 92

'Gypsys Tramps & Thieves,' 31, 50, 70–2, 75, 76, 79, 81, 82, 84, 86, 89, 97, 109, 134, 185–6, 200, 226, 232

Half-Breed, 91–2, 96, 97

'Half-Breed,' 90–1, 134, 186, 226

Hallström, Lasse, 191

Ham, Warren, 139, 144

Heart Of Stone, 178–81, 183, 189

'Heart Of Stone,' 182, 194, 200, 246

Heart Of Stone tour, 184–7, 226

'Hell On Wheels,' 135, 137, 140

Higgins, Brian, 219

Hinton, Eddie, 54

Hollywood Walk Of Fame, 214

Hoskins, Bob, 191

Howard, James Newton, 144

100 Club, 19

'I Found Someone,' 172, 173, 174, 176, 185, 226

'I Got You Babe,' 15–18, 19, 21, 23, 27, 37, 40, 43, 47, 48, 75, 77, 84, 177, 185, 193, 200, 201

I Paralyze, 148–50, 171, 172

'I Paralyze,' 148–9

'I Still Haven't Found What I'm Looking For,' 225, 240

'I Walk On Gilded Splinters,' 55, 63

I'd Rather Believe In You, 107

'If I Could Turn Back Time,' 179, 181, 183, 186, 187, 194, 198, 200, 201, 202, 226, 239, 242

If These Walls Could Talk (TV miniseries), 211, 212

'I'm No Angel,' 185, 187

Imperial Records (label), 27, 30, 35, 48, 49, 51, 52, 53

In Case You're In Love, 36–8, 84

Inner Views, 49

It's A Man's World, 204–8, 212, 237

'It's A Man's World,' 204

'It's Gonna Rain,' 17, 23, 25, 75

Jacobs, Ron, 17

Jewison, Norman, 166–70, 192, 211

John, Elton, 93, 104, 144, 145, 146, 171, 202, 235, 248

'Just Like Jesse James,' 179, 182, 242

Kalodner, John, 171, 174, 177–8, 180, 193, 195, 200, 201

Kapp Records (label), 68, 75, 82, 86

Kenna, Elgin, 184

Kennedy, Jackie, 26, 66

Kennedy, John, 8, 25

Kilmer, Val, 161, 168

Kinks, The, 29, 33
Kinnear, Walt, 252–3

LaPiere, Gilbert, 8
Larrabee Sound Studios, 108
'Laugh At Me,' 21, 32–3, 34, 77
Lauper, Cyndi, 239
Lester, Richard, 24, 41
'Letter, The,' 13, 22, 84
Letterman, David, 175–7, 203, 213, 230
Levine, Larry, 12
Liberty Records (label), 27, 69, 81, 82–3, 84
'Little Man,' 37, 38, 84
Live At The Mirage, 187–8
Live In Las Vegas Volume 2, 92–3
'Living In A House Divided,' 79
Living Proof, 236–8
Living Proof: The Farewell Tour, 238–43, 247, 248
Lloyd, Emily, 191
'Long Distance Love Affair,' 107
Look At Us, 21–3, 26, 30, 84, 109
Lopez, Jennifer, 243, 257
'Love And Understanding,' 196, 198
Love, Darlene, 12, **114**, **123**, 173, 184
Love Hurts, 195–8, 199
'Love Hurts,' 100
Love Hurts tour, 199

Madonna, 7, 174, 202, 206, 216, 259
McCallum, David, 39, 40
McCartney, Paul, 91–2, 147, 203, 247
McGuinn, Roger, 28
Mackie, Bob, 67, 72, 91, 104, 106, 139, 143, 145, 184, 198, 249, 250
Mama Was A Rock And Roll Singer—Papa Used To Write All Her Songs, 87–89
'Mama Was A Rock And Roll Singer—Papa Used To Write All Her Songs,' 88
Man From U.N.C.L.E., The (TV show), 39–40

Mason, Bonnie Jo, 12–13, 27
Mask (movie), 159–62, 166, 167, 189, 192, 210
MCA (label), 68, 72, 82, 86, 96, 97, 98, 200
Meat Loaf, 130, 147–8, 200
Melcher, Melissa, 9, 11
Melcher, Terry, 28
Mermaids (movie), 190–4, 199, 210, 222, 242
Metro (production team), 215–19, 233–5, 237
Monkees, The, 37, 41, 45
Moonstruck (movie), 166–70, 190, 192
Muscle Shoals Sound Studio, 54–5, 100, 110
'Music's No Good Without You, The,' 234, 237–8
Musso, Johnny, 68–9, 75, 76–7, 78, 96

'Needles And Pins,' 10, 17, 29
Newton John, Olivia, 148
Nichols, Mike, 155–9, 161, 211
Nicholson, Jack, 151, 153, 162–4
'Not Enough Love In The World,' 204, 207
not.com.mercial, 232–3

Old Grey Whistle Test, The (TV show), 111
'One By One', 205, 207, 212
Ortega, Kenny, 183–4

Page, Larry, 18
Paich, David, 85, 87, 92, 93, 95, 136, 144
Palminteri, Chazz, 209, 210–11
Parker, Colonel Tom, 40
Pfeiffer, Michelle, 162
'Pirate,' 109
'Plastic Man,' 37, 48
Player, The (movie), 194–5, 208, 222
Pregnolato, Denis, 51, 69, 77, 79, 87, 89, 92, 105
Presley, Elvis, 24, 40, 110, 204, 239
Prêt À Porter (movie), 208, 222
Prisoner, 136–7, 138, 144

Quaid, Dennis, 164

Ready Steady Go! (TV show), 18
Reagan, Ronald, 182
Reprise (label), 13, 27, 48
'Revolution Kind, The,' 33
Ricci, Christina, 191, 192, 194
'Ringo, I Love You', 12–13, 28
Rolling Stones, The, 15, 19, 91, 131
Rolling Stone (magazine), 49, 78, 102
Ronettes, The, 12, 99
Ronstadt, Linda, 151–2, 204
Rubini, Michel, 30, 77, 79, 87
Russell, Kurt, 157, 158
Russell, Leon, 67, 69, 80
Ryder, Winona, 190, 191, 192, 194

Sambora, Richie, 172–3, 178, 180, 185, 197
Sammeth, Bill, 183
Sanchez, Doriana, 241, 248
Sanders, George, 42–3, 44, 45, 46
Sarandon, Susan, 162–3, 194, 209, 223
Sarkisan, John Paul (Cher's father), 5, 6, 7, 23, 231
Sasha, Kenny, 137, 139
'Save Up All Your Tears,' 196, 198
Seger, Bob, 186
Shaw, Sandie, 29, 37
'Shoop Shoop Song, The,' 193, 199–200, 226, 242, 250
Silkwood (movie), 156–60, 166, 169, 242, 255
Silkwood, Karen, 156, 158
Silverman, Fred, 66
Simmons, Gene, 130, 134, 196
Simpson, Jessica, 243–4
'Song For The Lonely,' 236, 237–8, 239, 240
Sonny Comedy Revue, The (TV show), 104
Sonny & Cher Comedy Hour, The (TV show), 66–7, 72, 74–5, 76, 81, 84, 85, 86, 91, 95, 97, 104, 105, 185, 239

Sonny & Cher Show, The (TV show), 105–8, 129, 177
Sonny & Cher Live, 77–8, 79, 81
Sonny Side Of Cher, The, 30–2
Spears, Britney, 243–4
Specialty Records (label), 10, 13, 22
Spector, Phil, 10, 11–12, 13–14, 15, 16, 17, 22, 27, 30, 70–1, 94, 98–9, **114**, 221
Spector, Ronnie, 12, 16, 179
Springfield, Dusty, 46, 54, 70, 149
Springsteen, Bruce, 186
Stars, 98–100, 107, 172, 197
Stoltz, Eric, 161
Stone, Bob, 70, 81, 88
Stone, Brian, 13, 15, 22, 29, 32, 35
Streep, Meryl, 156, 157–8, 169–70, 254, 255
'Strong Enough,' 215, 217, 222
Stuck On You (movie), 252–3
'Sun Ain't Gonna Shine Anymore, The,' 205, 207, 208
Sun, Chastity, 53, 92, 95, 107, 111, **117**, **123**, 176, 177, 211, 213, 230–1
Superpak (Volumes One & Two), 82–4
Super Bowl XXXIII, 225
'Superstar,' 67, 80
Suspect (movie), 164–5

Take Me Home, 132–5, 139, 144
'Take Me Home,' 134, 146
Take Me Home tour, 140
Taupin, Bernie, 93, 145
Taylor, Mark, 215–19, 234
Tea With Mussolini (movie), 222–4, 253
Thomas, James, 234
3614 Jackson Highway, 52, 54–6, 63, 64, 67, 69, 78, 131
Top Of The Pops (TV show), 18
Toto, 144, 148, 174, 196
Turner, Tina, 203, 205
Two The Hard Way, 108–9, 131
Two Of Us, The, 83, 84, 85
Tyler, Bonnie, 173, 178, 180, 196

Universal (label), 68
Updike, John, 162
U2, 225–6, 240

Vaughn, Robert, 39
Vault Records (label), 13
VH1 Divas (TV special), 239

'Wah-Wah Watson,' 132
'Walking In Memphis,' 204, 205, 207, 208, 210, 250
Walter Reed Medical Center, 244–5
Warhol, Andy, 36
Warner Bros (label), 15–16, 98, 100, 108, 109, 110, 201, 206, 215, 219, 221, 232, 233, 237, 238
Warren, Diane, 172, 173, 178–9, 180, 196, 218, 256–7, 260
Washington Journal (TV show), 244–5
Wavra, Brad, 243
'Way Of Love, The,' 73, 79
'We All Sleep Alone,' 173–4, 185, 200, 218, 226, 240
Webb, Jimmy, 99, 135
Wexler, Jerry, 51, 53–4, 55, 56, **116**
'What Now My Love,' 33, 48, 77
'Where Do You Go,' 30
White, Maurice, 173
Wild On The Beach (movie), 24–5, 39
Will & Grace (TV show), 251–2
Witches Of Eastwick, The (movie), 162–4, 167, 189
With Love, Chér, 49–51
Wonder, Stevie, 31, 93
Wondrous World Of Sonny & Cher, The, 32–4
Wrecking Crew, the, 71

Yates, Peter, 164–5
'You Better Sit Down Kids,' 49, 50, 55, 76, 93
'You Haven't Seen The Last Of Me,' 256–7

Zeffirelli, Franco, 222–3

PICTURE CREDITS

Jacket front Everett Collection/Rex Features; **113** Michael Ochs Archives/Getty Images; **114** Ray Avery/Getty Images; Time Life/Getty Images; **115** Jack Robinson/Hulton Archive/Getty Images; **116** Michael Ochs Archives/Getty Images; **117–18** CBS Photo Archive/Getty Images; **119** Michael Ochs Archives/Getty Images; **120** CBS Photo Archive/Getty Images; **121** Ron Galella/WireImage; **122** NY Daily News Archive/Getty Images; **123** Richard Corkery/NY Daily News Archive/Getty Images; **124** Joe McNally/Getty Images; **125** Taro Yamasaki/Time Life Pictures/Getty Images; **126** Peter Still/Redferns/Getty Images; Ethan Miller/Getty Images; **127** Jon Super/Redferns; **128** Kevin Winter/Getty Images.